The Twelve-Step
Facilitation Handbook

The Twelve-Step Facilitation Handbook

---

*A Systematic Approach to Recovery
from Substance Dependence*

Joseph Nowinski
Stuart Baker

 HAZELDEN®

Hazelden
Center City, Minnesota 55012-0176

1-800-328-9000
1-651-213-4590 (Fax)

www.hazelden.org

© 1992, 2003 by Joseph Nowinski and Stuart Baker

Originally published by Lexington Books 1992. Originally titled *The Twelve-Step Facilitation Handbook: A Systematic Approach to Early Recovery from Alcoholism and Addiction.*
Published by Jossey-Bass, Inc., Publishers 1998
Published by Hazelden Foundation 2003—with updated preface, new introduction, and updated references

ISBN: 1-59285-096-0

07 06 05 04 03 6 5 4 3 2 1

Cover design by David Spohn

Hazelden Publishing and Educational Services is a division of the Hazelden Foundation, a not-for-profit organization. Since 1949, Hazelden has been a leader in promoting the dignity and treatment of people afflicted with the disease of chemical dependency.

The mission of the foundation is to improve the quality of life for individuals, families, and communities by providing a national continuum of information, education, and recovery services that are widely accessible; to advance the field through research and training; and to improve our quality and effectiveness through continuous improvement and innovation.

Stemming from that, the mission of this division is to provide quality information and support to people wherever they may be in their personal journey—from education and early intervention, through treatment and recovery, to personal and spiritual growth.

Although our treatment programs do not necessarily use everything Hazelden publishes, our bibliotherapeutic materials support our mission and the Twelve Step philosophy upon which it is based. We encourage your comments and feedback.

The headquarters of the Hazelden Foundation are in Center City, Minnesota. Additional treatment facilities are located in Chicago, Illinois; Newberg, Oregon; New York, New York; Plymouth, Minnesota; St. Paul, Minnesota; and West Palm Beach, Florida. At these sites, we provide a continuum of care for men and women of all ages. Our Plymouth facility is designed specifically for youth and families.

For more information on Hazelden, please call 1-800-257-7800. Or you may access our World Wide Web site on the Internet at www.hazelden.org.

for Maggie, Rebecca, and Gregory with love, from J. N.

and

For Mar-c, Aaron, and Maya:

Thank you for your inspiration and support—from S. B.

Contents

Part V. Termination 173

The Termination Session 175

Preface

Alcoholics Anonymous (AA) is a program of hope and renewal that was born of despair and decay. Its birth came at a moment in history, marking a nexus of personal and historical forces. At that time, the ethic of radical individualism that had dominated American culture was straining under the weight of war and economic depression. It was a time when many ambitious and individualistic men, like Bill Wilson, had experienced failure as a result of personal excess and hubris, as well as larger forces beyond their control. It was a time ripe for quantum change of the sort that AA offered. Proof that AA was an idea whose time had come is the growth it has experienced since its initial struggles.

AA at its most elemental level can be thought of as a method for helping those who wish to drink no more to do so, one day at a time. It is a program of attraction that holds no prejudice against those who would deal with their drinking through some other means. AA was—and at heart still is— a program for those who want it: for those men and women who believe that they've tried everything else they want to try, and who now have a desire to stop drinking.

But AA and its sister twelve-step programs like Narcotics Anonymous (NA) offer nothing less than a program of personal transformation. Through its twelve steps and its twelve written (and many other oral) traditions, AA marks a pathway to profound changes in outlook, lifestyle, and spirituality for those who would pursue it. It provides guidelines for change on multiple levels, including behavior, thinking, values, relationships, and spirituality. Members of the fellowship, which is open to virtually anyone, are free to partake of as much or as little of the richness of the program as suits them.

From its inception in a few seminal groups of middle-class white male drunks in Ohio and New York, AA has grown into an international and multicultural fellowship of men and women, young and old. It has given rise to similar fellowships for drug addicts, overeaters, and others who suffer from compulsive self-destructive behaviors, and it has become a virtual culture unto itself. Evidence of this is that twelve-step fellowships possess their own coherent spiritual philosophy, backed up by a body of common wisdom that is readily accessible. They are guided by an elaborate system of ethics, rites, rituals, and traditions. They've developed their own language of a sort, and have proved capable of adapting themselves over time to widely disparate social and cultural conditions. Finally, through sponsorship, twelve-step fellowships have a means of passing down their values, wisdom, and traditions to newcomers. Each and every AA old timer is testimony to the vitality of the AA culture, as well as a carrier of that culture.

Is AA for everyone? To the extent that it is so pragmatic and flexible, the answer is probably yes. Were they to drop any preconceived ideas or prejudices they might hold toward AA, it is unlikely that anyone could not find something personally useful in it. On the other hand, as a "treatment" for alcoholism it remains to be seen if AA will stand the test of time, for surely it will continue to thrive only if its members find it useful. In terms of facts we know that approximately 40 percent of AA members who are sober and active in the program for less than a year will remain sober and active for a second year.[1] Unless and until a more effective method is found, clinicians working with men and women who have symptoms of alcoholism or drug dependence—or who simply wish to stop drinking or using in their own interest—might do well to help facilitate their active involvement with AA and its sister twelve-step programs like NA.

The Twelve-Step Facilitation Handbook incorporates material originally developed for Project MATCH, a national collaborative study of alcoholism treatment funded by the National Institute on Alcohol Abuse and Alcoholism. The twelve-step facilitation manual developed for use in Project MATCH was also used in a study of treatment of concurrent alcohol and cocaine abuse sponsored by the National Institute on Drug Abuse. Both studies employed a patient-treatment matching design, intended to assess what kind of treatment works best with what kind of patient. When this book was originally published in 1992, Project MATCH had reported one-year post-treatment outcome results on 90 percent of its 1,726 subjects.[2] The data showed that Twelve-Step Facilitation (TSF) was effective in significantly reducing drinking behavior and that this improvement was sustained at the time of the twelve-month follow-up assessment. Furthermore, TSF was found to be equally effective with moderate and severe problem drinkers. Overall, the Project MATCH results suggest that twelve-step oriented manual-guided intervention for alcohol abuse and alcoholism can be an effective treatment across a range of client demographics, personality variables, and problem severity.

We are grateful to the twelve-step facilitators who participated in these studies for the valuable feedback they provided. We would also like to acknowledge the support and encouragement of Kathleen Carroll in the process of developing the original twelve-step facilitation manual. In addition, we are grateful to Pat Owen, Dan Anderson, and Fred Holmquist of the Hazelden Foundation for their thoughtful feedback regarding our early work. Finally, we wish to thank the following people who reviewed and provided valuable comments on various drafts of the original twelve-step facilitation manual: William Miller, Tom Babor, Ronald Kadden, Bruce Rounsaville, Ellie Sturgis, Carlo DiClemente, Dave Barrett, Sandy Rasmussen, and Charlie Wilber.

Introduction

1. Twelve-Step Programs

Though many models of treating alcoholism and addiction exist,[1] by far the best-known is the twelve-step approach, which originated with Alcoholics Anonymous (AA). (For the twelve steps of AA, please refer to Appendix B.) Ironically—and no doubt partly because it originated outside the medical and mental health establishments—AA and its sister programs such as Narcotics Anonymous (NA) have been the subjects of relatively little systematic study. Similarly, academic curricula in medicine, psychiatry, clinical psychology, social work, and family therapy typically offer little or no systematic training or education in the twelve-step approach to recovery from substance dependence.

The goal of this book is to educate professional counselors and therapists in twelve-step principles of recovery, and to present a systematic approach to facilitating early recovery through involvement in a twelve-step recovery program.

The facilitation program presented here is intended to be used as a guide in the clinical treatment of persons who manifest significant symptoms of alcohol or other drug dependence according to *DSM-IV-TR*.[2] It is designed to be flexible enough to allow for individual treatment planning. It can be used as a primary treatment modality for persons who have never previously been exposed to a twelve-step program like AA or NA, or it can be used for people who have already had such exposure, either in previous treatment or through voluntary involvement in AA or NA. Though the book is written for use in one-on-one, individual facilitation sessions, the methods described can be readily adapted to a group treatment format as well. Twelve-step facilitation may also be used as an adjunct to individual psychotherapy, family therapy, or marital counseling. In these cases, though, the authors advise facilitators to take heed of the AA adage: "First Things First." When designing a comprehensive treatment plan for an active addict, other significant issues may need to be put "on hold" until active addiction has been arrested and recovery started. As a rule of thumb, six to nine months of uninterrupted sobriety, combined with active involvement in a twelve-step program are, sensible preconditions for working on personal, family, vocational, or relationship issues.

Our intent is to provide a flexible structure for treatment that will enable facilitators to define relatively specific goals and assess patients' ongoing progress toward meeting those goals in a straightforward manner.

Symptoms of Substance Dependence

The primary qualifications for a patient's entry into a twelve-step facilitation program is clinical evidence of dependence—the loss of his/her ability to effectively control his/her use of one or more mood-altering substances, including alcohol. In particular, three symptoms in relation to such substances need to be clinically evaluated; tolerance, loss of control, and continued use despite clear negative consequences of that use. All three of these symptoms are discussed in detail in the chapter on Core Topic 1, assessment. Briefly, patients should be considered candidates for twelve-step facilitation if they manifest all of the following:

• *Tolerance.* The symptom of tolerance develops early in the addiction process. Tolerance refers to the condition in which the mood-altering effects of a substance are habituated with continued use. The drinker or user experiences a diminishing emotional impact or mood swing from the same dose of alcohol or drug over time. As a result, s/he must consume more of a substance, or a more potent form of the substance, or a different substance, in order to achieve the same mood swing. Tolerance therefore appears to drive or motivate increasing alcohol or drug use.

• *Loss of Control.* Loss of control refers to a pattern of progressively ineffective self-control over substance use. The alcoholic or addict cannot reliably predict how much of a substance s/he will use, will not be able to reliably stop once s/he has started drinking or using, and/or will tend to substitute or combine substances in order to stay drunk or high. Loss of control is a cardinal behavioral indicator of addiction. As one alcoholic patient put it, "As an alcoholic, I never wanted one drink. I wanted to get drunk as quickly as I could, and I wanted to stay drunk as long as I could. I might start out with gin, but I'd end up drinking mouthwash if that was all I could get my hands on."

• *Continued Use Despite Negative Consequences.* Chronic substance abuse leads inevitably to progressively severe negative consequences in a variety of critical areas, including the alcoholic's or addict's physical, emotional, social, vocational, and spiritual well-being. Alcoholics and addicts become depressed, alienated, sick, tired, and unreliable. They have accidents and get into fights, lose their jobs, exploit and manipulate others in the interests of continuing their use, and spend money foolishly. Many a marriage has been sacrificed to the alcoholic's or addict's "relationship" with his/her substance(s) of choice. The "insanity" of alcoholism and addiction is the alcoholic's or addict's continued use of the substance in the face of worsening consequences.

Patients who manifest all three of these symptoms should be considered candidates for a twelve-step facilitation program, regardless of what other diagnoses may be relevant.

Recovery versus Cure

Alcoholics Anonymous, Narcotics Anonymous, and twelve-step programs modeled on them assume that there is no *cure* for alcoholism or drug addiction. In speaking of recovery from addiction, they emphasize the concepts of "arrest" and "recovery" as opposed to "cure." As the AA and NA Big Books indicate:

> We realize that we are never cured, and that we carry the disease with us for the rest of our lives. We have a disease, but we do recover.[3]

> We have seen the truth demonstrated again and again: "Once an alcoholic, always an alcoholic." Commencing to drink after a period of sobriety, we are in a short time as bad as ever.[4]

The facilitation program described in this book is intended to be consistent with the patient's active involvement in the AA/NA fellowships. These fellowships are based on the assumptions that alcoholism and drug addiction are chronic, progressive illnesses of unknown etiology that affect the body, mind, and spirit; that they are characterized by a person's inability to reliably control his/her use of alcohol and/or drugs; and that the only effective remedy for them is abstinence from the use of all mood-altering substances. This book adheres to the concepts set forth in the Big Book (*Alcoholics Anonymous*[5]) and the "Twelve and Twelve" (*Twelve Steps and Twelve Traditions*[6]).

The AA fellowship of peers that evolved from the early work of Bill Wilson and others is based not on any motion of cure, but on the idea that one's addiction can be arrested through the help of one's fellow addicts. The twelve steps of AA are therefore not a treatment program but a suggested pathway for ongoing *recovery*. The essence of this recovery pathway is a changed lifestyle (habits and attitudes) and a gradual spiritual renewal.

In the AA/NA view, once a person is addicted, s/he is always addicted; sustaining sobriety therefore requires constant vigilance. The goal is for the recovering alcoholic or addict to become actively involved in a program that will help him/her avoid taking the first drink or drug dose that will re-ignite his/her compulsion to drink or use without limit. Twelve-step fellowships such as AA and NA provide vehicles for such vigilance.

Since cure is impossible, the best the alcoholic or addict can hope for is daily sobriety. Recovery is therefore undertaken "one day at a time," and the recovering alcoholic or addict is justifiably grateful for each day of sobriety. Recovery is experienced anew every day. Its enemies are complacency and forgetfulness. Relapse occurs well before the first drink is taken or the first drug is used. Relapse begins when ongoing, active recovery stops. It begins when alcoholics and addicts feel "safe" enough to stop going to meetings. It begins when they stop remembering the harm they did to others and to themselves as a consequence of their addiction; when they start to forget what it was like to lose their jobs and their friends, to ruin their relationships and their health, and to feel hopelessness and self-hatred.

Recovery can be considered a spiritual journey inasmuch as recovering alcoholics and addicts progressively change not only their habits but their values and attitudes. As recovery progresses, their isolation gives way to involvement, their alienation to faith, and their arrogance and grandiosity to humility and gratitude. Most (though not all) recovering persons eventually come to believe in some "Higher Power" to whom they can pray, look for guidance, and turn over their conscious wills. The twelve steps are a guide to the spiritual journey that is recovery.

The AA/NA Way

Rarely have we seen a person fail who has thoroughly followed our path.[7]

The overall goal of this program is to facilitate patients' active participation in the AA/NA fellowships. It regards active involvement—"working the program"—as the primary factor responsible for sustained sobriety; therefore, involvement in AA and/or NA is the desired outcome of this facilitation program.

According to the AA/NA view, alcoholism and addiction are chronic progressive illnesses that, if not arrested, may lead to insanity or death. Addiction is characterized by a loss of one's ability to control (limit) one's use of one or more mood-altering substances. AA puts it this way:

We alcoholics are men and women who have lost the ability to control our drinking. We know that no real alcoholic ever recovers control.[8]

The NA view of drug addiction parallels the AA view of alcoholism.

> As addicts, we have an incurable disease called addiction. The disease is chronic, progressive and fatal.[9]

Like all chronic illnesses, alcoholism and addiction have specific and predictable effects (symptoms) on individuals and a predictable course. In addition to their physical effects, alcoholism and addiction affect their victims on the cognitive, emotional, social, and spiritual levels as well. Addiction is a story of a steady decline in overall functioning, to the point of "bottoming out":

> We reached a point in our lives where we felt like a lost cause. We had little worth to family, friends or on the job. Many of us were unemployed and unemployable. Any form of success was frightening and unfamiliar. We didn't know what to do. As the feeling of self-loathing grew, we needed to use more and more to mask our feelings. We were sick and tired of pain and trouble. We were frightened and ran from the fear. No matter how far we ran, we always carried fear with us. We were hopeless, useless, and lost. Failure had become our way of life and self-esteem was non-existent. Perhaps the most painful feeling of all was the desperation.[10]

One important AA/NA tradition is that alcoholics and addicts share in meetings their personal stories of decline through addiction. The purpose of their "speaking" or "story-telling" at meetings is not to boast about their drunken exploits or to garner sympathy. The purpose, rather, is for everyone to be reminded of their own experience of decline, so that complacency and forgetfulness do not have a chance to set in: to help old-timers remember the way life was for them before their own recovery; and to help newcomers identify with AA or NA. Only first names are used at meetings (some of which are open to non-alcoholics and non-addicts). The process of mutual sharing is governed by certain procedural traditions. For example, it's customary not to interrupt or question a speaker. After a speaker is finished, the group simply expresses its thanks, after which members are free to share their thoughts and feelings based on their own experiences. A member may relate to the group that a speaker's talk reminded him/her of the way addiction had affected his/her own family life.

Alcoholism and addiction are also characterized by the phenomenon of "denial," or resistance to accepting the essence of addiction—the failure of one's own willpower and the loss of one's personal control.

> Most of us have been unwilling to admit we were real alcoholics. No person likes to think he is bodily and mentally different from his fellows. Therefore, it is not surprising that our drinking careers have been characterized by countless vain attempts to prove we could drink like other people.

Who cares to admit complete defeat? Practically no one, of course. Every natural instinct cries out against the idea of personal powerlessness. It is truly awful to admit that, glass in hand, we have warped our minds into such an obsession for destructive thinking that only an act of Providence can remove it from us.

Denial of our addiction kept us sick, but our honest admission of addiction enabled us to stop using.[11]

AA and NA make no commitment to a particular etiological model of addiction. Rather, they limit their conceptual schema to two related descriptive concepts: loss of control and denial. Addiction consists of alcoholics' and addicts' inability to reliably stop drinking or using once they have started, and by their unwillingness to accept that reality.

Once he takes any alcohol whatever into his system, something happens, both in the bodily and mental sense, which makes it virtually impossible for (the alcoholic) to stop.

We tried limiting our usage to social amounts without success. There is no such thing as a social addict.[12]

Spirituality and Pragmatism

Historically, AA and the fellowships modeled on it consistently repeat two themes—spirituality and pragmatism—in their programs for recovery.[13] All twelve-step programs share a common commitment to faith in a "Higher Power" as a key to recovery. Members are encouraged to conceptualize this Higher Power in any way they choose, as long as it represents a power greater than their own willpower, which is regarded as insufficient to conquer addiction. The Higher Power thus represents something other than willpower, in which members may place their hope and faith, for the ability to stay sober.

Twelve-step programs present recovery from alcoholism and addiction as a process of spiritual renewal, part of which involves a "surrender" to this Higher Power.

It is when we try to make our own will conform with God's that we begin to use it rightly. . . . Our whole trouble had been the misuse of willpower. We had tried to bombard our problems with it instead of attempting to bring it into agreement with God's intention for us.

The great fact is just this, and nothing less: That we have had deep and effective spiritual experiences which have revolutionized our whole attitude toward life, toward our fellows and toward God's universe. The central fact of our lives today is the absolute certainty that our Creator has entered into our hearts and lives in a way which is indeed miraculous. He has commenced to accomplish those things for us which we could never do by ourselves.

My Higher Power, at first, was the N.A. Fellowship. It represented goodness and caring, and I trusted those recovering addicts. But eventually, the time came when I was alone, in the middle of the day with no meeting, and I wanted to use. I saw that I needed a Higher Power that would be with me twenty-four hours a day, just as my addiction is with me twenty-four hours a day. I began to pray. . . .

You can, if you wish, make A.A. itself your "higher power." Here's a very large group of people who have solved their alcohol problem. In this respect they are certainly a power greater than you. . . . Surely you can have faith in them.[14]

Despite their strong spiritual base, however, twelve-step programs are remarkable for their lack of religious dogma. Although they promote spirituality, AA and NA are not religious organizations; rather, they are fellowships or societies of peers who are connected by their common addiction and guided by common traditions, not by religious credos. Moreover, as spiritual as AA and its sister programs are, they are marked by a striking pragmatism: an absence of religious dogma and a tolerance for doing pretty much "whatever works" for a given individual in order to avoid taking the first drink that will trigger loss of control. AA is a program of pragmatism and action as much as it is one of faith and meditation.

Here, we tell only some methods we have used for living without drinking. You are welcome to all of them, whether you are interested in Alcoholics Anonymous or not.

Our drinking was connected with many habits—big and little. Some of them were thinking habits, or things we felt inside ourselves. Others were doing habits—things we did, actions we took.

In getting used to not drinking, we have found that we needed new habits to take the place of those old ones.

"Easy Does It"—but do it![15]

A Democratic Tradition

The counselor wishing to conduct a twelve-step facilitation program must be aware of and respect the diversity of twelve-step fellowships. Today it is easy to find AA/NA groups specifically for women, for men, for gays and lesbians, for young people, for older people, for clergy, and for professionals. There are twelve-step groups for any number of cultural and ethnic groups and religious denominations, from Native Americans to Hispanics to Asians. Though all share a common view of alcoholism, addiction, and recovery as stated in the official literature, the meetings that these groups organize and run necessarily vary greatly in character.

What accounts for the pluralism that is a hallmark of the twelve-step movement? In part, the adaptability of AA and other twelve-step programs may come from their strongly democratic foundation, the basis for which is embodied in the twelve traditions. Consider, for example, tradition three:

> The only requirement for AA membership is a desire to stop drinking. You are an AA member if you say so. You can declare yourself in; nobody can keep you out.[16]

This tradition sets the stage for virtually anyone to feel welcome within the fellowship on the basis of a common problem. It invites people with alcohol and drug problems to see beyond their differences, while at the same time respecting those differences.[17]

Furthermore, AA manifests a clear and distinct dislike for personal power, embracing instead a strong preference for simple democracy. Consider the following comment:

> In the world about us we saw personalities destroying whole peoples. The struggle for wealth, power, and prestige was tearing humanity apart as never before.[18]

The AA response to unbridled ambition and radical individualism was to create a fellowship based on anonymity, governed by simple democratic principles that emphasize respect for the individual, humility, and avoidance of the accumulation of personal power. This is reflected in the way that AA groups are expected to begin:

> Being the founder [of a new AA group], he is at first the boss. Who else could be? Very soon, though, his assumed authority to run everything begins to be shared with the first alcoholics he has helped. At this moment, the benign dictator becomes the chairman of a committee composed of his friends. These are the growing group's hierarchy of service—self-appointed, of course, because there is no other way.
>
> Now [after the group has existed for a while] comes the election. If the founder and his friends have served well, they may—to their surprise— be reinstated for a time. If, however, they have heavily resisted the rising tide of democracy, they may be summarily beached. In either case, the group now has a so-called rotating committee, very sharply limited in its authority. In no sense whatever can its members govern or direct the group. They are servants.[19]

AA/NA traditions specifically eschew organizational control beyond the most democratic level of the individual group:

> Any two or three alcoholics gathered together for sobriety may call themselves an AA group provided that as a group they have no other affiliation.

> Each AA group [is] an individual entity, strictly reliant on its own conscience as a guide to action.[20]

These traditions are supported by another tradition that holds that each AA/NA meeting should be essentially autonomous and financially self-supporting.[21] No approval is needed from any centralized organization in order to start an AA/NA meeting; nor are meetings monitored or centrally controlled in any way.

> Our society has no president having authority to govern it, no treasurer who can compel the payment of any dues, no board of directors who can cast an erring member into outer darkness.[22]

With these sorts of traditions to guide them, is it surprising that twelve-step programs have adapted well—indeed proliferated—in an era characterized by the emergence of gender, sexual, and cultural consciousness?

Within this democratic framework, the agenda for a twelve-step meeting can be virtually whatever the group decides it should be, provided the focus is on staying sober. Some meetings are "speaker" meetings, in which members take turns telling their stories. Other meetings are "speaker-discussion" meetings, where the telling of a personal story is followed by a discussion of some significant theme. Some meetings limit their agendas to discussing certain steps; others focus on a particular book. Some groups emphasize spirituality and prayer, while others prefer to focus on men's or women's issues in recovery. Many cultural groups have adapted the AA concept of a Higher Power to suit their own religious beliefs and traditions.

The traditions at the foundation of AA/NA fellowships have fostered a richness and diversity that have made the twelve-step model accessible to a truly remarkable range of cultural groups. "Twelve Steppers" are connected not only by their common view of addiction as an illness marked by loss of control and hopelessness—for which the only hope is to be found in cooperative effort and mutual support—but by their traditions of democracy and pluralism.

> I'll always be grateful to N.A. for taking me from the depths of my addiction and giving me life. A life that is full of love and true concern for others. These are feelings that I never thought could be possible for me. As long as I take it easy and make a commitment with my Higher Power to do the best I can, I know I will be taken care of today. I've come to believe in miracles for I am one.
>
> —"An Indian Without a Tribe," *Narcotics Anonymous*

2. Twelve-Step Facilitation and Other Modalities

Much has transpired since the initial publication of *The Twelve-Step Facilitation Handbook* in 1992. A steadily expanding body of research continues to build a bedrock of empirical support for Twelve-Step Facilitation (TSF) as an effective treatment for people with substance abuse disorders. At the same time, strong interest has emerged among clinicians in correlating different treatment modalities, including TSF, with the trans-theoretical model of change developed by Prochaska and DiClemente.[23] The major finding of Project MATCH, that twelve-step, motivational, and cognitive-behavioral approaches can all be effective treatments[24], has also stimulated interest in how these approaches can be integrated to form a holistic treatment model. In this introduction to the second edition of the Handbook, I will explore each of these areas of interest.

TSF, Stages of Change, and Motivational Enhancement

In the stages-of-change approach to treating substance abuse, motivation for change is defined in terms of a client's readiness to change.[25] According to this model, there are five stages in the change process. An important implication for treatment planning is that a counselor using this model needs to accurately assess a client's relative position along this continuum of five stages to determine those interventions that are most appropriate to utilize.

A person at the first stage of change, *pre-contemplation*, does not believe a problem exists, and therefore probably doesn't not intend and is not likely to be motivated to change. Assuming that the counselor perceives a problem and the need for change, the appropriate intervention for the pre-contemplator according to the motivational enhancement (versus confrontational models) is to provide information. An example would be to point out some obvious consequences of abusing alcohol or other drugs.

A person at the second stage of the change process, *contemplation*, has moved from unawareness, or denial, of having a problem, to a state of ambivalence about the problem and the need for change. At this stage the counselor may use motivational interviewing techniques to engage the client in a two-sided dialogue about the relative merits of changing versus not changing. For substance abusing clients, that might entail a dialogue about what has happened as a direct result of their drinking and other drug use and what is likely to happen if they continue, versus cutting down or stopping altogether.

From *contemplation* the change process moves to the *decision* (sometimes referred to as *determination*) stage which, as the name implies, is the point at which a decision to change is made. Two therapeutic goals at this stage are, (1) to strengthen the client's determination and self-confidence, and, (2) to help the client to choose a course of action that is likely to succeed.

In the *action* stage, whatever plan the client has decided on is implemented. Often this plan (for example, "cutting back" on drinking) will not match the counselor's goals. However, when working with clients who are at this stage of change, it is important for the counselor to reinforce *any* effort to change, as well as all progress the client makes. Alternative plans may be suggested by the counselor, but under the motivational enhancement model, the client must experience any revised plan of action as the product of a collaborative relationship with the therapist if motivation is to be maintained.

Once change has been initiated, it needs to be maintained, which takes us to the *maintenance* stage. When working with clients who are in the maintenance stage, the counselor's goals are to counsel on relapse prevention strategies and to continue to reinforce any positive consequences associated with changes that have been made.

As originally conceived, TSF was divided into three components: (1) a core program, which covers assessment, acceptance, surrender, and getting active in AA and NA; (2) an elective program, which includes genograms; enabling; people, places, and routines; emotions; moral inventories; and relationships; and (3) a conjoint program, which covers enabling and detaching. TSF also includes guidelines for conducting a structured termination session. The intent was to devise an intervention that allowed for flexibility in implementation. Counselors could develop individualized treatment plans by tailoring TSF to the individual client's level of substance abuse and the extent to which they had already made some progress toward recovery. For example, a counselor working with someone who has just come out of out of a treatment program who expresses acceptance of his or her alcoholism, and who is abstaining from drinking and attending AA meetings regularly, could be expected to devise a treatment plan that touches on the core topics and reinforces them, but which then moves on to one or more topics in the elective program. Conversely, when confronted with actively drinking clients who express the belief that it is just "bad luck" that they have been mandated into treatment, the treatment plan would no doubt be anchored in the core program.

Clinical experience in Project MATCH and subsequent clinical trials that utilized TSF suggest that the topic in the elective program that is most often incorporated into a treatment plan that emphasizes core topics is the one dealing with *People, Places, and Routines.* Also, for the majority of clients seeking treatment, the one recovery task that must be emphasized repeatedly is for the client to attend one or more Twelve-Step support group meetings between therapy sessions.

Table 1 provides some guidelines for clinicians who are interested in devising TSF treatment plans that are coordinated with the stages-of-change model. The quotations cited under each stage of change are taken from the book *Alcoholics Anonymous*, or the "Big Book," which is the text book for the fellowship Alcoholics Anonymous and is also used as a core text in TSF. The suggested interventions associated with each stage are taken from the core, elective, and conjoint programs of TSF.

TABLE 1
TSF and Treatment Planning
Stages of Change Considerations

Stage of Change	Recommended TSF Interventions
PRECONTEMPLATION "He is positive he can handle his liquor, that it does him no harm. He would probably be insulted if he were called an alcoholic" (p.109)	ASSESSMENT: Alcohol/Drug History Inventory of Consequences GENOGRAMS
CONTEMPLATION "He is remorseful after serious drinking bouts and he tells you he wants to stop. But when he gets over the spree, he begins to think once more how he can drink moderately next time." (p.109)	ASSESSMENT: Tolerance Loss Of Control ENABLING (Elective & Conjoint Programs)
PREPARATION "We admitted we were powerless over alcohol that our lives had become unmanageable." (Step One)	ACCEPTANCE PEOPLE, PLACES, ROUTINES EMOTIONS DETACHING (Conjoint Program)
ACTION "Came to believe that a Power greater than ourselves could restore us to sanity." (Step Two) "Made a decision to turn our will and our lives over to the care of God *as we understood him*." (Step Three)	SURRENDER GETTING ACTIVE IN AA/NA Meetings Telephone Therapy
MAINTENANCE "Having had a spiritual awakening as the result of these steps, we tried to carry this message to alcoholics, and to practice these principles in all our affairs." (Step Twelve)	MORAL INVENTORIES RELATIONSHIPS GETTING ACTIVE: Sponsor Service Work

The stages-of-change model can be useful in guiding and supporting counselors in both designing and persisting with their treatment plans. For example, the appropriate level of intervention for a client who is stuck at the pre-contemplation stage is basically an ongoing assessment, which involves a collaborative effort to monitor consequences of use, and to encourage AA or NA attendance. If counselors become frustrated with a lack of progress and attempt to move ahead too quickly, they are likely to provoke more resistance than cooperation. Or, the client may attempt to placate the therapist by temporarily complying with recommendations. A better strategy is to persist in the assessment process and engage the client in an ongoing monitoring of use and its consequences. The therapist can also continue to suggest that the client attend AA or NA, perhaps with a goal of simply listening. Then, when (and if) the counselor senses that the client is ready to contemplate change, treatment can proceed to the next level of TSF topics, and so on. This approach can help to reassure counselors who may feel that they should be moving faster or making more progress with a resistant client. In such instances resistance is redefined in terms of readiness for change, which in turn guides the appropriate TSF intervention.

TSF and the Different Dimensions of Change

Recovery from substance dependence can also be conceptualized as a process of change that can move forward within each of several different dimensions of a person's life. There can, for instance, be social/behavioral, cognitive, and spiritual correlates of change and recovery. This type of recovery model can be a useful tool for counselors using TSF. It is based on the assumption that different clients may make changes at different paces in each of the different dimensions. Seen from this perspective, comprehensive treatment incorporates goals and strategies drawn from cognitive-behavioral therapy as well as TSF and motivational enhancement therapy.

Table 2 presents a schematic for how recovery can be conceptualized in terms of domains of change and recovery.

TABLE 2
TSF and the Process of Change
Dimensions of Recovery

Dimension	Core Process	Key Concept	Markers
SOCIAL/ BEHAVIORAL	Bonding	Getting Active	Active Participation Peer Group Shift
COGNITIVE	Acceptance	Denial	Steps 1 and 2
SPIRITUAL	Spiritual Awakening	Surrender	Steps 3-12

Rather than representing a template for treatment planning, the above can be used as a guide by counselors who wish to monitor their therapeutic efforts and the progress of their clients' recovery. One could hypothesize that a recovery that is based on significant changes in all three dimensions would be more robust than one that relies primarily on changes in only one. However, this hypothesis remains to be empirically tested. In the meantime, counselors using TSF might pause at times in the treatment process to reflect on whether their intervention is overly weighted in one dimension and the extent to which the topics they choose to address, and the recovery tasks they assign, reflect some degree of balance across the three dimensions of change. By working to promote change in each of the three dimensions, they may be able to facilitate a more robust recovery.

Social/Behavioral Dimension of Recovery

The goal of the counselor's interventions in the cognitive dimension is to facilitate the client's bonding to a twelve-step fellowship. Markers for change include progressive participation in a fellowship, along with a shift in one's primary social network away from those who use or support the use of alcohol or other drugs, and toward a group that supports sobriety. It should be noted that while TSF is a treatment program, AA and NA are not treatment programs. Rather, from their inception, their primary therapeutic function has been relapse prevention. AA and NA exist, first and foremost, to offer group support and practical guidance (e.g. Big Book study, sponsors, and step work) that provide two fundamental recovery skills: how to avoid drinking or using drugs, and what to do next if you have a slip. Changing behavior patterns and establishing ties to others who share the same goals have always been the main roles that AA and NA have played in the lives of recovering people.

Through the process of assigning recovery tasks, the counselor promotes change in the social/behavioral dimension using a shaping approach. Change in this dimension can begin simply by getting the client to attend meetings, and may gradually progress to deeper levels of involvement and bonding, including speaking at meetings, getting a sponsor, volunteering for service work, and socializing before and/or after meetings.

Cognitive Dimension of Recovery

Recovery can not only be measured in terms of changes in behavior and one's social network, it can also be measured in terms of changes in one's thinking. The first and second steps of AA and NA challenge alcoholics and addicts to change their thinking about the role that alcohol or other drugs have played in their lives. This change process can be thought of in terms of movement from *denial* toward *acceptance*. TSF provides the counselor with guidelines for how to approach denial, how to discuss the complex issue of powerlessness, and how to promote hope and positive expectations for change. These are the cognitive changes that form the basis for the first two steps of AA, and which in turn set the stage for motivation and behavioral change. In this regard, some have argued that behavioral change that is made in the absence of cognitive change may reflect mere compliance[26] as opposed to change that is driven by true acceptance and belief.

Spiritual Dimension of Recovery

Although the primary focus of twelve-step support groups is relapse prevention, the founders of AA believed that alcoholism is a spiritual as well as a physical illness and they were keenly interested in healing the spiritual wounds caused by addiction. Accordingly, steps 3 through 12 of AA and NA could accurately be described as a blueprint for personal insight, growth, and healing—which the AA founders believed went hand and hand with having a spiritual awakening. TSF does not provide guidelines for helping clients explore all 12 Steps. It does, however, provide guidelines for exploring such spiritual concepts as a higher power and dealing with the guilt and shame that usually hinders a client's healthy understanding of that concept. To that end, TSF also includes guidelines for beginning the process of conducting a personal moral inventory (Steps 4 and 5), and making amends, when appropriate, for harm done to others as a result of alcohol or other drug use (Steps 8 and 9).

AA and NA, through their literature and the oral traditions and lore passed on through the groups, are rich in advice that can help to transform a life of hopelessness and moral compromise into one that is built on self-respect and honesty.

Another core AA text, *Twelve Steps and Twelve Traditions*, sums up well this idea of a spiritual awakening and demonstrates the hope that is so necessary to motivate clients to go through the hard work that is required in working a twelve-step program of recovery.

> When a man or a woman has a spiritual awakening, the most important meaning of it is that he has now become able to do, feel, and believe that which he could not do before on his unaided strength and resources alone. He has been granted a gift which amounts to a new state of consciousness and being. He has been set on a path which tells him he is really going somewhere, that life is not a dead end, not something to be endured or mastered. In a very real sense he has been transformed, because he has laid hold of a source of strength which he had hitherto denied himself. He finds himself in possession of a degree of honesty, tolerance, unselfishness, peace of mind, and love of which he had thought himself quite incapable of.[27]

The Dimensions of Change and MET

The dimensions of change model can be useful to clinicians who wish to incorporate the techniques of Motivational Enhancement Therapy (MET).[28] One of the prime tenets of MET is that change is more likely to occur if counselors take pains to avoid evoking resistance, for example by pressuring clients to embrace ideas they are not ready to entertain (such as, powerlessness over alcohol), or do things they are not ready to do (such as, get a sponsor). Instead of pressuring clients in any way, MET recommends "rolling" with resistance, which is to say avoiding excessive confrontation, pressure, or arguing.

By using the dimensions of change model, counselors can roll with resistance first by *recognizing it* and, second, by *shifting the focus* of a therapy session to a different dimension. For example, when a client shows a distinct reticence to discuss anything to do with spirituality, the treatment focus could shift to either the cognitive or the social/behavioral dimension. Conversely, a client who steadfastly resists the idea that she or he is powerless over alcohol (cognitive dimension) could be encouraged to attend and talk about AA meetings (social/behavioral dimension), or engaged in a discussion of whether she or he believes that people are capable of experiencing epiphanies that change their view of themselves and the course of their lives (spiritual dimension).

Alcoholics Anonymous did not evolve out of a coherent theoretical model of change. Rather, it is a fellowship that evolved out of a search for "what works." This includes its fundamental belief that abstinence is the only sane goal for someone who has lost control of their alcohol or other drug use. As such, we cannot expect AA or other twelve-step programs to conform to any particular model of change or therapy. On the other hand, one can readily see how many different models of treatment can be applied to achieve the goal of facilitating involvement in a twelve-step fellowship, which as we shall see below, greatly improves the prognosis for recovery.

Empirical Support for TSF and the Minnesota Model

Studies of AA participation have found that active involvement in twelve-step fellowships is associated with recovery from alcohol abuse[29][30][31]. TSF, which is informed by and consistent with what is more generally known as the Minnesota Model of substance abuse treatment,[32][33] as typified by the treatment program at one of its early developers, the Hazelden Foundation, was found in Project MATCH to result in significant and sustained reductions in drinking.[34] As compared to the cognitive-behavioral and motivational enhancement treatment models, TSF was more effective among subjects who measured lower in overall psychopathology, whereas there were no differences in outcome across treatments for those subjects who did score positively for psychopathology.[35] No gender or cultural differences in treatment effectiveness were found in Project MATCH, and subsequent research has confirmed that women and ethnic minorities are just as likely to attend twelve-step meetings—a defining feature of TSF when comparing the three modalities—as Caucasian males.[36]

A three-year follow up of subjects treated in Project MATCH found TSF to be significantly more effective than MET among patients whose social environments tended to support drinking.[37] These findings are consistent with one of the major goals of TSF, which is to alter drinkers' lifestyles, including their social environments. Similarly, research has supported the idea that cognitive changes, such as the notion that controlled drinking is not possible for the alcoholic, and that recovery requires a life-long commitment to a twelve-step program, are associated with twelve-step meeting attendance and recovery.[38]

Some studies, including ongoing outcome studies carried out by Hazelden dating back to 1973, have demonstrated the effectiveness of Hazelden's treatment program, which shares much in common with TSF. Based on the key measure of relapse rates alone, Hazelden compares positively across the board with outcomes found in meta-studies of the research literature.[39]

In Project MATCH the effectiveness of TSF was not mediated by drinking severity, suggesting TSF may be applied to mild and moderate drinkers, as well as those traditionally thought of as alcoholics. In addition, several of the studies on the effectiveness of the Minnesota Model report reduced drinking or drug use as an outcome for a significant portion of the treated populations. However, although it would appear that patients need not necessarily be dependent on alcohol in order to benefit from TSF, and that outcomes for the Minnesota Model range from reduced use to abstinence, AA and NA advocate abstinence, as opposed to controlled use of alcohol or drugs, as the desired long-term goal for those people whose drinking experience is marked by a series of failures to effectively moderate use.

This brief summary of research lends strong support for the effectiveness of TSF and compatible Twelve-Step oriented interventions. It should be noted, though, that TSF, as well as the treatment program offered at Hazelden, are well-developed, structured approaches, with specific goals and objectives. They also offer clear guidelines for conducting the therapeutic relationship. Other treatment programs may claim to be twelve-step based; however, to the extent that these programs diverge from TSF, it cannot be guaranteed that they will yield results similar to those reported above.

At this point new research using the Twelve-Step Facilitation model appears regularly. For the most recent studies, the reader interested in empirical data is referred to www.projectcork.org on the Internet.

Part I
Overview of the Facilitation Program

Goals and Objectives

Goals

This facilitation program has two primary goals (which generally relate to the first three steps of Alcoholics Anonymous). They are "acceptance" and "surrender." These steps, we believe, form the basis for early recovery from alcoholism and addiction.

Acceptance

By acceptance, we mean the breakdown of the illusion that the individual, through willpower alone, can effectively and reliably limit or control his/her use of alcohol and/or drugs. Acceptance takes several forms in twelve-step programs:

- acceptance by the patient that s/he suffers from a chronic and progressive illness characterized by compulsive use of alcohol and/or drugs;
- acceptance by the patient that his/her life is (or is becoming) unmanageable as a result of alcohol or drugs;
- acceptance by the patient that s/he has lost the ability to effectively control his/her drinking or using through willpower alone; and
- acceptance by the patient that since there is no effective way to reliably control his/her use, the only viable alternative is complete abstinence from the use of alcohol and drugs.

Surrender

Surrender involves a willingness to reach out beyond oneself and to follow the program laid out in the twelve steps. Surrender includes acknowledgement by the patient:

- that there is hope for recovery—sustained sobriety—only through admitting the reality of his/her loss of control;

3

- that recovery requires having faith that some Higher Power can help him/her when willpower has been defeated by alcoholism or addiction;
- that fellowships of fellow addicts, such as AA and NA, have helped millions of alcoholics and addicts to sustain their sobriety; and
- that his/her best chances for success are to live the twelve steps and become actively involved in a twelve-step fellowship.

Objectives

These two major program goals are reflected in a series of specific objectives, which are congruent with the AA/NA view of alcoholism and addiction. These specific objectives of recovery are:

Cognitive Objectives

- Patients need to understand some of the ways in which their thinking has been affected by alcoholism and addiction. For example, drinking and using often lead to rationalizing and lying, to one self as much as to others.
- Patients need to understand how their thinking may reflect denial (or "stinking thinking") and how their own rationalizations can contribute to continued drinking or using despite negative consequences. For example, many an alcoholic attributes DWI (driving while intoxicated) arrests to "bad luck"—or bad tires!
- Patients need to see the connection between their substance abuse and the negative consequences that result from it. These consequences may be physical, social, legal, psychological, financial, and spiritual. Many alcoholics and addicts are inclined to resist making causal attributions concerning their drinking or using. For instance, a self-employed cocaine addict may attribute his business failure to a bad economy, unfair competition, or bad employees rather than to his own cocaine-induced mismanagement.

Emotional Objectives

- Patients need to understand the AA/NA view of emotions and how certain emotional states (like anger, resentment, loneliness, and shame) can lead to drinking or using.
- Patients need to be informed about some of the practical ways that AA and NA suggest for dealing with emotions so as to minimize the risks of drinking and using.

Relationship Objectives

- Patients need to understand that alcoholism and addiction constitute "relationships" with mood-altering substances that eventually take precedence over relationships with people, such as friendships, family ties, and intimacies.
- Patients need to see that they systematically encourage the significant others in their lives to "enable" their own alcohol or drug use by helping them obtain alcohol or drugs, and/or by helping them avoid or minimize the negative consequences of their drinking or using.

Behavioral Objectives

- Patients need to understand how their powerful and cunning illness has affected their whole lives, and how many of their existing or old habits support their continued drinking or using.
- Patients need to turn to the fellowship of AA or NA and make use of the resources of those fellowships in order to change their addictive habits.
- Patients need to get active in AA or NA as a means of sustaining their sobriety.

Social Objectives

- Patients need to attend and participate regularly in AA/NA meetings of various kinds, as well as in AA/NA-sponsored social activities.
- Patients need to obtain and develop a relationship with an AA sponsor.
- Patients need to access AA or NA whenever they experience the urge to drink or use, or have had a "slip" (relapse), no matter how minor.
- Patients need to reevaluate their relationships with their "enablers" and with fellow alcoholics and addicts.

Spiritual Objectives

- Patients need to experience hope that they can arrest their alcoholism or addiction.
- Patients need to develop a belief and trust in a power greater than their own willpower.

- Patients need to acknowledge their own character defects, including specific immoral or unethical acts they have committed, and to recognize that they have done harm to others as a result of their alcoholism or addiction.
- Patients need to begin to heal their shame and guilt through sharing their moral inventory with another trusted person.

Program Overview

Organization and Structure

The facilitation program is organized into a core program, an elective program, and a conjoint program. It concludes with a termination session.

- *Core Program.* The core program consists of sessions devoted to four core topics. These are: assessment, acceptance, surrender, and getting active in AA or NA. The core topics should be covered in depth for all patients. In other words, they should be given priority in the therapeutic agenda. The facilitator may need to keep coming back to them, or spend more than a single session on one or more of them, as needed.
- *Elective Program.* This part of the program consists of six elective topics: genograms, enabling, people-places-routines, emotions, moral inventories, and relationships. The elective component of the program is designed to be more flexible, to permit the development of treatment plans that are "tailored" to the individual patient. Depending on an ongoing assessment of progress in the core areas, any of these elective topics may be covered. In addition, the facilitator should feel free to "split" sessions so as to cover both a core and an elective topic in the same session.
- *Conjoint Program.* The goal of the conjoint sessions is to educate the patient's partner about alcoholism or addiction; to introduce the twelve-step model and the concept of enabling; and to encourage the partner to make a commitment to attend six Al-Anon/Nar-Anon meetings of his/her choice. The goal is not to resolve long-standing relationship conflicts, improve communication, overcome sexual dysfunction, or teach conflict-management skills. These are appropriate goals for relationship counseling, not for twelve-step recovery programs.

We recommend that relationship counseling be postponed, however, if possible, until the patient has completed the facilitation program and the partner has attended several Al-Anon/Nar-Anon meetings. This is not to say that relationship concerns should be minimized or ignored by the twelve-step facilitator. On the contrary, the facilitator should clearly validate these concerns. Patients and their partners can be encouraged to prioritize their goals, but early recovery should be the first. The facilitator can assure the couple that an appropriate referral will be made once this initial goal is reached. As a rule of thumb, the facilitator may suggest that relationship counseling will be most useful once the patient has had three to six months of sobriety and is involved in a twelve-step program on some ongoing basis.

• *Termination.* The closing of the facilitation program is an important event. It involves assessments by both the patient and the facilitator, as well as the setting of future goals.

Duration of the Program

The facilitation program is intended to be used in a series of hour-long meetings over a brief period of time. As a guideline, we recommend the following treatment schedule:

- twelve to fifteen individual sessions with the patient, if s/he is single; or
- twelve to fifteen individual sessions, plus two to three conjoint sessions with the patient's partner, if s/he is in a relationship.

We recommend that the sessions be held weekly and that canceled sessions be rescheduled for the same week, if possible. This allows the facilitation program to maintain a degree of momentum. There is some danger of losing this momentum if the patient or the facilitator stretches out the program over an extended period. This is particularly true if twelve-step facilitation itself is the primary treatment. On the other hand, if the facilitation program is being integrated into a larger treatment plan, there is no reason why it cannot be extended over a somewhat longer period, as long as the continuity of the facilitation is maintained and as long as the facilitator continues to set and monitor meaningful recovery tasks for the patient.

If a patient's progress seems slow, it is to some extent a matter of clinical judgment whether that patient's progress is nevertheless meaningful or is negligible. It is also a matter of judgment whether a patient is avoiding dealing with his/her problem by attempting to shift the session agendas to focus on something other than drinking or using. In either case, regardless of how much progress has or has not been made, we do not recommend extending the facilitation program—assuming that twelve-step facilitation (i.e., early recovery) is the primary treatment goal—much beyond fifteen individual sessions. Rather, we recommend that the facilitation program be terminated and that patients be encouraged to "try it on their own" for a period of time thereafter—for example, three to six months. If patients find themselves unable to stay sober or clean after this period of time, and if they express positive interest in further facilitation, they may repeat the program or attend a series of "booster" sessions. If patients are simply unable to stop drinking or using despite their clear motivation to do so, and if they are in immediate danger of continued use, referral to a more structured treatment setting may be required. This has been our experience, for example, in some cases of long-standing alcohol and cocaine abuse and in some cases of addiction to crack cocaine.

Flexibility of the Program

Combining core topics and elective topics allows this program to be highly flexible with respect to planning for individual patients. It can be used with patients who have had no prior exposure to twelve-step programs; with patients who have never undergone treatment of any kind for alcoholism or addiction; and with patients who have had one or more intensive treatment experiences and/or extensive exposure to AA or NA. For patients who have had little or no treatment or prior exposure to twelve-step programs, we expect that the treatment plan would follow the format presented here most closely.

Although there is flexibility in treatment planning, the facilitation program itself is designed to be implemented in a fairly structured manner. For example, each session has a specific agenda. The topic of a session (whether core or elective) should be determined in advance of the session. The topic choice should reflect an assessment of the patient's progress and the facilitator's estimation of what would be most relevant at the time. It should not be determined spontaneously at the beginning of a session. Nor should the facilitator allow a session to meander from topic to topic. Each session should follow the format described in this book, beginning with a review of the previous week's experiences, proceeding to a presentation of new material, and ending with the assignment of recovery tasks. The patient should be asked to keep a personal journal throughout the duration of the treatment. Finally, the facilitator should be prepared to suggest specific readings drawn from official AA or NA literature. Each chapter contains a section called "Facilitator Notes" that discusses problems and issues that may arise in the session on a given topic.

Central to this program is that the facilitator should strongly encourage the patient to attend several AA/NA meetings each week. The goal is to get the patient to attend ninety meetings within ninety days. Patients should be encouraged to experiment with a variety of kinds of meetings ("step" meetings, "speaker" meetings, men's or women's meetings) and to eventually settle on a "home" meeting to which they make a commitment. Patients are also encouraged to read the Big Book (*Alcoholics Anonymous*) and/or the NA Big Book (*Narcotics Anonymous*), as well as other AA publications such as *Living Sober* and *Twelve Steps and Twelve Traditions*, during the course of the program.

The Journal

We strongly advise that patients maintain a personal journal during the program. It should be used to record the following:

- all AA/NA meetings the patient attended (include the date, time, and type of meetings)
- the patient's personal reactions to and thoughts about the meetings
- the patient's reactions to the suggested readings
- "slips" (occasions when the patient has taken a drink or used a drug) and what s/he did about it—that is, what "action" was taken
- the patient's reactions to recovery tasks
- the patient's cravings or urges to drink or use, and what s/he did about them—what action was taken

The journal should be reviewed by the facilitator in the review at the start of each session.

Emergencies

When working with patients who are actively drinking or using, or whose sobriety is compromised by slips (relapses), it is not uncommon for a facilitator to be confronted by various emergency situations or to be contacted by a patient or a family member as a result of a crisis. Typical examples of such crises include the patient:

- getting drunk or high;
- getting arrested for driving while intoxicated;
- having a family dispute as a result of drinking or using;
- experiencing sudden, intense urges to drink or use;
- feeling depressed about being an alcoholic or addict, or about having a slip;
- getting into trouble on the job as a consequence of drinking; and

- needing medical detoxification as a consequence of a binge or an overdose.

Patients with emergencies of a psychiatric nature (such as suicidal thinking, acute psychosis, violence, or self-injury) may require an emergency evaluative session, either with the facilitator or at an emergency mental health service or hospital emergency room. Intervention by the latter may be necessary. Such patients' continued involvement in the facilitation program should be reviewed after the crisis has passed. In general, medical detoxification is not grounds for termination, as long as the patient is willing to continue with the program. A decision to admit a patient to an inpatient treatment program, on the other hand, has obvious implications for continuing an outpatient twelve-step facilitation. Nor should psychiatric emergencies lead to termination of the facilitation program unless they are so severe that hospitalization is required. These ground rules are consistent with the third AA tradition that "the only requirement for A. A. membership is a desire to stop drinking."[1]

As a general rule, family and relationship issues that are presented as crises are best deferred until the patient is no longer actively drinking or using ("First Things First"). The facilitator may need to take some time, however, to evaluate a crisis before making that recommendation. Spouse abuse and child abuse are crises that require immediate action. In other family or relationship issues, family members and partners should be encouraged to avail themselves of the resources of twelve-step programs such as Al-Anon and Nar-Anon until the patient has achieved some stable sobriety, prior to undertaking marital or family therapy.

Session Format

What follows is an overview of the intended "flow" of a typical facilitation session in this program.

First Session: Introduction and Assessment

In the first session the facilitator introduces the program and provides an overview of it (including its goal of active involvement in AA or NA); helps the patient to evaluate his/her level of alcohol and/or drug involvement; introduces the AA/NA view of addiction; defines the respective roles and responsibilities of the facilitator and the patient; and attempts to engage the patient's motivation to stay clean and sober. The first session, like the termination session, has a unique format. Also like the termination session, it is intended to be longer (approximately an hour and a half) than the regular facilitation sessions, which should run the standard hour.

Facilitation Sessions: Core and Elective Topics

Over the course of the approximately fifteen facilitation sessions, all four core topics should be covered, plus as many elective topics as can be reasonably covered in that period of time. The facilitator may plan for the elective topics in collaboration with a clinical supervisor, a clinical team, or a colleague. We recommend that the facilitator tentatively select three or four elective topics to pursue after evaluating the patient's progress at around the third or fourth facilitation session.

The format for these sessions is as follows:

Review. Beginning with the second session, each session starts off with the facilitator "checking in" with the patient—briefly reviewing the patient's experiences since the last session, with special emphasis on drinking or using. This opening portion of each session (roughly ten to fifteen minutes) is crucial. During this time it is important for the facilitator to set the agenda for treatment by avoiding protracted discussions of collateral issues (such as work, relationships, and children). The facilitator should keep the focus as much as possible on drinking or using, and on following up on recovery tasks. In addition to the patient's self-report, reading journal entries can be very helpful for the checking-in process, as well as for evaluating ongoing progress and establishing recovery tasks.

During the review period, specific mention should be made of all the patient's clean and sober days. These are legitimate causes for recognition and sincere congratulation: "So you didn't drink [or use] for the past five days. That's great!" Strong urges to drink or use that the patient reports should be discussed openly and nonjudgmentally. Similarly, slips—times when the patient drank or used—need to be approached nonjudgmentally, as events that can be acknowledged and discussed openly without the patient fearing recrimination. Slips should be thought of and interpreted as times when the "powerful, baffling and cunning" illness of alcoholism or addiction overcame the patient's willpower.

In dealing with relapses, the facilitator's overriding goal is to encourage honesty in the therapeutic relationship and to open it to effective communication. The facilitator may need to stay vigilant for any tendency to evaluate his/her own success in terms of the patient's sobriety, and to not let this undermine honesty in the facilitator's relationship with the patient. As desirable as sobriety is, urges and slips are both to be expected. They are not cause for excessive disappointment, much less despair, on the part of either the facilitator or the patient. The appropriate response to a slip is: "What can you do now so that you won't drink [or use] for the rest of today?"

In addition to briefly reviewing sober days and slips, the review time should be used to talk about the patient's reactions to the readings and to meetings that s/he attended since the last session. If the patient attended no meetings or seems to be resisting going to them, the reasons for this resistance should be explored.

Presenting the New Material. Following the review, each session moves on to cover the main focus: a core or elective topic. These are described in detail in this book. Although in introducing these topics the facilitator plays the perhaps uncomfortable role of teacher in some respects, it is important for the facilitator to help the patient understand the new concepts in terms of his/her personal experience. The goal, in other words, of presenting new material is for the facilitator to make it "come alive" for the individual patient through discussion and example.

Recovery Tasks. Each session should end with the facilitator making specific suggestions—recovery tasks—for the patient to do between sessions. These tasks include:

- a mutually agreed-upon list of AA/NA meetings to be attended;
- suggested readings from conference-approved literature (see below);
- other suggested readings, including pamphlets, meditation books, and materials that the facilitator would recommend as pertinent to the individual patient.

When a facilitator "assigns" a patient a recovery task in a twelve-step-oriented program like this one, it is important to keep in mind that AA and NA themselves prefer the word *suggestion* to the word *rule*. Sponsors (see the chapter on Getting Active) too, may offer advice, but no good sponsor will "prescribe" behavior. The specific strategies for staying sober are as varied as the people who make up AA/NA fellowships. The bottom line in evaluating suggestions is that "what works" for the individual alcoholic or addict is the best advice—meaning how s/he has succeeded in staying sober, one day at a time.

In keeping with the spirit of AA and NA, facilitators in this program should avoid giving patients "homework" in the sense of giving them "assignments" or telling them what they "have to" do. The AA/NA traditions tell us that it is better to share with a particular patient "some things that other alcoholics [or addicts] have found helpful in your situation," without pressing the patient for the kind of commitment that, say, behavioral therapies might. This boils down to the facilitator making suggestions rather than prescribing behavior: giving the patient the choice—and the responsibility—to do what works for him/her.

The recovery tasks the twelve-step facilitator suggests should be consistent with the guidelines in AA/NA-approved publications. For example, strategies for dealing with urges and slips that are consistent with AA and NA might include:

- calling an AA or NA friend on the telephone
- going to an AA/NA meeting (or another meeting, or a different meeting)
- going to an AA/NA social event
- calling the patient's sponsor
- calling the AA/NA Hotline
- changing a habit pattern (doing something other than what the patient would usually do when he/she wanted to drink or use)
- distracting himself/herself (such as by going to a movie or visiting a friend)
- praying or meditating
- relaxing
- exercising
- reading the Big Book or the NA Big Book, or other AA/NA material

Recovery tasks should not only be consistent with AA/NA traditions and be couched as suggestions, they should be specific. The facilitator should make a point of following up on suggested tasks at the beginning of the next session.

Needless to say, the facilitator should be thoroughly familiar with all the conference-approved literature (see below). Moreover, he/she should be familiar with the locations, times, and types of AA/NA meetings that are available in the area, when giving a patient recovery tasks that involve going to meetings or reading.

Termination Session

The final session has its own goals and an agenda somewhat different from that of the other sessions. Since recovery is an ongoing, lifelong process, and since relapses are common among addicts and alcoholics, the termination session is intended not only to assess progress but to establish ongoing recovery goals and to leave the door open, as it were, to booster sessions in the future. The material in the chapter on termination provides more specific information.

Official AA and NA Literature

Since their inception, twelve-step programs like AA have emphasized reading, particularly the Big Book (*Alcoholics Anonymous*) and the Twelve and

Twelve (*Twelve Steps and Twelve Traditions*) as a way of understanding these fellowships, their views of addiction and recovery, and the ideas that organize them. The facilitation program in this book incorporates reading materials to augment the material covered in sessions. Toward this end, all patients should be asked to obtain the following books:

- *Alcoholics Anonymous*, 4th ed. (New York: Alcoholics Anonymous World Services, 2001).
- *Twelve Steps and Twelve Traditions* (New York: Alcoholics Anonymous World Services, 1952).
- *Living Sober* (New York: Alcoholics Anonymous World Services, 1975).

In addition, patients whose problems involve drug abuse or dependency should be advised to get a copy of the NA Big Book:

- *Narcotics Anonymous*, 5th ed. (Van Nuys, CA: Narcotics Anonymous World Services, 1988).

Contrast with Other Treatment Approaches

The facilitator using this program may find it useful to know what its basic assumptions are, so as to be able to understand how it differs from other approaches to the treatment of alcohol and drug problems.

Specific assumptions associated with this treatment program include the following:

- Alcoholism and addiction are chronic, progressive illnesses with predictable symptoms and a predictable course: Life becomes unmanageable due to alcohol or drugs.
- Willpower alone is not sufficient to overcome alcoholism or addiction: The alcoholic or addict is effectively powerless over his/her own compulsion to drink or use.
- The alcoholic or addict has permanently lost the capacity to control his/her drinking or using: that is, once an alcoholic or addict, always an alcoholic or addict.
- Alcoholism and addiction affect the body, mind, and spirit, producing "insanity."
- The only viable alternative for the addict or alcoholic is total and lifelong abstinence from alcohol and drugs.
- Even a single drink or use can trigger the alcoholic's or addict's craving

for alcohol or drugs and lead to a renewed cycle of compulsive drinking or using.

- The individual has the best chance of staying sober over the long run if s/he:
  - accepts his/her loss of control,
  - accepts the need to abstain permanently from all mood-altering substances, and
  - reaches out to fellow addicts through AA or NA for help in staying clean and sober.
- Faith in some Higher Power—a source of strength outside the individual—plays a more powerful role in recovery than does personal willpower.
- Encouraging patients to actively work the twelve steps of AA and NA is the primary goal of treatment, not teaching any skill.
- The patient is better served if s/he can be taught and encouraged to utilize the fellowships of AA and NA and their resources (meetings, hotlines, sponsors), rather than rely on the facilitator or any significant other as a means of sustaining sobriety.
- The ultimate goal of the alcoholic or addict is to resist taking the first drink or drug, one day—or even one hour—at a time.

Facilitator Guidelines

To maximize the effectiveness of this manual-guided facilitation, it is important that the facilitator make every effort to follow the format laid out in this handbook. The facilitator should decide before each session the topic to be covered (whether core or elective). The facilitator should be thoroughly familiar with the contents of a session prior to beginning it.

Apart from variations in individual therapeutic style among facilitators, the facilitator should generally attempt to pose questions and cover concepts the way they are presented in this book. We recommend that, in addition to the entire core program, the facilitator cover as many electives as is reasonable over the span of twelve to fifteen sessions.

Role of the Facilitator

The first responsibility of the facilitator is to determine the patient's level of involvement with alcohol or drugs or both. If a thorough assessment reveals clear symptoms of alcohol or drug dependence, the role of the facilitator is then to explore the patient's acceptance or denial of this dependence, to explain basic twelve-step concepts, and to promote the patient's active involvement in the AA/NA fellowships as the preferred means of staying clean and sober. Throughout this program, the facilitator assists the patient, through a combination of support and confrontation, in working through all resistances that s/he has to taking the action necessary to staying clean and sober. This is best accomplished when the facilitator is prepared to perform all the following functions in the context of the patient-facilitator relationship.

Educate and Advocate

The facilitator acts as a resource and advocate of the twelve-step approach to recovery. The facilitator:

17

- explains the AA/NA view of alcoholism and addiciton as chronic progressive illnesses marked by loss of control (unmanageability) and denial;

- helps the patient assess the extent to which alcohol or drug use has made his/her life unmanageable;

- identifies denial as it is reflected in the patient's attitudes toward drinking or using and in his/her behavior;

- introduces several of the twelve steps and their related concepts, and helps the patient to understand key twelve-step themes and concepts (such as denial and unmanageability) by pointing out experiences in the patient's life that illustrate them;

- introduces, explains, and advocates reliance on the AA/NA fellowships as the foundation for recovery, or clean, sober living;

- explains how to make use of various AA/NA resources (like hotlines, meetings, and socials) for recovery;

- explains recovery as an ongoing process of "arrest"—as opposed to "cure"—for alcoholism or addiction;

- explains the role of a sponsor (see chapter on Getting Active) and helps the patient to identify what s/he should look for in a sponsor; and

- answers questions to the best of his/her ability about material found in the Big Book, the Twelve and Twelve, the NA Big Book, and other readings.

Provide Guidance and Advice

The facilitator actively and systematically encourages the patient's involvement in AA and/or NA. The facilitator:

- monitors patient involvement in AA or NA and promotes a progression toward greater involvement, such as by:
  - suggesting meetings that require increasing personal involvement, such as "step" meetings and "closed discussion" meetings, rather than "open speaker" meetings;
  - encouraging patients to volunteer for basic service work, such as making coffee and setting up for or cleaning up after meetings;
  - identifying appropriate AA/NA social events, and encouraging the patient to attend them; and
  - encouraging the patient to get phone numbers of AA/NA friends and call them between meetings.

- assists the patient in locating meetings and provides appropriate support for getting the patient to attend and participate. This support can include:
  - problem solving around issues like transportation and child care;
  - role playing how to ask for phone numbers, volunteer for responsibilities, approach potential sponsors, and the like.
- clarifies the respective roles of facilitator and sponsor, and refuses to become a sponsor while helping the patient to find one; and
- suggests recovery tasks that will enhance the patient's successful integration into the AA/NA fellowships.

Provide Empathy and Motivation

The facilitator makes specific efforts to empathize with the patient and to motivate him/her to abstain from the use of all mood-altering substances. The facilitator:

- demonstrates an empathic understanding of the patient's feelings of shame, anger, anxiety, and guilt about substance abuse and the problems it has caused;
- empathizes with the patient's resistance to accepting his/her own loss of control and his/her need to abstain from using all mood-altering substances;
- reinforces each and every day of sobriety, and supports the patient's motivation to stay clean and sober one day at a time;
- provides "detached caring," such as by:
  - supporting the patient after a slip, while encouraging him/her to take action to stay sober for the rest of that day;
  - supporting the patient's decision to do "whatever it takes" to stay clean and sober;
  - empathizing with the patient's feelings of loss associated with "giving up" alcohol and drugs; and
  - supporting the need for the patient in sobriety to deal with long-standing issues and wounds that may have contributed to his/her substance abuse initially.

Desirable Facilitator Characteristics

Familiar with AA/NA Programs

A twelve-step facilitator, as a professional whose goal is to facilitate and encourage the patient's active participation in AA and/or NA, need not be in recovery from alcoholism or drug addiction personally. What is essential, however, is that s/he be knowledgeable of and comfortable with the process of twelve-step recovery as described in AA/NA–approved literature.

The facilitator's self-disclosure of his/her own recovery status is a subject that often arises in twelve-step approaches. As a rule, we encourage facilitators to be frank regarding their personal use of mood-altering substances, past or present, including alcohol. We regard it as appropriate for patients to want to know this, as well as the facilitator's personal experience, if any, with AA, NA, Al-Anon, Nar-Anon, or any other twelve-step program such as Adult Children of Alcoholics (ACOA).

While we support honesty and reciprocity in the facilitator-patient relationship, we also believe it is inappropriate for a facilitator to engage in protracted discussions of his/her own alcohol/drug history, whether s/he is in recovery or not. We suggest limiting such discussions to brief but honest responses to the patient's questions. In short, we suggest that the facilitator "keep it simple" when disclosing his/her own experiences with alcohol or drugs, while encouraging the patient to talk to others at AA/NA meetings.

For reasons that should be self-evident, we urge again that the facilitator who is not in recovery but who is planning to use this manual-guided approach make a commitment to attend several open AA/NA meetings and several open Al-Anon/Nar-Anon meetings, and to read all the conference-approved literature recommended for patients. In addition, to be maximally effective both as a resource and as a facilitator, the facilitator should develop a network of AA/NA contacts—men and women who are active in AA and/or NA, and upon whom the facilitator can call to help get a shy or ambivalent patient to those first meetings, to give patients information about particular meetings, to provide directions, and the like. Persons who have been sober and active in AA for at least a year are candidates for doing this type of "twelfth-step" work as part of their own recovery. Facilitators can develop working relationships with their contacts by going to meetings on a regular basis, or by networking with recovering persons they know personally.

Is Active, Supportive, and Involved

Twelve-step facilitators should work toward being active, conversational, empathic, and nonjudgmentally confrontational (that is, frank but respectful) during facilitation sessions—as opposed to being merely reflective, detached, and interpretative. The facilitator avoids "lecturing" the patient, talking more than the patient talks during sessions, or chastising the patient for his/her attitudes or behavior. Rather, the facilitator should be prepared to establish a collaborative and supportive relationship with the patient. Indeed, some sense of "bonding" between patient and facilitator may be appropriate.

The twelve-step facilitator helps the patient understand and identify his/

her denial as it is revealed in his/her decisions, words, and actions. The facilitator confronts the patient consistently in a frank but respectful manner about his/her attitudes or behaviors that support drinking or using; consistently encourages the patient to get involved in the AA/NA fellowships; and helps the patient to understand key AA/NA concepts in terms of his/her own experience.

Facilitators should recognize that many twelve-step concepts allow for individual interpretation by the patient. Indeed, patients can and should interpret AA/NA concepts in the light of their own experience. What one person may see as an "unmanageable" life, for example, may not seem so through the eyes of another. One person's Higher Power may not be another's—and so on. This pluralism is consistent with AA/NA traditions, which not only allow but actively encourage individual interpretation within broad guidelines. What is most important is not whether patients interpret twelve-step concepts in identical ways, but the end result: acceptance and surrender—admitting to unmanageability and becoming active in AA and/or NA. Patients need to be encouraged to do "whatever it takes" and "whatever works" in order to stay clean and sober each day.

The twelve-step facilitator should be familiar with basic AA/NA traditions and introduce them, along with various slogans, as they become appropriate during the program. These slogans—"Easy Does It," "One Day at a Time," "Fake It Till You Make It," "Turn It Over," and so on—should be thought of not as cliché abstractions but as statements of practical wisdom that are firmly grounded in the real-life experiences of many recovering persons. The successful twelve-step facilitator utilizes these slogans judiciously and gives them meaning by connecting them to the individual patient's experience.

Empathy is an important part of any therapeutic relationship, and twelve-step facilitation relationships are no exception. Addiction is an illness of isolation. An alcoholic or addict is more likely than not to have progressively lost most if not all the meaningful relationships in his/her life, to have become more and more alienated, and to feel more and more ashamed. Alcoholism and addiction undermine people's self-esteem to the point that they feel worthless, hopeless, and unlovable. Reaching out for support requires a leap of faith and represents a true act of courage, since the addict expects to be rejected by others. In many instances s/he tests the facilitator's own capacity to care. His/her low self-esteem may be reflected in obvious depression: alternatively, it may be concealed beneath a veneer of arrogance and grandiosity. The challenge for the facilitator is to be compassionate without being put off by defensive arrogance, and to care without taking on responsibilities that are rightly the patient's.

In the complex psychological climate that addiction creates, the facilitator-patient relationship becomes seminal. It represents the prototype for the kind of relationships that the patient will (hopefully) eventually cultivate through AA and/or NA. Successful management of the facilitator-patient relationship requires an ability on the part of the facilitator to balance genuine caring with healthy detachment. The facilitator needs to demonstrate empathy and concern while avoiding becoming, in effect, the patient's total "recovery program." The professional whose work is firmly anchored in twelve-step traditions will successfully balance the relationship by allowing the patient to feel a sense of connection while actively promoting the development of ever more connections through AA or NA. As the first "successful" relationship that the alcoholic or addict may have had for many years, even a brief facilitation relationship can represent a true watershed in many patients' lives.

Is Focused

This program aims to facilitate change in a relatively short time. It becomes a therapeutic challenge to the facilitator to cover as much ground as is reasonable, given the particular circumstances of a patient's case. To do this, the facilitator needs to be able and willing to focus the treatment and to stay on task.

At the beginning of each session, in reviewing the work of the previous week, issues relevant to the patient's life can be expected to come up. The patient should be given time to articulate his/her problems and concerns, and to feel heard by the facilitator. At the same time, it is important for the facilitator to keep in mind that the structure of this program does not allow him/her to "follow the patient" entirely—that is, to pursue therapeutic agendas apart from the facilitation program's agenda. In the light of this, it is the facilitator's responsibility to keep sessions focused on sobriety-related issues and to avoid getting off the track into lengthy discussions of marital problems, job problems, parenting problems, and the like. In such cases, the facilitator is wise to invoke the "First Things First" slogan from AA, the "first thing" being to attain a degree of sobriety as the foundation for all other change and growth.

Establishing sobriety may very well have beneficial "spillover" effects into many other aspects of the patient's life. Some problems may even resolve themselves "spontaneously" through sobriety; others may not—but they should be given attention later on, not during the program. No matter how pressing these issues may seem at the moment, they can usually be put on hold until some stable sobriety is achieved, as long as the facilitator recognizes them and affirms that they are indeed important in the meantime. Indeed, rushing prematurely into potentially explosive issues such as a strained marriage or alienated family relations can effectively undermine the patient's recovery before it gets established, and the facilitator may point this out. The addict or alcoholic's first and foremost recovery goal should be to get active in AA and/or NA: "Don't drink or use, and go to meetings."

Sustaining sobriety for a minimum of six months is a sensible precondition for addressing other problems of living.

Some patients may persistently try to shift the focus of the facilitation sessions from drinking or using to an issue that they regard as more important—to divert the agenda to discussions of relationships, work, or family problems. One appropriate response to such patients' efforts is to assure them that they will be referred to an appropriate consultation following completion of the twelve-step facilitation program, should these issues continue to be of concern. Another response is to discuss how a patient's efforts to shift the focus onto these issues might reflect denial (or avoidance) of his/her most important problem—drinking or using. One form of denial is "minimizing and maximizing"—that is, understating the importance of drinking or using, while simultaneously overstating the importance of something else.

Relies on AA and NA

In this program it is the AA/NA fellowships, not the individual facilitator, that are the major agent of change. Involvement in AA or NA—including regularly attending a variety of meetings and social activities, using the telephone to connect with AA/NA friends on a regular basis, and developing a relationship with a sponsor—is preferable to relying on the facilitator (who will, after all, be unavailable once the program is completed) as a means of staying sober. Similarly, the patient should generally be encouraged to rely more on the resources of his/her preferred fellowship than on the facilitator in times of crisis.

The facilitator's first response to a patient's crisis, aside from offering sympathy, should be to encourage him/her to call an AA/NA friend or sponsor, or to go to a meeting as soon as possible. If the facilitator sees the need to schedule an emergency session to deal with a crisis, the goals of this session should be:

- to help the patient assess the crisis in terms of its threat to his/her sobriety;
- to establish priorities—"First Things First"—and determine what the patient can do immediately in order to stay sober;
- to identify courses of action that are consistent with the AA/NA approach to recovery; and
- to solve the crisis by relying on AA or NA.

Crises or emergency calls from the partners or family members of patients can be handled in a similar manner. Al-Anon and Nar-Anon provide ongoing sources of support for persons related to alcoholics and addicts.

The facilitator should be familiar with the times and locations of these various meetings, and if possible should cultivate a network of Al-Anon/ Nar-Anon contacts who can be called upon to talk to a family member in crisis, and who can help get that person to a meeting.

In dealing with partners and family members, the facilitator should keep in mind the "Three C's" of Al-Anon[1]: "You didn't *Cause* the disease, you can't *Cure* it, and you can't *Control* the alcoholic's behavior." What family members can do is turn to the fellowships of Al-Anon and Nar-Anon for help in learning to "detach with love" from the alcoholic or addict.

Suggests Medical Treatment

Some patients need medical evaluation for possible detoxification. Such evaluations should be provided for by the facilitator in advance of beginning this program. The need for detoxification does not necessarily imply a need for a more structured program than the one described here. As a rule of thumb, the patient's motivation and progress are better indicators of twelve-step facilitation than is his/her medical status at the outset of treatment.

Confronts

In the context of this program, facilitators can best think of confrontation as "sincere and honest mirroring." The most appropriate form of confrontation is for the facilitator to share frankly but respectfully what he/she sees the patient doing. Most often, this involves confronting the patient about some form of denial.

Confrontation that is patronizing or harsh, or that implies that the patient has a character defect (such as a lack of willpower or immaturity), rather than being caught up in a powerful, baffling, and cunning illness, is apt to be unproductive in the long run. The facilitator needs to keep in mind the following goal of confrontation:

> Confrontation is a way to help a patient see his/her behavior in perspective. It reflects the patient's resistance to accepting the reality of his/her loss of control and the resultant unmanageability that addiction creates in his/her life (Step 1).

Here are two examples of the preferred mode of confrontation:

Facilitator: "What you're saying is that you can't find the time to go to a meeting. I hear you saying that lots of other things are more important to you than going to a meeting. I see that as denial, meaning some resistance on your part to accepting that you've lost control over alcohol [or drugs]. It seems that way to me because if you really accepted your limitation—the fact that your life is unmanageable because of drinking [using]—and your need to abstain completely from alcohol [or drugs], then hardly anything would be more important than getting active in a program that offers you hope. I think you'd find the time to go for 'treatments,' even every day of the week, if you had a potentially terminal illness and if treatment meant the difference between life and death. That's the way it is with alcoholism [or addiction]. It's an illness, it's chronic, and it's progressive. It can and does lead to a premature death. How do you feel about that?"

Facilitator: "You've told me again that you think you need to cut down on your use of alcohol and marijuana, but that you don't believe you need to quit using either one altogether. Another way of saying that is, you believe you can control your use— that you aren't addicted. After all, addiction means an inability to reliably control use. Addiction leads to negative consequences that get worse and worse. The Big Book and the NA Big Book are filled with personal stories of alcoholics and addicts who thought they could control their use. Often it's only when their willpower has been totally defeated— and after they've lost an awful lot—that they're ready to admit to being addicted. I see a pattern of progressively worse consequences in your life. For example, ————. I also know that you've already made many attempts to stop or cut back your using and drinking. Do you think you might be like all of those men and women who didn't want to face the truth? What would it take to convince you that you can't control your drinking and using, and that your only sane choice is to give them up?"

Slogans

Although Alcoholics Anonymous and Narcotics Anonymous are spiritual fellowships, they are eminently practical in their approaches to staying clean and sober. The practical wisdom and the spirituality of AA and NA are captured in many of their slogans. These slogans represent more than "bumper-sticker psychology"; they reflect practical wisdom that is as valuable as any to be found in literature.

The twelve-step facilitator should not only be familiar with many twelve-step slogans but should actively use them in the course of the facilitation program to promote involvement in AA or NA and to advise patients on how to handle difficult situations. The better a patient understands the meaning of each slogan, the better s/he will be at applying it on a day-to-day basis.

A few key twelve-step slogans are described here. Many more can be found in the various books and pamphlets oriented toward twelve-step recovery, and through going to meetings.

"One Day at a Time"

Recovery is best thought of as a journey undertaken one step at a time. The patient's goal is to avoid taking the first drink, and to stay sober one day at a time. Anniversaries of sobriety are important, but what is most important is whether the patient drinks today, not whether he/she drank yesterday or will drink tomorrow.

"First Things First"

If the alcoholic or addict does not stay sober, nothing else will matter, since s/he may end up homeless and destitute, in jail, or prematurely dead; meanwhile, alcoholism or drug addiction will continue to undermine his/her body, mind, spirit, and relationships, making the overall quality of life progressively worse. Although everyone, including alcoholics and addicts, has multiple commitments, obligations, and responsibilities in life, the *first* commitment of the alcoholic or addict must be to sobriety. S/he must be prepared to make whatever hard decisions are necessary in order to stay clean and sober. Sponsors and fellowship friends are especially helpful in making sensible decisions and keeping first things first.

"Fake It Till You Make It"

Not everything in AA/NA fellowships will appeal or necessarily make sense to the recovering person, particularly in the early stages of recovery. "Fake It Till You Make It" admonishes the alcoholic or addict to be humble: to sometimes follow advice on faith at first, in the belief that it will prove beneficial in the long run. This includes going to meetings, working the steps, doing what one's sponsor advises, and so on. A good example of this is calling the sponsor. Sponsors often ask newly recovering people to make brief daily contact, even by telephoning for only a minute or two to say hello. They are asked to do this regardless of how they are feeling and of whether they "have the time." Though the long-term benefits of building such habits and connections are easy to see, men and women in early recovery sometimes don't see the purpose of "checking in" and may even resent having to do it. Often they think of sponsors as people to call only in times of dire distress or intense craving, or after a slip. To this, the good sponsor will simply say: "I suggest you do it anyway, even if it doesn't make sense to you right now."

"Easy Does It"

The recovering person needs to learn how to cope with stress without resorting to drinking or using drugs. Our society promotes "compensatory" substance use—the use of mood-altering substances to reduce anxiety and frustration—through its mass media. In effect, this slogan urges the recovering person to manage stress by limiting its sources: by avoiding "overloading the plate" and by learning to relax. The retreat-like atmosphere of many residential treatment facilities is conducive to such relaxation.

"Live and Let Live"

This slogan advises the recovering person to accept that which cannot be changed, as opposed to trying to "play God or therapist," which only creates stress. Things that are better accepted than challenged include the reality of one's own alcoholism or addiction; certain family or marital problems; other people's personalities; past mistakes and transgressions; decisions that have already been made; situations that must be endured; and injustices that must be suffered.

"Turn It Over"/"Let Go and Let God"

As statements of spiritual faith, these slogans challenge us to face the fact that good intentions and honest effort alone will not always succeed in getting us what we want. At the same time, they ask us to believe that evil and brutishness, injustice and cruelty, will not necessarily win out in the end. These statements advocate neither passivity nor hopelessness; on the contrary, they express the belief that things can work out for the best in the long run, if we have faith. They help us to recognize that while we are responsible for making an effort to get what we need, we cannot control the final outcome of that effort.

Dealing with Technical Problems

When dealing with technical problems like the following ones, the facilitator's goal is to determine if the patient is still interested in and capable of participating in the facilitation program. We encourage facilitators to discuss technical problems with their colleagues or supervisors as well.

Patient Is Consistently Late for Appointments or Consistently Cancels Sessions

In general, the facilitator should begin by exploring the reason the patient was late, or missed or rescheduled a session. Listen carefully for evidence of denial—for statements such as: "I think I can do this on my own," "I don't think my problem is as bad as you seem to think it is," "I don't believe I've lost control of my drinking," "I was busy and forgot about our session," and the like. When denial seems to be the issue, the facilitator should identify it and interpret it straightforwardly as part of the illness of alcoholism or addiction.

Alcoholics and addicts should be expected to manifest denial. They may not manifest denial consciously or verbally; they may unconsciously "act out" denial in their behavior, or by making various and sundry excuses for not going to meetings, or by not following through on suggested readings. Denial often takes the form of chronic lateness and repeated cancellations of sessions. If this pattern emerges but the patient refuses to own up to it as denial, try to engage him/her in a frank and nonjudgmental discussion of his/her reservations about the program. If the pattern continues, a more open discussion of his/her motivation for recovery may be helpful.

Patient Comes to Sessions Drunk

Do not proceed with a session if the patient shows up apparently under the influence of alcohol or drugs. If possible, test the patient for alcohol use, or take a urine sample for later testing. Regardless of what s/he says, if you believe s/he has been using or drinking, ask him/her to call the AA/NA Hotline, an AA/NA friend, or his/her sponsor, if possible, to arrange for transportation home. If the patient is not willing to do this, have him/her call a significant other to arrange transportation home. As a last resort, rely on police for transportation. Do not allow an intoxicated patient to leave with car keys. Do not get into a protracted discussion of the slip with a patient who is drunk or high. Some patients who arrive drunk may require immediate medical evaluation and referral for detoxification.

Patient Resists Going to Meetings

Listen for statements that reflect denial: "I couldn't get a babysitter," "I was bogged down with work," "I lost the list you gave me," "I don't relate to those people," "I'm bored," and the like.

Resistance usually involves making excuses for not going to meetings, or criticizing AA or NA or their members. The facilitator should interpret this respectfully as denial, as evidence of the patient's unwillingness to do "whatever is necessary" in order to stay clean and sober. Denial is driven by a refusal to accept one's own loss of control and by the fact that alcohol or drugs are making the patient's life progressively more unmanageable. Treatments for many chronic illnesses (such as renal disease) are inconvenient and at times uncomfortable, but they are a matter of life and death. So is recovery.

Refusing to go to meetings can also take the form of "bargaining" with the illness: "I won't drink or use, but I won't go to meetings either." Such "white-knuckle" approaches to sobriety are usually setups for failure, since they rely on willpower alone rather than group support and faith in a Higher Power. Help the patient who is bargaining in this way to explore whatever feelings or attitudes underlie his/her resistance to reaching out for help.

We encourage the facilitator to patiently persist in trying to get the patient to make specific commitments to meetings. Use an AA/NA meeting schedule to identify specific meetings that would be appropriate. Never terminate a patient for refusing to go to meetings—to do so would be inconsistent with AA/NA traditions.

A patient's resistance to attending AA/NA meetings does not invariably reflect denial of his/her alcoholism or addiction. For some, it may simply reflect a fear of failure or social shyness. The facilitator should help the resistant patient clarify his/her reasons for declining active involvement in AA/NA and work from there. Role-playing potential interactions in advance of a meeting or enlisting the help of an AA/NA contact person can be extremely helpful in getting a shy or anxious person to break the ice.

Patient Uses a Substitute Substance

Substance substitution is a symptom of addiction, and if the patient reports using a substitute for his/her "substance of choice," it should be so interpreted. Addicts and alcoholics cannot "safely" use any mood-altering substances. Nor should they be allowed to believe they can—for two reasons. First, use of a substitute substance will reduce the patient's resistance to using his/her "substance of choice." Second, there is a definite risk of cross-addiction (or multiple addiction) if the patient turns to a substitute mood-altering substance.

Patient Appears Clinically Depressed or Psychotic

Mild depression may be a symptom of the patient's withdrawal or an appropriate response to his/her "acceptance"—to admitting to the loss of his/her control over alcohol or drugs. Severe depression or other psychopathology may require referral to alternative treatment. In these instances, twelve-step facilitation may need to be deferred.

Any suicidal ideation and psychotic thought patterns that the patient manifests need to be evaluated immediately. The facilitator should provide for emergency psychological evaluation by a qualified professional, preferably one who is experienced with alcohol and drug abuse treatment.

Part II
The Core Program

I n order to expose patients to the key twelve-step concepts, the facilitator needs to be sure to cover all four core topics thoroughly. These four topics should be introduced in the order in which they appear in this handbook:

- Core Topic 1: Assessment
- Core Topic 2: Acceptance
- Core Topic 3: Surrender
- Core Topic 4: Getting Active in AA or NA

Core Topic 1, the assessment, should be covered completely in the first facilitation session, but it is permissible to spend more than one session on the other core topics. It may be necessary to refer back to one or more of the core topics from time to time, even in a session devoted to an elective topic.

Session Format

After the initial session, all sessions (core and elective) should follow the following format:

- Review (approximately 10 minutes)
  - Review of journal
    - Note what AA/NA meetings the patient attended since the last session.
    - Discuss the patient's reactions to those meetings.
  - Review of slips
    - Did the patient drink or use at all?
      - What did the patient use?
      - Where?

31

- When?
- With whom?
  - What, if anything, did the patient do to try to stay clean and sober after the slip?
  - What AA/NA resources could the patient use in the event of a future slip?
- Review of urges to drink or use
  - When and where did the patient have urges?
  - Who was the patient with?
  - How did the patient handle the urges?
  - What AA/NA resources could the patient call on in the event of a future urge to drink or use?
- Review of sober days
  - Every day of sobriety deserves recognition and praise, yet without going so far as to promote false confidence or complacency.
- New material (approximately 30 minutes)
  - Introduction of new concepts or material for discussion.
  - Questions and reactions are elicited and discussed.
- Recovery tasks (approximately 10 minutes)
  - Meetings: Which meetings will the patient attend between now and the next session?
  - Readings: What should the patient read before the next session?
  - Other suggestions: What people, places, and routines might the patient change or avoid in the interest of sobriety?
- Summary (approximately 5 minutes)
  - What was the gist of today's discussion (in the patient's own words)?
  - Does the patient understand the recovery tasks that have been suggested? Is s/he willing to follow through on them?

Facilitator Notes

Meetings

The patient should be expected to attend AA/NA meetings on a daily basis, and the facilitator should negotiate down from that expectation only with reluctance. Seek specific commitments from the patient in this regard, and follow up by checking the patient's journal entries. The goal is for the patient to attend ninety meetings in ninety days. This is common advice to new members of AA and NA. Daily attendance serves to establish new habits and involvement in a twelve-step fellowship at the same time as it provides firm support for the patient during the crucial early days of recovery. Although daily attendance is the facilitator's sincere goal, he/she should avoid scolding the patient who commits to something less and no more. Explain the rationale for the "ninety and ninety" commitment without alienating the patient. Use current AA/NA meeting schedules to select meetings held at times and locations convenient for the patient. Encourage the patient to call on an AA/NA member to help him/her break the ice and get to those first few meetings. The facilitator may utilize his/her own network of AA/NA contacts for this purpose. Reassure the patient that this is "twelfth-step work" and is part of all twelve-step programs. It will not be a burden imposed on members but will be welcomed.

Slips

When the patient tells the facilitator that s/he has slipped, the facilitator's goal is not to admonish but to find out in a straightforward and sympathetic manner how the patient handled the slip and to tell him/her what s/he could do next time that would be consistent with AA and NA, such as:

- calling a hotline (listed in the white pages under Alcoholics Anonymous and Narcotics Anonymous);
- going to a meeting;
- calling someone the patient met at a meeting (an AA/NA friend).

Some people prefer the word *relapse* to *slip*. Either word may be used, although the former seems to have more severe connotations than the latter.

Reticence

A certain amount of reticence is normal for patients in the beginning. The facilitator should expect patients to resist the idea that they are alcoholic or addicted, to agree to go to meetings only reluctantly, to question twelve-step concepts, and to find fault with meetings. The Big Book is filled with stories of people with just these attitudes (and worse), who eventually went on to lead productive, sober lives.

It's natural to engage patients in discussions about their questions and concerns, but the twelve-step facilitator should not feel obligated to "sell" the AA/NA program to the patient. Keep in mind that in AA/NA tradition, patients are always free to "try it their way" if the twelve steps do not appeal to them. Therefore, arguments are to be avoided. Perhaps the best way to present the twelve-step approach to a new patient is by saying, "This program has helped millions of men and women around the world stop drinking and using and stay sober. I'd like to introduce the program to you, explain it, and facilitate your giving it a try. I'm not here to force you to do anything. In fact, there's a saying that originated within AA, that goes like this: 'Try our program for ninety days; if you decide you don't like it, we'll refund your misery.' "

Core Topic 1: Assessment

The first facilitation session may be expected to last between one and a half to two hours. It has several objectives:

- to introduce the patient to the AA/NA view of alcoholism and addiction;
- to help the patient assess his/her level of alcohol and/or drug involvement (including symptoms of dependency);
- to explain this twelve-step facilitation program; and
- to engage the patient's willingness to participate actively in the program—in other words, "to give AA [or NA] a fair try."

Introductions

The facilitator should begin by establishing a friendly rapport and getting basic background information from the patient.

Getting Acquainted

Many psychotherapists prefer a formal surname-only relationship with their patients. But a first-name basis is appropriate here and is more consistent with AA/NA practice, as well as with the twelve-step tradition of informality. Therapists who are uncomfortable with this prospect might simply give it a try; after all, they are asking their patients to give many new things a try. We suggest opening questions like the following:

- "Hello. My name is _____. And yours?"
- "Were you able to find your way here all right? Any major transportation problems?"
- "How does this meeting time work out for you?"
- "Where do you live?"

- "Do you live alone, or with someone else? Who?"
- "Are you in a relationship now? Are you married, living together, or living separately? What's your spouse's [or partner's] name?"
- "Do you have any children? How old are they? Do they live with you?"
- "Are you working? Where? What do you do?"

Getting an Initial Impression of How the Patient Is Feeling

The facilitator's next task is to find out how the patient is feeling by asking questions like:

- "What circumstances led up to your being here today?"
- "Did someone refer you to me [or this program]?"
- "How do you feel about being here today? Are you nervous? Upset? Angry? I hope you'll make yourself comfortable. And I hope this meeting will be useful to you."

Explaining Confidentiality

It is important for the facilitator to assure the patient that everything that passes in the program's sessions will be confidential. The facilitator might say:

> *Facilitator:* "First of all, before we even begin, I want to make sure that you understand that anything you tell me, either today or any other time, is strictly confidential. In fact, the federal government has passed laws specifically protecting your rights to privacy and confidentiality. No information about your alcohol [or drug] history, or about your treatment, can be released to anyone without your specific permission, in writing. I am not even permitted to tell anyone that I've met you or know who you are. That's true both during and after your treatment with me. I have to keep my records secure, apart from any other records. Also, not even a general release of information for medical or mental health records is enough to permit me to release any information about your alcohol [or drug] use. Is this all clear to you? Do you have any questions at all? I'd be glad to answer them as best I can."

Explaining the Agenda

The next subject of discussion is the agenda. The facilitator should briefly outline it by saying something like:

> *Facilitator:* "I'd like to explain what I hope we can accomplish in this meeting. First, I'd like to get some background information on your previous treatment experience, so that I have a better sense of you as an individual. Then I'd like us to work together to assess your own level of involvement with alcohol [or drugs], to see if that involvement is harmful at this time. This is something we need to do together. If you answer my questions honestly, I'll be able to give you an honest impression of where you're at with alcohol [or drugs]. That information could be valuable in helping you to decide what you can and perhaps should do for yourself. After that, I'd like to take a few minutes to explain my approach to helping people who want to stop drinking [or using drugs], which is basically a twelve-step approach. You may or may not already know about this. Last, I'll give you an idea of how this facilitation program works, including what my role would be and what yours would be. All this will probably take about an hour and a half, though other sessions would be an hour long. Do you have any questions about anything so far?"

Previous Treatment Experience

Having briefly established the patient's reasons for being in treatment and having outlined the goals of the assessment session, the facilitator moves on to assess the patient's previous experiences, if any, with alcohol and/or drug treatment, by asking a series of questions.

- To determine whether the patient has previously been in an alcohol or drug rehabilitation program, or any other treatment program for drinking or drug abuse:
  - "Have you ever gone for help about your drinking [or drug use] before today?"
  - "If you have been in treatment before, give me a quick rundown of those experiences:
    - "Where and when did they occur?"
    - "How long were you in the program(s)?"

- "What was the orientation or philosophy of the program(s)?"
- "What did you learn about yourself and your drinking from those treatment experiences?"
- "How long did you stay sober [or clean] after each of those treatment experiences?"
- "In your opinion, why did you go back to drinking [or using]?"

- To determine what, if any, experience the patient has had with AA or NA:
  - "Have you ever gone to AA [or NA]? How many times?"
  - "Approximately how many AA [or NA] meetings have you attended in the last year?"
  - "When was the last time you went to a meeting?"
  - "Did you have a sponsor? When was the last time you spoke with him [or her]?"
  - "Why did you stop going to AA [or NA]?"
  - "In your period of sobriety, what were the circumstances of your relapse? How did you react to your relapse?"
    - "How did you feel?"
    - "What did you do?"

- To assess how the patient has attempted to control or stop his/her alcohol or drug use, aside from rehabilitation, AA, or NA:
  - "Have you tried to control or stop your drinking [or using] on your own? What did you do?"
  - "What has been the longest period of time, over the past year or so, that you've gone without having a single drink [or using one time]?"

- To assess what the patient's interest in this program is:
  - "Do you believe you have a problem with alcohol [or drugs]?"
  - "Are you interested in doing something about your drinking [or using]? If so, why?"
  - "Do you think you need help with your drinking [or using]? If so, why?"
  - "Do you believe you need to stop drinking [or using] altogether?"
  - "How would you feel about the idea of giving up alcohol [or drugs]?"
  - "What's your gut feeling about being here today? What do you hope to get out of it? What are your concerns about being here?"

Taking an Alcohol/Drug History

An alcohol/drug history is a chronological account of a patient's use of mood-altering substances. It shows patterns of his/her use (such as increases or changes in preference), as well as life events and transitions associated with the onset of his/her use or with significant changes in using habits. The therapeutic goal of taking a patient's alcohol/drug history is to develop a diagnosis with the patient based on information that s/he has provided and to share it with the patient. An effective alcohol/drug history can facilitate acceptance (AA Step 1) by identifying a progression of symptoms and problems associated with drinking or using. The alcohol/drug history can help the patient draw a connection between his/her alcohol or drug use and its negative consequences (such as a sense that life is becoming unmanageable as a result of using alcohol or drugs).

There are many approaches to doing an alcohol/drug history, but we suggest that the facilitator begin by jotting down a list of all the mood-altering substances the patient admits to having used regardless of how often he/she used them or how long it has been since he/she used them last. This can be done by asking an open-ended question:

Facilitator: "I need to know about all of the mood-altering substances you've ever used, including alcohol, even if you've used them only once. I'd like to make a quick list of them. Can you tell me all the different substances you've tried?"

Regardless of what the patient volunteers, we recommend that the facilitator go over whatever list the patient gives and specifically inquire about his/her use of each of the following:

- marijuana ("pot," "weed")
- cocaine ("coke," "crack")
- amphetamines ("speed," "ice," "uppers")
- barbiturates ("downers")
- prescription drugs (Valium, Librium, etc.)
- hallucinogens ("LSD," "acid," "shrooms," etc.)
- heroin ("horse")
- inhalants (glue, "rush," etc.)

The facilitator can then introduce alcohol/drug history as follows:

Facilitator: "I'd like to spend some time with you doing an alcohol and drug history. The purpose of this is to help us identify together the patterns of your use over time, as well as to see how the use of alcohol and possibly other mood-altering substances may be having an impact on your life.

"It's important that you be honest with me about this information, which is confidential. In addition to asking you what you've used, when you first used it, and how your habits may have changed over time, I'll also be asking you to tell me something about what was going on in your life at the times when your drinking or using increased. I'll also be asking you about how whatever you've used affected you, positively and negatively, at different times.

"Okay. Why don't we start with the first mood-altering substance you ever tried. What was that? How old were you, as best you can remember, when you first tried it? Where and when did you use it?"

After getting this initial information, we suggest moving on to asking about the next (and the next) substances used. This will give the facilitator a quick overview of the kinds of substances the patient used and the ages of first use:

- "Okay, what was the next substance you remember using?"
- "How old were you when you first used _____?"
- "Can you tell me what the circumstances were?"

Once the facilitator has gained an overview of all of the mood-altering substances the patient has used, when s/he first used them, and what the circumstances were at the time of first use, the session proceeds to filling in the history, using the patient as a guide. Starting with the age of onset (first use), the facilitator should ask the patient when his/her use of a substance either increased or decreased significantly. Note the substances whose use dropped, and when and why, as well as substances whose use decreased. Next, take time to query the patient about significant events and changes in his/her life (such as relationship and family issues, developmental milestones, job changes, births and deaths) that correlate with changes in his/her drinking and using patterns:

- "What was going on in your life at that time?"
- "Where did you live, and who did you live with? How did you get along with each other?"
- "What were you doing [school, work, etc.] at that time? Were there any significant changes in your family?"
- "Are there any personal experiences, good or bad, that stand out in your mind about that time in your life?"

Last, the facilitator should inquire about the emotional and behavioral effects that alcohol or other substances had at different times in the patient's life:

- "How did _____ make you feel at that time?"
- "Did you ever have any negative emotional reactions to _____?"
- "Did _____ change the way you acted in any way? How?"
- "Did using _____ ever get you into any trouble on account of how it affected your behavior?"

What follows is a brief example of an alcohol/drug history.

Substance/ Age	Type/Amount	Frequency	Effects	Events
Alcohol/11	beer/sips from Dad's beer can	weekends	sick & giddy	none
Alcohol/13	beer/1–2 cans	2–3 times a week	grown-up & "cool"	parents separated
Marijuana/14	1–2 joints	weekends	relaxed	doing bad in school
Marijuana/16	ounce/week	4–5 times a week	"mel- low"	fighting a lot with my mother
Alcohol/18	six-pack	daily	tired & angry	girlfriend left me

We recommend that the facilitator use a large sheet of paper for taking notes. We also recommend giving a copy of the completed history to the patient for his/her personal use and reflection.

Negative Consequences

Having established the patient's alcohol/drug history, the facilitator should work with the patient to determine the nature and chronology of the negative consequences that have been associated with that use. Again, this should be a collaborative effort. We suggest an introduction such as the following:

Facilitator: "Let's take a few minutes to look at some of the issues, problems, and conflicts that you've experienced over these past several years. Let's begin with your physical health."

Negative consequences can be divided into several categories, and the facilitator should make an effort to cover all of them.

Physical Consequences

Make a point of listing all medical problems, as well as accidents or injuries, that correlate with the use of alcohol or drugs, such as:

- hypertension (high blood pressure)
- gastrointestinal (digestive) problems
- sleep disorders: insomnia, unrestful sleep, early waking
- weight loss, gain, or fluctuation
- auto, home, or job accidents or injuries
- emergency room visits
- blackouts
- passing out
- heart problems
- diabetes
- liver disease

Legal Consequences

List all legal consequences correlated with substance abuse, including:

- DWI (driving while intoxicated) arrests
- arrests for disorderly conduct
- arrests for possession of illegal substances
- problems encountered in the military related to alcohol or drugs (veterans only)
- illegal activities for which the patient was not caught.

Social Consequences

The facilitator should carefully inventory all social consequences of alcohol or drug use, including:

- job problems, such as excessive sick leave; poor, declining, or uneven performance evaluations; being fired; being forced to undergo treatment
- marital problems, such as chronic conflicts over drinking or using; conflicts over money spent on alcohol or drugs; conflicts over deceit, unreliability, infidelity, or abuse; breakdown of marital communication and intimacy
- conflicts with children or relatives over use
- problems functioning effectively as a parent
- loss of old friends correlated with alcohol or drug use.

Sexual Consequences

Though seldom discussed, alcohol and drug abuse are commonly associated with sexual dysfunction and trauma, including:

- problems of arousal (impotence in men, dyspareunia in women)
- orgasmic dysfunction (anorgasmia in women, delayed ejaculation in men)
- loss of sexual desire
- sexual behavior that the patient would not choose to engage in if sober
- sexual victimization or exploitation (rape, prostitution, pornography).

Psychological Consequences

The facilitator should ask the patient about symptoms of depression or other psychological disorders that he/she may be experiencing, such as:

- insomnia or disturbed sleep (such as waking up consistently in the middle of the night)
- appetite disorders, especially loss of appetite
- irritability or moodiness
- suicidal thoughts
- loss of motivation, drive, or interest
- memory problems (especially "forgetfulness")
- disorientation
- impulsivity
- aggressiveness
- confused thinking

Financial Consequences

The facilitator should ask the patient specifically about his/her current financial status and problems s/he may have had over the past few years, including:

- creditor problems, such as overextended credit, revoked credit cards
- mortgage or rent problems
- delinquent loans
- problems "making ends meet"

- fines
- legal fees associated with alcohol or drug-related arrests (particularly among cocaine and heroin abusers).

Once the inventory of negative consequences is completed, the facilitator should summarize it aloud to the patient. Do this partly to get concurrence and partly to elicit negative consequences that may not have been mentioned so far.

The final step in taking this inventory is to test the patient's willingness to see a connection between these negative consequences and his/her drinking or using—in other words, to attribute at least some of the personal problems listed above at least partly to drinking or using.

> *Facilitator:* "I'm interested to know if you see any connection between any of these problems you've had, and alcohol [or drugs]. What do you think? Do you think that drinking [or using] contributed in any way to any of these problems? Which ones? How much did it contribute? Do you believe that any of these could have been avoided if you weren't drinking [or using] at the time? Which ones? What consequences of alcohol [or drugs] use have you suffered recently?"

Assessment of Tolerance

Another symptom of alcohol and drug dependency that the facilitator should assess in the first session is the patient's level of tolerance, or the tendency to require progressively larger amounts of a mood-altering substance to produce the same physical and emotional effects. Tolerance drives the user of a mood-altering substance to use more of the substance, or a more potent form of it to experience the same "mood swing." The facilitator should ask questions like the following to determine the extent to which the patient has developed a tolerance to any substances:

- "Does it take more _____ [alcohol, drug name] now than it used to for you to get really drunk [high]?"
- "Have you noticed that your ability to 'tolerate' _____ has gotten greater over time—in other words, that you can use more _____ now without it affecting you as much as it did when you first used it?"
- "On the average, how much _____ does it take now for you to get drunk [high]? How much did it used to take?"

Assessment of Loss of Control

Loss of control is the third major area that must be evaluated diagnostically. As the Big Book states, it is a hallmark of addiction:

> The fact is that most alcoholics, for reasons yet obscure, have lost the power of choice in drink. Our so-called will power becomes practically non-existent. We are unable, at certain times, to bring into our consciousness with sufficient force the memory of the suffering and humiliation of even a week or a month ago. We are without defense against the first drink.[1]

Symptoms of loss of control over alcohol or drug use include:

- repeated failures in efforts to stop drinking [or using]
- failed efforts to control or restrict use, such as:
  - drinking [or using] only on weekends
  - drinking [or using] only certain forms of a substance (drinking only wine or beer instead of "hard liquor," say, or smoking only "home-grown" marijuana)
  - limiting, the amount consumed ("no more than _____").

The following passages from the Big Book and the NA Big Book may be useful in helping patients understand this aspect of loss of control. The facilitator may want to read them aloud to the patient.

> Here are some of the methods we have tried: Drinking beer only, limiting the number of drinks, never drinking alone, never drinking in the morning, drinking only at home, never having it in the house, never drinking during business hours, drinking only at parties, switching from scotch to brandy, drinking only natural wines, agreeing to resign if ever drunk on the job, taking a trip, not taking a trip, swearing off forever (with and without a solemn oath), taking more physical exercise, reading inspirational books, going to health farms, accepting voluntary commitment to [hospitals]—we could increase the list ad infinitum.

> When I got out, I made a promise to myself to limit my heroin use to the weekend. I didn't know anything about addiction. Little did I know that it was the first fix that started me.[2]

Substance Substitution

Addicted persons typically have a "substance of choice"; however, if deprived of his/her substance of choice the alcoholic or addict will substitute another one sooner than stay sober. It is important for the facilitator to ascertain the extent to which the patient prefers substance substitution to sobriety. Questions like the following can be helpful:

- "What kind of alcohol [or form of marijuana or cocaine] do you prefer?"
- "What do you usually do if you can't get the kind you like the best?"
- "What would you do if you couldn't get any _____? Would you use something else, or stay sober?"
- "What's your 'back-up' if you can't get any _____?"

"Stashing"

Alcoholics and addicts are known to go to great lengths to safely hide a supply (a "stash") of alcohol or drugs. To determine whether this is part of a patient's pattern, ask questions such as these:

- "Have you ever been tempted, or have you ever actually hidden some _____ somewhere, so that no one else could find it?"
- "Where do you keep your stash of _____?"
- "Why do you feel a need to keep some _____ hidden?"
- "Have you ever bought a little extra _____, to have just in case your supply runs low?"

Preoccupation

Preoccupation refers to the alcoholic's or addict's tendency to ruminate about alcohol or drugs. As use becomes habitual, the alcoholic's or addict's life gradually "accommodates"[3] to using in such a way that nonusing activities drop out of the lifestyle and relationships become secondary to the self-absorbed act of drinking or using. With the following questions the facilitator can get at the extent to which the patient is preoccupied with drinking or using:

- "Do you find yourself daydreaming about having a drink [or getting high] while you're at work [or school], or anticipating having a drink [or getting high] on the way home from work [or school]? Give me a couple of examples."
- "Do you find yourself distracted ('out of it') at times because you're thinking about having a drink [or getting high]? Can you give me an example?"
- "Have you ever skipped work [or school] in order to stay home and drink [or get high]? When was the last time you did that?"

- "Do you get upset or feel uptight if you see that your supply is getting low? What do you do then?"
- "Do you find that most of your social activities center on getting drunk [or high] with other people?"

Drinking or Using Alone

Though drinking and using usually start out as social activities, as addiction sets in the social agenda gives way to the compulsion to get intoxicated or high. Addicts no longer need to socialize in order to justify or facilitate their use; on the contrary, they become progressively more socially isolated as a consequence of their obsession with getting and staying high. The facilitator's simple and straightforward questioning about when and where the patient uses will shed light on how important his/her social agenda is, versus his/her desire to use.

"Chasing"

Alcoholics and addicts are typically in a hurry to get high. Unlike nonaddicts, alcoholics and addicts do not feel "normal" being sober. The dysphoria associated with sobriety, along with the obsession to drink or use, drives the addict to "chase" his/her high. For the addict, "the sooner, the better" is the modus operandi. With questions such as the following, the facilitator can evaluate chasing:

- "Have you found yourself having an urge to 'guzzle' drinks [or 'chase' a high], meaning wanting to get high as quickly as possible?"
- "What's the first thing you do when you get home?"
- "Do you ever drink [or use] before you go out, so that you have sort of a 'head start' on getting high?"
- "Has your enthusiasm for getting high led you to drink [or use] more than you had intended? How often have you gotten 'carried away' that way?

Diagnosis

Using information obtained from the alcohol/drug history as well as the other information gathered above—on negative consequences correlated with use, tolerance, and loss of control—the facilitator needs to share with the patient, in a frank and respectful manner, a diagnosis. It is vitally important to emphasize to the patient that this diagnosis is based on information provided directly by the patient. One way to do this is to say: "It seems to me, based on the information you've given me, that you have a number of symptoms." Then go down the list.

- Tolerance. Explain, using specific examples from the patient's self-reported experience.
- Loss of control. Give supportive evidence, based again on the patient's self-reported experience.
- Continued drinking despite negative consequences. Summarize the negative consequences, as per the patient's self-reported experiences.

"Taken together," the facilitator might continue, "this information— that you've given me yourself—suggests that you can't effectively control your use of _____. Basically, your inability to control your use is what it means to be an alcoholic [or addict]. How do you feel about that idea? Does it seem to fit the facts as you've described them to me? What's your own opinion at this time?"

Alternatively, a dignosis based on the very same self-report data can be correlated to a Jellinek Chart. Two such charts, one for men and one for women, are included in Appendix A of this book. Based on analyses of case histories, Jellinek Charts present a visual image of the course of alcoholism in terms of symptoms and phases. (They can be adapted to drug use fairly easily.)

If you choose to use a Jellinek Chart to share a diagnosis, once again be certain that you can document your case by references to the patient's self-reported experiences. It can be approached in this way:

Facilitator: "Let me give you this chart to look at. I have a copy, too. It's based on research, and it shows the course of alcoholism. It shows how symptoms progress, and how alcoholism eventually ends in obsessive drinking. [I think you can see how pretty much the same picture emerges from drug abuse.] Based on what we've talked about today, I honestly believe that your use of _____ at this time places you at the _____ stage of use. Let me give you my reasons for believing that, based on what you've told me today. Then I'd like to know what your own opinion is."

Either way a diagnosis of alcoholism or drug addiction is shared with the patient, it will very likely evoke some emotional and intellectual reactions from him/her. If it does not, it is highly probable that the patient is choosing not to share his/her feelings and opinions with the facilitator in an open and honest way. We do not recommend that the facilitator challenge this reticence in a confrontational or skeptical manner at this point. The patient will be asked to give some thought to the diagnosis between now and the next session (see "Recovery Tasks" below), and the issue can be followed up on at that time.

Providing a Program Overview

The facilitator should now review the twelve-step facilitation program, being sure to cover each of the following points:

Sessions

Contract with the patient for a specific number of sessions—we recommend between twelve and fifteen, including this first session—before proceeding further. If the patient prefers not to commit to such a large number of sessions, contract to evaluate his/her progress after a certain number of sessions (six to eight).

Explain that another part of the program involves two to three conjoint sessions with the patient and his/her spouse or partner, if the patient has one.

Objectives

Explain that the facilitator will work with the patient to achieve the following objectives:

- to understand the AA/NA view of alcoholism and addiction: that these are chronic, progressive, and potentially fatal illness that cannot be cured but that can be arrested so long as a person who has the illness is willing to follow some suggestions based on the experiences of alcoholics and addicts who have successfully stopped drinking or using;
- to understand how AA and NA "work": what the ground rules are, how to find meetings, what meetings are like, what a sponsor is and how to get one, and the like;
- to understand some of the key twelve-step concepts, such as denial and surrender, as well as the meaning of many of the AA/NA slogans; and
- to learn how to use AA and/or NA as resources for staying clean and sober one day at a time.

Responsibilities of the Facilitator

The facilitator should make it clear that he/she is there to:

- educate, support, advise the patient;
- act as a resource person and "coach" to facilitate the patient's understanding of alcoholism and addiction, AA/NA fellowships, and their twelve steps to recovery; and
- help the patient focus on staying sober one day at a time with the help of AA and/or NA.

Responsibilities of the Patient

The facilitator should explain that he/she expects the patient to:

- attend all sessions;
- come to sessions sober;
- keep a journal;
- make an honest effort to follow through on all recovery tasks that you suggest (see below); and
- be honest (including about slips and urges to drink or use).

Ask the patient to try to arrive five minutes or so early for each session, beginning with the second session, so that you will have a few minutes to review his/her journal in advance. Making this request helps to emphasize the importance of the journal, and also allows you to plan specific recovery tasks with respect to meetings and suggested readings.

Recovery Tasks

Recovery tasks are specific suggestions that the facilitator makes at the end of each session. They should be followed up on at the outset of the next session. Two areas where specific recovery tasks should always be suggested are:

- how many AA and/or NA meetings the patient will attend between sessions, with the goal for initial recovery being the equivalent of one meeting a day, or ninety meetings in ninety days;
- what readings the patient might read before the next session.

In addition to the above, the facilitator may wish to make suggestions about specific meetings (or types of meetings) the patient might consider attending, and about how the patient can go about "getting active" in AA meetings.

Suggested Recovery Tasks

The following recovery tasks may be suggested for the first facilitation session.

Do an honest self-assessment. Ask the patient to spend some private time thinking about this session, in particular about the information s/he provided to the facilitator. Ask the patient to reflect on his/her alcohol and drug history and to make some notes in his/her journal concerning any thoughts or feelings s/he has, between now and the next session, about this session, about his/her history, and about the diagnosis the facilitator has offered.

Attend an AA and/or NA Meeting. Give the patient a current schedule of AA/NA meetings that are held in his/her geographic area. If the patient lives and works in two different areas, give him/her the schedules for both areas. (*Note:* These schedules can also be obtained by calling the AA/NA information lines listed in the white pages of your telephone book). If the patient has symptoms of dependency on alcohol and other drugs, recommend that s/he attend both an AA and an NA meeting. Help the patient select the specific meeting(s) that s/he will attend between now and the next facilitation session. Make a note of this in writing for follow-up purposes, and make sure that the patient writes it down in his/her journal as well.

Start a personal journal. Give the patient a "journal" to keep. A composition book is fine for this purpose. (*Note:* Though it is of course possible to ask the patient to purchase a journal, we recommend giving one directly to the patient.) Ask him or her to make a note of any AA/NA meetings s/he attends [including dates and times] as well as his/her unedited thoughts and reactions to them. Encourage the patient to be completely honest about both positive and negative feelings about the meetings, as well as his/her reactions to readings in the AA/NA literature.

Start reading. Recommend that the patient purchase the following publications:

- *Alcoholics Anonymous* (the Big Book) and/or
- *Narcotics Anonymous* (the NA Big Book);
- *Twelve Steps and Twelve Traditions* (the Twelve and Twelve)
- *Living Sober*

Ask the patient to begin to read these books as soon as possible, and make any specific suggestions you like with respect to them, keeping in mind the patient's reading level and the amount of time that s/he can reasonably be expected to devote to reading. Chapters 1, 2 and 5 of the Big Book are useful for those who are completely unfamiliar with AA. Similarly, the first four chapters of the NA Big Book provide a good introduction to NA. Pages 1–7 of *Living Sober* are a good introduction for both alcohol and drug users to some of the practical aspects of recovery.

Stay sober today. Ask the patient if s/he is willing to make a decision not to drink or use for the rest of that day. If the patient expresses such a willingness, thank him/her and express your approval of that decision. If you like, explain that this is the way that twelve-step programs like AA and NA work: Alcoholics and addicts commonly say not that they have decided to "quit" drinking or using, but that they have decided not to drink or use today. This is the spirit of the one-day-at-a-time approach to recovery, and if the patient understands that, you will have helped him/her take a big step in the right direction.

Wrap-Up

End this first session by checking once again the patient's willingness to follow through on all of the suggested recovery tasks. Help him/her to articulate any resistance you detect, and be empathic. After all, not everyone will like the idea of having to do so much "work" to stay sober. Encourage the patient to do as much as s/he can, but keep the primary emphasis on attending AA/NA meetings. Remember, this is the bottom line of recovery: "Don't drink [or use] today, and go to meetings." If necessary, the facilitator should use his/her clinical judgment and therapeutic skill so that the patient may achieve a set of mutually agreed upon goals.

Facilitator Notes

Compliance

The primary purpose of the first session is to engage the patient's interest in voluntarily committing to this twelve-step facilitation program. Utilizing excessive pressure, threat, or coercion toward this end is likely to elicit a false commitment at best. This false commitment is called "compliance."[4] The compliant patient is "talking the talk" of recovery—most likely to please or placate the facilitator—but s/he is not "walking the walk" of recovery, in the sense of being truly motivated to the give the AA/NA approach an honest try. Facilitators in this program are advised to take a direct, non-judgmental, and educative approach to confronting the patient on this matter. They should stick to the facts as they see them, and not allow themselves to be talked out of their interpretation of those facts. At the same time, they should "respect" the patient's resistance to accepting the idea that s/he is "powerless" over alcohol or drugs.

The facilitator should consistently rely upon the alcohol/drug history; the self-reports of tolerance, negative consequences, and loss of control; and the Jellinek Chart as the basis for confronting the patient firmly and frankly on his/her current situation. Since alcoholism and addiction are primary disease processes, the facilitator should have confidence that the patient has already struggled to control his/her drinking use, and should attempt to elicit evidence of this struggle in a direct but supportive and sympathetic way. Similarly, the facilitator can discuss slips frankly yet sympathetically by noting that they are the result of a disease that is more powerful than individual willpower.

Faced with a resistant patient, the facilitator should attempt to consistently provide feedback to him/her about:

- how the patient's life is becoming increasingly unmanageable due to alcohol or drug abuse; and
- how his/her individual efforts have not proven effective in stopping or "controlling" that use over the long run.

The facilitator, in turn, should resist temptations to be distracted from the main subject of this program, which is the patient's alcohol or drug use and involvement in AA or NA. Keep in mind that the primary goal here is twelve-step facilitation, not psychotherapy. Concurrent issues such as marital problems, job problems, post-traumatic stress, and depression can be initially handled by encouraging the patient to make use of fellowship resources such as meetings, social events, peers, and sponsors.

Finally, in this program, it is important that the facilitator accept the concept that addiction to alcohol or drugs is a "no-fault illness."[5] Alcoholism and drug addiction are diseases that cannot be overcome by simple willpower. Nor is it the addict's "fault" that s/he has this illness. Therefore, for the facilitator to induce guilt over the patient's alcoholism or addiction is as inappropriate as it is to make someone feel guilty over having heart disease or diabetes. Perhaps the patient could have done things differently with respect to prevention, but once the illness is there, it cannot be willed away. At the same time, there is no cure for alcoholism or addiction; there is only a method for arresting the process of addiction. That method is active participation in the twelve-step programs of Alcoholics Anonymous and Narcotics Anonymous.

While addicts are not responsible for their illness, however, they are responsible for their recovery. Addicts cannot blame anyone else for their illness—or assign responsibility to anyone else for their recovery.

Core Topic 2: Acceptance

R ecovery from alcoholism and addiction, like every great and difficult journey, begins by taking the first step. The facilitation session devoted to the core topic "acceptance" introduces Step 1 of AA and NA and discusses the following key concepts:

- powerlessness
- unmanageability
- denial

One goal of this session is to elicit from the patient a willingness to extend two decisions that s/he made at the end of the first session: to not drink or use today, and to attend AA/NA meetings. If those decisions were not previously made, the facilitator should pursue that issue in this facilitation session.

Stages of Acceptance

The first step, as it appears in Alcoholics Anonymous and Narcotics Anonymous, reads as follows:

> We admitted we were powerless over alcohol—that our lives had become unmanageable.

> We admitted we were powerless over our addiction, that our lives had become unmanageable.[1]

In both of these versions, Step 1 is a complex statement. At its heart lies the idea of accepting one's own personal limitation and loss, as embodied in the words *powerless* and *unmanageable*. These statements of limitation and loss can evoke a range of emotional and intellectual reactions in patients. At the core of many of these reactions, and driving them, is a resistance to accepting limitation and loss. This resistance is commonly referred to in the literature on grief as *denial*.[2]

The reactions to limitation and loss that men and women typically have run the gamut from anxiety to depression to anger. People employ all sorts of intellectual defenses against facing up to their loss and limitation. The loss that alcoholics and addicts must confront is the loss of their control over drugs or alcohol. The limitation imposed upon them is the need to abstain—to give it up forever. Other losses are associated with recovery from alcoholism or addiction; they include the loss of the ability to rely on a mood-altering substance for comfort, as a means of coping, and as a vehicle for socializing and recreating. Alcoholics and addicts contemplating recovery are usually also aware of the potential necessity of limiting or possibly eliminating their contact with friends whose continued use would pose a threat to their recovery.

It is rare that human beings accept any limitation, let alone one of this scope, with equanimity. More typically acceptance comes only gradually, after considerable emotionality and much defensiveness.

Acceptance—Step 1—can be thought of as the process by which patients come to terms with the limitations and losses imposed on them with alcoholism and addiction. The process of acceptance can be broken down into a series of stages, as follows:

- Stage 1: "I have a problem with alcohol [or drugs]."
- Stage 2: "Drinking [or using] is gradually making my life more difficult and is causing more and more problems for me."
- Stage 3: "Since I have lost my ability to effectively limit my use of alcohol [or drugs], the only alternative that makes sense is to give it up."

When discussing Step 1 with the patient, the facilitator may find it useful to keep these "stages of acceptance" in mind and to work toward the goal of helping the patient achieve acceptance in these stages. Remember that virtually all alcoholics and addicts have experienced a personal struggle for control over one or more mood-altering substances. The initial reasons for their drinking or using may be myriad, but the final common pathway for all of them is the struggle to control or limit their use, and their final common denominator is the defeat of their personal willpower by the compulsion of addiction. Along the way, their self-esteem erodes and their isolation grows. It is rare that addicts share their struggle while it is happening.

As a result of wounded pride, the patient is more likely than not to respond defensively when the facilitator's words strike close to home. The facilitator needs to be cognizant of the erosion of character and the sensitivity that addiction creates, while at the same time having the courage to be frank.

Powerlessness

Powerlessness is the essential quality that defines addiction, though it is not always helpful for the facilitator to confront the addict with the stark reality of his/her powerlessness—at least, not initially. But all alcoholics and addicts must ultimately come to terms with their powerlessness over their compulsion to use alcohol or drugs. The more symptoms of dependency they exhibit, the more that powerlessness is a fact of life.

Bob and Kathy are a couple who had been married for twenty years. They came to see the first author, in his capacity as a marital counselor. Though initially obscured by discussions and arguments about money, children, and sex, it became apparent after a while that Bob had a significant drinking problem that needed to be evaluated. He was asked to come in individually for two sessions to talk about this.

It turned out that Bob had several signs of alcohol dependency. He had a powerful tolerance, he drank daily, and he had experienced a number of drinking-related negative consequences—not the least of which was his seriously strained marriage. In addition, he was in trouble at work as another negative consequence of his drinking, a problem he'd kept from his wife.

At first, Bob was reluctant to shift the focus of therapy from his troubled marriage to his drinking. The marriage counselor assured him that his concerns about his marriage were legitimate and would be dealt with; but first, the counselor said, he needed to do something about his drinking or risk losing his job and possibly even his marriage.

Bob's private struggle for control over his alcohol consumption is a testament to stubborn determination as much as it is a classic story of the power of addiction. Having started out as a youth barely twelve years old by sipping beers he stole from the refrigerator, Bob had been drinking continuously for thirty years. Things didn't get bad, he said, until after he was married and the kids were born. Two things happened then. First, he felt obligated to stay in a job that paid well but that he had previously intended to leave. Second, his relationship with Kathy, in his words, had become "diluted" by the demands of family life.

It was around this time—after his younger child, a daughter, was born—that Bob developed the habit of having "a cocktail or two" every night after work, before dinner. For a long time Kathy went along with this, though she noticed that "a cocktail or two" eventually became three, four, or more. She didn't much care for alcohol herself, and she had little personal experience with it in her own family. Out of naïveté, she supposed Bob's ability to "drink others under the table"—in other words, his tolerance—was a good thing. Ironically, she also believed that Bob's ability to "hold his liquor" was a sign that he could not become addicted.

As time went on, addiction gradually set in. Instead of eating in the company cafeteria, Bob found himself going out for lunch two or three times a week. He'd have a couple of beers every time. By the time he got home, he was anxious to "relax"—his euphemism for having cocktails. Kathy and the kids soon found that anything that stood between Bob and his cocktails made him irritable. He didn't want to be "bothered" with their problems until he was "relaxed." Of course, by the time he was "relaxed," Bob was also intoxicated. That made him emotionally unstable and prone to losing his temper. So the rest of the family learned to avoid him. Kathy took to solving most of the household problems by herself, or else she let them go. The kids, meanwhile, led their own lives and had minimal communication with their father.

Though he was very hesitant to admit it for a long time, privately Bob had struggled long and ultimately unsuccessfully to control his drinking. He hadn't wanted to be like his own father—a "quiet drunk" whose drinking was less flamboyant than Bob's but who had "liked his liquor" no less, and who had also been socially isolated and a "nonfactor," as Bob described him, within the family.

The various methods that Bob used in his effort to control his drinking sounded like something right out of the Big Book: drinking only wine, drinking only beer (no cocktails) at lunch, drinking from a smaller glass, adding more ice cubes to his cocktails, and so on. All the while he was conscious on some level that he was gradually losing control, yet he continued to convince himself that he was really all right. Not until he was caught with liquor on his breath at work was Bob's shell of self-deceit finally and abruptly shattered.

To begin the discussion of Step 1, the facilitator should read one or both of the first steps aloud and then talk to the patient about them, making sure to cover the following points:

- "What do these statements mean to you?"
  - "How do they make you feel emotionally?"
  - "What thoughts do you have in relation to them?"
- "How do you relate to the concept of powerlessness? What kinds of things can people be powerless over in their lives?"
- "Can you see how some people might be 'powerless' over alcohol or drugs?"
- "Have you ever felt powerless over something in your own life? What was it?"
- "At this point, do you believe that you can control your use of alcohol [or drugs]? What makes you believe this?"
- "How have you attempted to limit or stop your use up until now?"

• "How powerful is your urge to drink [or use] as compared to your determination not to?"

Discussing Powerlessness

In explaining powerlessness, it may be helpful to say something like this to the patient:

> *Facilitator:* "Step 1 is basically a statement of personal limitation. In other words, 'accepting' powerlessness over alcohol or drugs is much like having to accept any other personal limitation— something you either can't do or have to give up doing. Some people who have a hard time relating to Step 1 as it is written, because of this idea of being powerless, understand it better if they think of it in terms of 'limitation.'
>
> "Can you think of times in your life when you were confronted by a limitation of some sort? It could be physical, intellectual, economic, or whatever. It was something that you wanted to do but couldn't, or else that you liked doing but had to stop. What was it?"

Alternatively, the facilitator can approach powerlessness this way:

> *Facilitator:* "One way to think of powerlessness as it applies to addiction is to compare a person's willpower—their ability to make a decision and stick to it—to their urges to drink or use drugs. AA and NA tell us that, in alcoholism and addiction, even the most powerful people lose this struggle eventually. Gradually, over time, the urge to drink or use becomes a compulsion that overcomes individual willpower. Stories in the Big Book and the NA Big Book tell us that this can happen to even the most determined individuals. That's what the first step challenges us to own up to."

Finally, if the patient continues to have difficulty relating to the concept of powerlessness as it applies to his/her drinking or using, reading the following story, adapted from the Big Book may be helpful:

> Our behavior is as absurd and incomprehensible with respect to the first drink as that of an individual with a passion, say, for jay-walking. He gets a thrill out of skipping in front of fast-moving vehicles. He enjoys himself for a few years in spite of friendly warnings. Up to this point you would label him as a foolish chap having queer ideas of fun. Luck then deserts

him and he is slightly injured several times in succession. You would expect him, if he were normal, to cut it out. Presently he is hit again and this time has a fractured skull. Within a week after leaving the hospital a passing car breaks his arm. He tells you he has decided to stop jay-walking for good; but within a few weeks he breaks both legs.

On through the years his conduct continues, accompanied by his continual promises to be careful or to keep off the streets altogether. Finally, he can no longer work, his wife gets a divorce, and his friends laugh at him. He tries his best to get the jay-walking idea out of his head. But the day comes when he races in front of a fire engine, which breaks his back. Such a man would be crazy, wouldn't he? The fact is that alcoholics, for unknown reasons, have lost the power of choice in drinking, much as the man in this example has lost the power of choice over jay-walking. However intelligent we may have been in other respects, where alcohol [or drugs] has been involved, we have been strangely insane.[3]

Follow this up by engaging the patient in a discussion of this story. Ask questions like:

- "Can you relate to the idea of compulsion presented in this story?"
- "Would you say that jay-walking was 'out of control' in this case?"
- "Can you see how in this example the compulsion was more powerful that the man's willpower?"
- "Have you known anyone who had a compulsion or an obsession that they couldn't control? Have you?"
- "Can you see how some people are as out of control of their drinking as this man was out of control of his jay-walking?"

Conclude the discussion of powerlessness by exploring the patient's prior reactions to limitation.

Facilitator: "Typically, people do not react to limitation calmly; instead, they resist or deny it.

- "Can you relate to not wanting to think about having to face up to and live with some personal limitation in your past? Or feeling mad or uncomfortable about it? When was that? What was the limitation? How did you resist accepting it?"
- "Would you say that limitation has been easy or difficult for you to accept?"

Unmanageability

Another key concept that the facilitator should present in this core topic session is *unmanageability*. As addiction progresses and the alcoholic or addict's lifestyle progressively accommodates to drinking or using,[4] compounding negative consequences gradually undermine the overall quality of his/her life. It is not unusual for work and personal relationships both to become strained, for job evaluations to get worse, and for children to "act out" in various ways. Legal difficulties and financial problems further complicate the alcoholic's or addict's life; meanwhile, s/he is less and less motivated to deal with them.

By the time Bob and Kathy came for marital therapy, he had managed to fall two years behind on his income tax returns and owed the government several thousand dollars. According to Kathy, the house they lived in was "falling apart faster and faster" on account of maintenance projects that he refused to hire someone else to do but kept putting off doing himself. Their son, who had just turned eighteen, was failing half of his courses in college; meanwhile, his daughter "hated" Bob and alternately fought with and ridiculed him. He had not gotten a merit raise for three years at work, and his job evaluations, which had once been outstanding, were now routinely average. His boss was openly critical of him, and Bob was convinced that the man was out to get him. Worst of all, he had been called on the carpet as a result of having alcohol on his breath, and he had been warned that a second such incident would lead to disciplinary action. On top of all this, Kathy was sexually turned off to him, which left him feeling frustrated and filled with self-pity.

Like Bob's life, every alcoholic and addict's life is a story of increasing unmanageability. To facilitate the patient's understanding of it on a personal level, the facilitator should engage the patient in a historical review of his/her life's unmanageability. If necessary, "prompt" the patient's memory with information gathered during the first session.

Facilitator: "Can you think of any ways in which your life become less manageable in recent years?"

The facilitator may want to list ways the patient's life has become increasingly unmanageable on a blackboard or a flipchart:

1. _____

2. _____

3. _____

4. _____

Denial

No other kind of bankruptcy is like this one. Alcohol, now become the rapacious creditor, bleeds us of all self-sufficiency and all will to resist its demands. Once this stark fact is accepted, our bankruptcy as going human concerns is complete.[5]

Denial refers to the emotional and intellectual difficulties that people typically encounter in facing a personal limitation or loss. With respect to alcoholism and addiction, denial is a difficulty in facing and accepting the loss of one's control over drinking or using, as well as the necessity to give it up for good. This is what this core topic—and Step 1—is all about. It is usually a very intense experience, to say the least.

Limitation and loss cause pain, and it is normal for people to try to protect themselves from pain. One of the easiest ways to protect oneself is to deny the reality of the limitation or loss. Limitation and loss arouse feelings of anxiety, anger, shame, sadness, inadequacy, and/or guilt. They pose a decided threat to self-esteem. Any or all of these factors can motivate an individual to avoid—deny—coming to terms with or accepting a personal limitation such as addiction.

Bob tried to avoid coming to terms with his loss of control over drinking as fiercely as any alcoholic might. His first line of defense was to get angry whenever anyone, such as his wife or his children, brought up the subject. After blowing up, he'd usually change the subject and launch into an attack on the other person, or complain long and loudly about some other problem, like finances or his annoying in-laws. In response to the ever-growing list of household maintenance chores that were going undone, he pleaded fatigue—after all, he said, he worked hard all week and needed the weekends to "unwind."

Not surprisingly, Bob's denial extended to his outward behavior, and even inward, to his own thought processes. He went out of his way to associate with men who drank as much as or more than he did, then comforted himself by comparing the level of his own use and theirs. Of course, he concluded that his drinking was merely "average" (and therefore "normal") among his peers. At times when he felt guilty pouring himself that fifth or sixth martini, he'd tell himself that he "deserved" it—because of the stress of having to endure an unsatisfying job. His troubles at work he wrote off to a combination of bad luck and a vindictive boss, and his increasing tendency toward sexual impotence he attributed to his wife's rejection of him and her "preoccupation" with the children.

In these and other ways, Bob was able to fend off the complaints of others, as well as his own nagging conscience. Meanwhile the quality of his life and his own health steadily declined. It was only when he faced disciplinary action at work, when his wife talked about separation, and when his doctor discussed impotence and early symptoms of diabetes, that Bob reluctantly took a hard look at his drinking and his ability to control it.

Discussing Denial

To start discussing denial, the facilitator should ask the patient how it feels to think about being "powerless" over alcohol or drugs. Help the patient to articulate both emotional and intellectual reactions:

> *Facilitator:* "What is it like to be powerless? How does it make you feel?"

1. _____
2. _____
3. _____

Anger, anxiety, and depression are typical reactions to loss and limitation. Acceptance of alcoholism, like acceptance of any limitation, is a grief process. Anger, anxiety, and sadness are part and parcel of healthy grieving, so reassure the patient that these would be normal, indeed healthy reactions.

> *Facilitator:* "What do you think about the idea of being out of control of drinking [or using]?"

1. _____
2. _____
3. _____

Loss of control also invites a variety of protests, from an intellectual questioning of the concepts of addiction and alcoholism, to feelings of guilt and shame over the addiction. Guilt and shame have strong emotional components, but they are also associated with specific negative thoughts about the self: the idea that one has done something wrong, or that one is inadequate or inferior. Try to elicit both the affective and the cognitive aspects of shame and guilt that can be associated with Step 1.

Forms of Denial

Next, the facilitator should describe and explain the various forms that denial takes:

Simple Denial. Simple denial amounts to a blunt refusal to face facts, to look at one's own behavior, or be open to an experience. Examples include:

- refusing to discuss drinking or using;
- resisting doing a serious alcohol/drug history;
- refusing to acknowledge the real consequences of drinking or using;
- rejecting clear evidence of tolerance; and
- refusing to go to AA/NA meetings.

Minimizing and Maximizing. In this form of denial, the individual minimizes his/her own drinking or using and their consequences by drawing false comparisons to the drinking or using that others do. Examples are:

- understating the negative consequences of one's own drinking or using, while exaggerating the drinking or using problems of others; and
- accusing others of exaggerating one's own use or its negative consequences.

Avoidance. In this form of denial, alcohols or addicts avoid coming to terms with their problem by becoming socially isolated from friends or family, or both. Another way to avoid the problem is to become excessively busy, such as by working a lot or devoting an extraordinary amount of time to an activity or hobby.

Rationalizing. This form of denial involves finding excuses for drinking or using. Some common rationalizations for drinking or using include:

- work, family, or marital stress;
- depression or anxiety;
- physical pain, discomfort, or insomnia.

Aside from excusing their own drinking or using, many people find excuses for not following up on suggested recovery tasks, especially going to meetings or actively participating in them. It can be helpful to anticipate these rationalizations. They include:

- being too busy at work;
- being too busy at home;
- not having a babysitter;
- not having transportation; and
- being too shy to speak up.

Distracting. One of the most effective forms of denial is distracting oneself and others whenever the issue comes up. Alcoholics and addicts can be remarkably creative at coming up with distractions. In these sessions, the facilitator may try to discuss tolerance and negative consequences, for example, only to find himself/herself lured into a discussion of the patient's marital problems, unhappy work life, or problem children. The facilitator's efforts to discuss the core topic may be turned into debates over the exact nature of addiction; suggestions about meetings might get sidetracked into soliloquies on the merits of self-help groups versus psychotherapy, or discussions on a recent article in the newspaper on the treatment of addiction. Instead of talking about what needs to be done, such as going to meetings, the patient may attempt to distract the facilitator by complaining about their inconvenient times or locations, about the kinds of people who go there, or about the AA/NA emphasis on spirituality.

The facilitator should be vigilant for such distractions and make efforts to shift the focus back onto what counts most.

Contrasting. One AA maxim says, "Identify, don't compare." This simple saying speaks to two truths about addiction. One is that in order to reach out for help, the addicted individual needs to identify with others. The second is that drawing contrasts is a good way for such an individual to avoid identifying. Twelve-step programs are all based on the fact that regardless of differences in sex, cultural background, or social status, all alcoholics and addicts share one thing: substance dependency. Their individual willpower has been defeated by their addiction, and sobriety—perhaps survival itself—depends on their willingness to reach out for the support of others like themselves.

Drawing unfavorable comparisons between themselves and other alcoholics or addicts, then using these contrasts as a reason not to give AA or NA a fair chance, is yet another form of denial. Contrasts that patients commonly make include all of the above (sex, culture, status), along with many more, such as education and politics ("I can't relate to the people at AA meetings"), spirituality ("I don't believe in God like you're supposed to in AA") and lifestyle ("I'm much busier than people who go to AA meetings"). Again, the facilitator should be alert for denial that takes the form of contrasting.

Pseudochoice. In this form of denial, the patient acknowledges his/her excessive use and the negative consequences of that use. But then s/he attempts to attribute these to choice rather than to addiction. An alcoholic may attribute his/her tendency to get falling-down drunk four or five times a week to having a "party personality," thereby implying or claiming that the behavior is voluntary—and therefore "under control." S/he may admit to having a substantial tolerance level, to getting into trouble at work, and even to getting arrested, then explain these symptoms of dependency away as reflections of a lively, rebellious personality.

Bargaining. When a patient bargains, it usually takes the form of agreeing to limit or control the amount of alcohol or drug used, or when it is used, or the type used. Bargaining can be thought of as denial by way of placating—either one's own conscience, or the expressed concerns of others.

Denial List

The facilitator should work with the patient to list some of the ways in which s/he may be using denial to fend off facing his/her powerlessness, loss, and limitation because of alcoholism or addiction:

1. _____
2. _____
3. _____

Once this list is finished, make a copy for the patient to keep, preferably on his/her person at all times. Ask the patient to review the list every few days and to refer to it when s/he feels reluctant to follow up on recovery tasks.

Overview of Twelve-Step Fellowships

Regardless of how familiar the patient professes to be with AA, NA, or other twelve-step programs, it is usually helpful for the facilitator to take a few minutes to cover several points of information.

Twelve-step fellowships like AA and NA were started by and for alcoholics and addicts who had tried their best to control their alcohol or drug use over many years, only to admit "defeat"—powerlessness and unmanageability—in the end. Along the way they employed all manner of defenses against facing the truth and tried all sorts of ways to "control" their drinking or using.

The fellowships of AA and NA were founded on these simple ideas:

- that some people, for some reason, simply cannot stop their use of alcohol or drugs by relying on individual willpower alone;
- that there is no "cure" for alcoholism or drug addiction—no "treatment" that will enable an alcoholic to drink "safely" or an addict to use "safely";
- that abstinence—staying clean and sober one day at a time—is the only viable option for alcoholics and addicts if they want to stop the steady decline that alcoholism and addiction create;
- that because willpower is no match for addiction, alcoholics and addicts

need to seek support from others in making whatever changes are necessary; and

- that the best source of support and advice for alcoholics and addicts is other recovering alcoholics and addicts who have found ways of leading clean and sober lives.

The facilitator should also review the main goals of AA and NA to make certain that the patient clearly understands the following:

- that the goal of AA is to avoid "that first drink," and that the goal of NA is to avoid using drugs "that first time";
- that AA and NA ask their members not to think about abstaining from drinking and using "forever," but to focus on deciding not to drink or use today; and
- that AA and NA are not looking for perfection—slips are less important than what one does about them.

Recovery Tasks

The following are the recovery tasks suggested for this session, on the core topic of "acceptance."

Meetings

The facilitator and patient should agree on how many and which AA/NA meetings the patient will attend before the next session. Review the patient's reactions to meetings that were already attended, and make specific suggestions about what meetings could be attended between now and the next facilitation session. Keep in mind the goal of encouraging the patient to commit eventually to attending ninety meetings in ninety days. Explore any resistance the patient's exhibits to going to meetings as a form of denial. Press for a maximum commitment, and make a note of exactly what meetings the patient says s/he will attend.

Reading

Suggested readings relative to this core topic are:

- Twelve by Twelve: pp. 21–24
- Big Book: "The Doctors Opinion," "Bill's Story," and "More About Alcoholism" and/or

- NA Big Book: "Who Is An Addict?" "Why Are We Here?" and "How It Works," pp. 3–8, 13–51
- *Living Sober*, pp. 7–10

The facilitator may make additional suggestions for readings as they seem appropriate for the individual patient. A particularly good pamphlet is "Grieving: A Healing Process."[6]

Journal

The patient should continue to make a note in the journal of meetings already attended, and to write down his/her frank reactions to those meetings, as well as to the readings.

Follow-Up: Unmanageability

Ask the patient to give further thought to the idea that alcohol or drugs make life unmanageable. Suggest that s/he make a list in the journal, in chronological order, of experiences and events that illustrate how his/her life has become gradually and increasingly unmanageable as a consequence of drinking or using.

Facilitator Notes

Denial

The main goal of this part of the facilitation program is not to explore, confront, or break down the patient's denial per se. The main goal here is to facilitate his/her active participation in AA and/or NA. The issue of denial becomes clinically relevant here only insofar as it presents itself as resistance to "getting active" in AA or NA. If there is little such resistance, there is little need to explore denial in depth. On the other hand, if a patient offers resistances that are similar to the forms of denial as they have been described here the facilitator needs to address them.

Approaching Denial as "Insanity." However it is conceptualized and whatever form it takes, denial should be thought of as an integral part of the illness of addiction itself. From the twelve-step perspective, addiction produces a kind of "insanity"—revealed in denial in its various forms. Alcoholism and addiction are "cunning" illnesses, one symptom of which is self-delusion about the problem. It is common wisdom within AA that it is an aspect of alcoholism itself that alcoholics convince themselves they aren't ill. From this point of view, the denial of illness is part of the illness itself. Indeed, one of the earliest symptoms of addiction is resistance to talking about one's drinking or using.[7]

In the "insanity" of addiction, alcoholics and addicts continue to drink or use by convincing themselves that "this time will be different"—that previous losses of control and previous negative consequences will somehow magically not happen again. Of course, the next time is never different from other times. The addict loses control and suffers some negative consequence all over again. The following passage from the Big Book illustrates denial in action:

> I went to my hotel and leisurely dressed for dinner. As I crossed the threshold of the dining room, the thought came to mind that it would be nice to have a couple of cocktails with dinner. That was all. Nothing more. I ordered a cocktail and my meal. Then I ordered another cocktail. After dinner I decided to take a walk. When I returned to the hotel it struck me a highball would be fine before going to bed, so I stepped into the bar and had one. I remember having several more that night and plenty next morning. I have a shadowy recollection of being in an airplane bound for New York, and of finding a friendly taxicab driver at the landing field instead of my wife. The driver escorted me about for several days. I know little of where I went or what I said and did.[8]

Such experiences are commonplace among alcoholics and addicts. Still, they convince themselves that "this time it will be different."

Another way in which alcoholism and addiction manifest their "insanity" is in the fallacious feeling of safety that addicts have while drinking or using. Another passage from the Big Book:

> I decided to drive into the country and see one of my prospects for [buying] a car. On the way I felt hungry so I stopped at a roadside place where they have a bar. I had no intention of drinking. I just thought I would get a sandwich.
>
> I sat down at a table and ordered a sandwich and a glass of milk. Still no thought of drinking. I ordered another sandwich and decided to have another glass of milk.
>
> Suddenly the thought crossed my mind that if I were to put an ounce of whiskey in my milk it couldn't hurt me on a full stomach. I ordered a whiskey and poured it into the milk. I vaguely sensed that I was not being any too smart, but felt reassured as I was taking the whiskey on a full stomach. The experiment went so well that I ordered another whiskey and poured it into more milk. That didn't seem to bother me so I tried another.
>
> That started one more journey to the asylum for Jim.[9]

So does addiction play out as cunning, baffling, and powerful.

One way of conceptualizing denial, then, is as "insanity," as represented in the above patterns of thinking. In this facilitation session, based on the patient's own accounts of his/her experiences, the facilitator can consistently point out the patient's delusional belief (delusional because it flies in the face of experience) that s/he can "safely" drink or use. Alcoholism and addiction are illnesses of the mind as much as of the body[10] insofar as alcoholics and addicts create the illusion that they drink or use by their own choice, when in fact their drinking or using is an obsession that lurks just beneath the surface of their consciousness and that, once released, leaves no room at all for their free will or conscious, rational choice. Seen from this perspective, a patient's resistance to accepting a diagnosis of alcohol or drug dependency, and continuing to think and act in ways that promote the illusion of self-control, are themselves aspects of alcoholism and addiction, just as surely as physical tolerance is.

The facilitator can interpret denial in terms of "insane" thinking and self-deception by offering comments such as the following at appropriate times:

> *Facilitator:* "Alcoholism is in fact an illness—an illness of the mind and of the body. It affects you physically. For example, you've had blackouts, you've developed a strong tolerance, and you crave alcohol. It also affects you mentally—the way you think—even when you're sober. When you went to that party last weekend, you convinced yourself that it would be okay to drink, as long as you only drank wine with dinner. Then you went home and got drunk on bourbon. That's the illness at work. It's called 'stinking thinking.' "

> *Facilitator:* "From the NA point of view, the fact that you don't want to go to meetings is just another symptom of the illness of addiction. You know from experience that once you start using, you can't stop. But you continue to convince yourself that you really don't have this obsession, that you can control your use of _____ without the help of NA, when the facts speak to the contrary. It's probably just a matter of time before you trick yourself into using again."

Approaching Denial as Part of Grief. Another way for the facilitator to approach denial is to describe it as a normal part of the grief process. People seem to be naturally disposed to deny their losses and limitations:

> Denial is a shock absorber for the soul. It's a normal, natural, instinctual response to loss.[11]

Alcoholism and addiction present us with losses and limitations. Step 1—this session's core topic of "acceptance"—asks the patient to acknowledge a "loss" of personal control over his/her drinking or using and a "loss" of his/her ability to manage his/her own life. Recovery means "losing" not only the mood-altering substances upon which the patient has come to depend, but very possibly a group of friends and a lifestyle that supported his/her addiction.

Though denial is natural and in a sense normal, it is dangerous for the alcoholic or addict who refuses to face the reality of his/her loss of control:

> Denial is serious. When alcoholics deny their disease, they continue drinking themselves to death. Drug addicts deny they have a problem, and get sicker.[12]

The facilitator may want to interpret this way of conceptualizing denial for the patient as follows:

> *Facilitator:* "I think that part of your unwillingness to go to meetings may be denial. I think there's a part of you that doesn't want to accept this limitation: That you're an alcoholic [or addict], that you've lost control, and that you have to give up drinking [or using]. That part of you wants you to avoid the truth, and it motivates you to avoid going to an AA [NA] meeting where you might have to face the truth."

Approaching Denial as Bargaining. A third way for the facilitator to approach denial, also consistent with the literature on grief, is to label it "bargaining." As it applies to Step 1 and the core topic of acceptance, bargaining is revealed in the patient's secret belief that s/he can "safely" drink or use, that s/he can in fact "control" his/her drinking or using.

This idea of bargaining is a natural part of our defenses against facing and accepting loss and limitation. To explore this idea with the patient, the facilitator may want to read the following passage to the patient:

> Bargaining is a desperate attempt to stay in control, to have things the way we want them. Trying to control our use is bargaining: "If I have only one or two drinks, it'll prove I'm in control and therefore not powerless. Bargaining keeps us from facing reality, and in that way, it's a form of denial."[13]

As a form of denial, bargaining is most evident when a patient with obvious symptoms of dependency "tempts fate" by having a drink or two, or by using drugs once or twice, between sessions. To pursue this, ask the patient questions like these:

- "So you had a couple of drinks this week. In making the decision to do that, were you trying to convince yourself that you're still in control?"

- "How would you interpret the fact that you drank [or used] last week in light of Step 1? Is there a part of you that won't accept having to give it up altogether?"

- "In your own mind, what did drinking [or using] this last time prove about your ability to control your use? How does this square with the negative experiences you've had in the past, and with your overall ability to control your use?"

Approaching Denial as an Internal Conflict. Some facilitators may find it helpful to approach denial by framing it as an internal conflict within the patient. Addicts can be thought of as people who have a "dual personality": Part of them wants to live a clean and sober life and enjoys sober consciousness (the "recovering personality"), while another part resists the idea of limitation, craves alcohol or drugs, and will do anything to get it (the "addict personality"). For the addict perceived as a dual personality, recovery represents an ongoing struggle between these two inner forces. The facilitator needs to identify the patient's recovering personality as it is revealed in the patient's actions and thoughts; to ally unequivocally with that recovering personality; and to assist the patient in strengthening it. At the same time, the facilitator needs to be vigilant for the addict personality, to point it out, and to help the patient work through his/her inner conflict.

In using this approach to denial, the facilitator should keep the following in mind in order to align effectively with the "recovering personality" within the patient:

- Alcoholism and addiction are more powerful than the patient's individual willpower (the recovery personality) alone. The addict personality—denial—will inevitably win out if the patient chooses to fight it without help from AA and/or NA.

- It is a normal human tendency to resist accepting limitation and to "test" limitation. This resistance feeds the addict personality and may be deadly to the patient in the long run.

- The addict personality is cunning and clever and will make every effort to lower the defenses of the recovering personality.

It can be helpful for the facilitator to have the patient objectify these two personalities, such as by writing out brief "personality sketches" of them or by giving them names. These names can then become a convenient shorthand between patient and facilitator: "I can hear _____ whispering in your ear when you think about going to that party, where all your old using friends will be."

Here are other interpretations consistent with this approach to denial:

- "You slipped because you fooled yourself into thinking you were safe. So you went to the bar to meet your old friends, thinking that you could do that and not drink."

- "The part of you that wants to deny your addiction tells you that you can control your use, that it was okay for you to have those cocktails at _____'s party. You fooled yourself into believing that you could limit your use, because you wanted to believe it."

- "I know you don't like to hear this, but I see your denial at work again. The part of you that still wants to drink—that doesn't want to let go of alcohol—was telling you that you *could* have that beer, and that you'd be able to stop there, even though experience proves you can't."

Whatever approach to denial the facilitator chooses to use, the goal is to help the patient understand and relate to it in the context of his/her own experience with drinking or using. Once that has been done, the facilitator can interpret the patient's resistance to getting involved in AA or NA in this light. This interpretation should be made as often as necessary in a frank and nonjudgmental manner.

Keep this phrase in mind throughout treatment: "Denial Never Sleeps." Some AA members compare being in recovery to "walking up a down escalator": As soon as the recovering alcoholic or addict becomes complacent and stops actively "working the program," the illness begins bringing him/her down once again. Recovery demands eternal vigilance—which is what active involvement in the AA/NA fellowships can provide.

Compliance

The facilitator should beware the patient who accepts a diagnosis of dependency or embraces Step 1 with equanimity. Among the many common reactions to loss and limitation, calm acceptance is not high on the list. More likely than not, the patient's calm acceptance is a cover for placating the facilitator. Many a patient who has relapsed soon after leaving an alcohol or drug rehabilitation program has confessed to not "buying" the idea of powerlessness and the need for abstinence in the first place. Many of these men and women concealed their doubts from public view. To say publicly, "My name is _____, and I am an alcoholic [or addict]" cannot be a genuine act of acceptance, many believe, if the person who says it is emotionally neutral.

True acceptance of loss and limitation—of powerlessness and unmanageability—is most likely to be an emotionally intense experience. Patients who too readily accept the implications of Step 1 for themselves and their lives may very well be merely "talking the talk" of recovery. Meanwhile, their actions reflect their true resistance to "walking the walk" of the twelve steps.

Core Topic 3: Surrender

Core Topic 3, surrender, is based on the second and third steps of Alcoholics Anonymous and Narcotics Anonymous:

> We came to believe that a Power greater than ourselves could restore us to sanity.

> We made a decision to turn our will and our lives over to the care of God as we understood him.[1]

If Step 1 involves "accepting the problem," Steps 2 and 3 involve "accepting the solution." The two go hand in hand, and together they form the foundation for recovery through involvement in the AA/NA fellowships. Whereas taking Step 1 requires coming to terms with loss and limitation, taking the next two steps challenges the patient to take a leap of faith: to believe that there is hope for arresting his/her addiction and for making life manageable again, and to place his/her fate in the hands of a power greater than his/her individual will. This leap is sometimes referred to as "surrender," in contrast to the resistance that characterizes the addict in denial.

Presenting the Material

In the session devoted to core topic 3, we recommend that the facilitator introduce this material by referring the patient to the chapters on Steps 2 and 3 in *Twelve Steps and Twelve Traditions*, suggesting this reading as a recovery task for the coming week. Then read Step 2 aloud to the patient and elicit his/her reactions to it. In approaching this discussion, emphasize the importance of keeping an open mind. Remember that what you are asking is that the patient give the twelve-step way a try, without getting hung up on issues of religious beliefs and without necessarily making a long-term commitment to it. Reassure the patient that twelve-step fellowships are open to people with a wide range of personal beliefs—in this case, the belief in some power greater than personal willpower.

First, Alcoholics Anonymous does not demand that you believe anything. All its twelve steps are but suggestions. Second, to get sober and to stay sober, you don't have to swallow all of Step 2 right now. Looking back, I find that I took it piecemeal myself. Third, all you really need is a truly open mind. Just resign from the debating society, and quit bothering yourself with such deep questions as whether it was the chicken or the egg that came first. Again I say, all you need is the open mind.

Of course, in facilitating this dialogue it is important that the facilitator keep as open a mind as s/he is asking the patient to have. Step 2 is rooted in the experiences of countless alcoholics and addicts that personal will-power alone is not sufficient to overcome true addiction. As the Big Book says,

> Lack of power, that was our dilemma. We had to find a power by which we could live, and it had to be a Power greater than ourselves. Obviously. But where and how were we to find this Power?
> Well, that's exactly what this book is about. Its main objective is to enable you to find a Power greater than yourself which will solve your problem. That means we have written a book which we believe to be spiritual as well as moral.[3]

A Higher Power

The particular manner in which the individual chooses to think of a power greater than the self is up to that individual. But twelve-step fellowships are founded on the assumption that recovery begins with acceptance of defeat (of one's own willpower), combined with a leap of faith in some greater source of strength.

> The pain [of addiction] forces us to seek a Power greater than ourselves than can relieve our obsession to use.
> The process of coming to believe is similar for most addicts. Most of us lacked a working relationship with a Higher Power. We begin to develop this relationship by simply admitting to the possibility of a Power greater than ourselves. Most of us have no trouble admitting that addiction had become a destructive force in our lives [Step 1]. Our best efforts resulted in ever greater destruction and despair. At some point, we realized that we needed the help of some Power greater than our addiction. Our understanding of a Higher Power is up to us. No one is going to decide for us. We can call it the group, the program, or we can call it God. The only suggested guidelines are that this Power be loving, caring and greater than ourselves.[4]

Whatever Higher Power the individual chooses to cast his/her faith in, it is vital to do so.

If you think you are an atheist, an agnostic, a skeptic, or have any other form of intellectual pride which keeps you from accepting what is in this book, I feel sorry for you. If you still think you are strong enough to beat the game alone, that is your affair. But if you really and truly want to quit drinking liquor for good and all, and sincerely feel that you must have some help, we know that we have an answer for you. It never fails, if you go about it with one half the zeal you have been in the habit of showing when you were getting another drink.[5]

The facilitator should review the above concepts (we suggest reading one or more passages aloud to the patient), then proceed to a discussion of what the second step means to the patient.

- "As a youth, who were your heroes? Who are they now?"
- "What, in your own words, are your most cherished values?"
- "Are you open to the idea that there may be a power or powers in the universe that are stronger than your individual willpower?"
- "What kind(s) of Higher Power(s) do you believe in? Are any of these powers benign and loving?"
- "Were you ever religiously active? When? When and why did you stop being active?"
- "Have you ever prayed? If so, when, and for what reason? When was the last time?"
- "When was the last time you called on a friend for help of any kind? What was the occasion?"
- "Have you ever trusted anyone in the past? If so, who? How did that work out?"
- "Who do you trust the most now, and why?"

Defiance and arrogance are personality traits commonly ascribed to alcoholics and addicts.[6] Unrecovering alcoholics and addicts are known for their capacity to be grandiose and self-centered—in effect, to believe in no power greater than themselves. Explain this to the patient, and follow up with a question or two.

- "Have you ever been told that you are arrogant? If so, what was the occasion, and how did you react?"
- "In what ways do you see yourself as acting in defiant, stubborn, or arrogant ways?"
- "Can you relate to how arrogant defiance could be a defense against facing up to the limitation of your alcoholism or drug addiction?"

AA and NA are open to individual interpretations of what "a power greater than ourselves" means; so too are they open to diverse interpretations of the "God" to whom alcoholics and addicts are asked to subordinate their wills in Step 3. No doubt the addition of the phrase "as we understood Him" and the spiritual pluralism it represents has been at least partly responsible for AA/NA's remarkable cross-cultural adaptability, as well as their ability to accommodate many people whose spiritual beliefs are tenuous at best. Here are only two examples of the many ways in which the God of AA and NA can be approached:

> My depression deepened unbearably, and finally it seemed to me as though I were at the very bottom of the pit. For the moment, the last vestige of my proud obstinacy was crushed. All at once I found myself crying out, "If there is a God, let Him show Himself! I am ready to do anything, anything!"
>
> Suddenly the room lit up with a great white light. It seemed to me, in the mind's eye, that I was on a mountain and that a wind not of air but of spirit was blowing. And then it burst upon me that I was a free man. Slowly the ecstacy subsided. I lay on the bed, but now for a time I was in another world, a new world of consciousness. All about me and through me there was a wonderful feeling of Presence, and I thought to myself, "So this is the God of the preachers!"

> In quiet moments of meditation, God's will can become evident to us. Quieting the mind through meditation brings an inner peace that brings us into contact with the God within us.[7]

Step 3 can be thought of as opening a locked door: moving away from hopelessness and isolation toward hope and help. The facilitator should pursue a discussion of the patient's willingness and readiness to take this step by asking the patient questions like these:

- "What does the idea of 'turning over' your will mean to you? Have you ever trusted another person enough to follow their advice blindly? Who was that, and what was the outcome?"

- "Can you believe that the experience of countless alcoholics and addicts can have relevance for them, and that part of recovering may involve following 'common wisdom' such as that found in the twelve steps?"

- "How willing are you to 'turn yourself over' to the twelve steps and try following that program for a while, doing what is asked of you without questioning?"

Another way the facilitator can approach Step 3 is through discussing the "cult of self-reliance"—the contemporary notion, popular in many quarters, that one can be totally responsible for oneself, without needing to rely on others to achieve personal goals. AA and NA are based on the idea of interdependence as opposed to self-reliance. They address the cult of self-reliance in this way:

> Now we come to another kind of problem: the intellectually self-sufficient man or woman. To these, many A.A.'s can say, "Yes, we were like you— far too smart for our own good. We loved to have people call us precocious. We used our education to blow ourselves up into prideful balloons, though we were careful to hide this from others. Secretly, we felt we could float above the rest of the folks on our brainpower alone. Scientific progress told us there was nothing man couldn't do. Knowledge was all-powerful. Intellect could conquer nature. Since we were brighter than most folks (so we thought), the spoils of victory would be ours for the thinking. The god of intellect displaced the God of our fathers.[8]

We suggest that the facilitator follow this line of thought, if it seems applicable, by asking the patient questions like these:

- "How much have you bought into the cult of self-reliance in your own thinking?"
- "What reactions do you have to the notion of dependency, as opposed to self-sufficiency, in life?"
- "How much have you become alienated from the idea of God as a result of having a faith in something else: science, intellect, or personal will-power?"

Wrap-Up

Finish this discussion of surrender by taking the time to elicit in detail any concerns or reservations the patient may have to this initial talk about Steps 2 and 3. Reassure the patient that reservations, especially ones about having "faith," are common (and quite acceptable within AA and NA), as the following passage suggests:

> You have convinced us that we are alcoholics [or addicts] and that our lives are unmanageable. Having reduced us to a state of absolute help-lessness, you now declare that none but a Higher Power can remove our obsession. Some of us won't believe in God, others can't, and still others who do believe that God exists have no faith whatever He will perform this miracle.[9]

Recovery Tasks

Suggested recovery tasks for this facilitation session are as follows:

Meetings

Decide with the patient which meetings s/he will attend before the next session. How many meetings is the patient willing to commit to generally. Is s/he willing to try to do ninety meetings in ninety days, as a way to "turning it over" to AA or NA?

Is the patient ready to try out different kinds of meetings, such as "step" meetings and "discussion" meetings? How about a women's or men's meeting?

If the patient resists going to meetings, how might this reflect the workings of denial?

Reading

Suggested readings for this session are as follows:

- The Big Book: "Bill's Story," "There Is a Solution," and "We Agnostics," and/or the NA Big Book, pages 22–26;
- Twelve and Twelve, pages 25–41; and
- *Living Sober*, pages 77–87.

Facilitator Notes

Stories of Other People's Experiences

Jennie was typical of women (and men) who have suffered abuse—she balked when she was confronted with Steps 2 and 3. Her distrust and cynicism stood in the way of her finding hope for herself, of finding a Higher Power in whom she could have faith, and of reaching out to others. The roots of her distrust are not hard to understand. Abandoned through divorce by her natural father, she was later sexually abused by a stepfather over a period of years. Her mother divorced the stepfather when she discovered the abuse, but Jennie's relationship with her by then was badly strained as well. When Jennie was fifteen, the one sibling to whom she had felt close, an older sister, was killed in a car accident. It is little wonder that Jennie had difficulty accepting the concept of a loving Higher Power—much less turning her life and will over to that power.

As a lesbian, Jennie was comfortable with her sexual orientation, but she was decidedly uncomfortable around men. Her partners seem to have been more dependent on her than vice versa and inclined to hold her in awe. Indeed, Jennie was an attractive, intelligent, and talented woman. She was also cross-addicted to alcohol and cocaine and was massively underachieving in virtually every aspect of her life.

Despite her air of erudite sophistication, Jennie was naive in many ways. Her facade of bravado covered up deep inner insecurities and an almost desperate dependency. At her mother's urging, she sought psychotherapy after yet another of a long string of brief emergency room detoxifications, and she was told that her best (and perhaps only) hope was not psychotherapy but to get to an AA/NA meeting immediately and to go to as many of these as necessary in order to stay sober, one day at a time.

Six months later, Jennie returned to the psychotherapist who had told her this, clean and sober. She told the therapist her story of recovery through AA and NA, explaining that the hardest step for her had not been admitting powerlessness. "No," she said, "Step 1 was easy for me. By then, I was ready to admit defeat. It was the solution I couldn't bring myself to swallow."

Jennie had already tried AA and NA before, and each time she'd had a mixed reaction. On the one hand, she had always liked the warm feeling of acceptance she got at meetings. On the other hand, it turned her off that men would sometimes approach her in a way that made her uncomfortable. "They would ask me to go for coffee," she said, "but all the time they were looking me up and down." This upset Jennie and made her angry. To complicate matters, she had a self-destructive tendency, no doubt connected in some way to her childhood abuse, to accommodate the man despite her own anger. Sitting there having coffee with a man she didn't want to be with and talking to him would make her feel trapped. This was especially likely to happen with men who came on in a way that was outwardly appropriate but whose private intentions she had reason to suspect. If she saw a man a second time, at another meeting, and if he approached her again, she slipped out the back door and never returned.

Later on, Jennie effectively solved this problem through a combination of assertiveness and networking. The first thing she did was to go to a couple of women's meetings. There she talked not only about her addiction but about her discomfort at the other meetings. She was encouraged to find a sponsor she could trust and to use the sponsor as a source of advice and support in both matters. She did—"I found me a beautiful, wise, and kind woman old enough to be my mother," she laughed—who helped her to break her self-destructive pattern over time.

But another thing that had originally bothered Jennie about AA and NA was the idea of God. All she heard, it seemed, was people talking about God. This made her almost as uncomfortable as the men who came on to her since she had nothing positive to say about either God or religion. She could not bring herself to believe in a God, she explained, that she regarded as "a sexist, vindictive male image—a way for men to worship themselves."

One day she was sitting in a meeting trying hard to overcome the desire to get drunk that had been nagging her all day, when an old man who had been sitting quietly next to her suddenly grunted aloud and shifted in his seat. "Well," he said after the person who'd been talking was finished, "speaking just for me, AA has nothing much at all to do with God. It has to do with staying sober, pure and simple. I get tired sometimes of listening to too much God-talk. It makes me shiver. AA is a place where I can go and be with sober people. It's been that way for me for eighteen years. If you want to stay sober, go to meetings; if that's not enough, then you live at meetings, like I did for about a year when I first got sober."

Jennie found herself moved by the simple honesty of his remarks, and she was touched when the rest of the group simply thanked the old man for sharing his thoughts. Then someone else spoke, and the meeting moved on. "That was it," said Jennie. "No arguing. No recriminations. That old guy could just say out loud that he thought God was unnecessary, and no one argued with him! No one kicked him out! That's when I realized that if AA could be a home for him, it could be one for me, too."

For Jennie, the Higher Power she could believe in turned out to be the group itself; its support and kindness; its ability to accept diversity, fault, and failure with love; its encouragement of honesty; and its collective wisdom. She had always felt different, alienated, and used, and she wanted more than anything to be accepted and respected. AA and NA gave her that, and her groups were all the Higher Power she needed to stay clean and sober (at least for the time that we knew her).

Twelve-step programs have a long and rich oral tradition. Telling personal stories of loss and recovery and reading about others' experiences with addiction are powerful ways that the lessons of AA and NA are learned. Sharing and discussing stories like Jennie's, or stories from the Big Book and the NA Big Book, or stories based on the facilitator's own experiences can be powerful tools in twelve-step facilitation. We strongly encourage facilitators to suggest that the patient read one or two stories as a recovery task after each facilitation session. Stories that are relevant to this session on Core Topic 3 include:

- NA Big Book: "If I Can Do It, So Can You"
- Big Book: "Our Southern Friend"

Progress versus Perfection

> The principles we have set down are guides to progress. We claim spiritual progress rather than spiritual perfection.[10]

This statement describes not only the AA/NA view of spirituality but the very heart of the twelve-step approach to addiction and recovery. What AA and NA seek and expect is progress, not perfection. They expect slips, denial, and resistance; they hope for long-term gains in behavior, thinking, and in outlook. They tolerate differences while looking for the common ground.

The facilitator should explore the patient's slips and failures to maintain the patient's commitment in light of these expectations. Engage the patient in a frank and open discussion of the slip, or discuss his/her reasons for not doing what s/he had agreed to do between sessions. Try to help the patient who has not kept a commitment to see how this might be a reflection of denial. What attitudes lie behind the patient's resistance? Does the patient make excuses, vacillate, ridicule, or find fault with the twelve steps? Does s/he entertain a secret belief that s/he is not really an alcoholic or addict? One of the most common forms of denial is to think of oneself as "different" from the people who go to meetings—"I'm not like those people." This becomes an excuse for not attending meetings at all. Of course, every patient is "different" from other alcoholics or addicts in some ways, and the facilitator can readily acknowledge this. The point, however, is not how AA/NA members differ but how they are the same—namely, in being unable to control their compulsion to drink or use. In what ways is the patient is similar to those who go to meetings, especially with respect to drinking or using? Does it make the patient uncomfortable to think that s/he may resemble "those other people" in this way? If others are worse off without attending meetings, can the patient imagine ending up that way too?

Explore the patient's attitudes, then counter them by using facts that have been established by the alcohol/drug history and other information that has emerged in the facilitation program. Do this in a respectful but frank manner: The patient has the right to resist, but you have the obligation to state the facts as you see them.

One Day at a Time

It is understandable that patients and facilitators alike are inclined to count consecutive sober days as a measure of success. But it is more consistent with the AA/NA view for the facilitator to congratulate the patient for staying sober today than to get overly involved in counting sober days. The goal is to stay sober today and not to worry too much about yesterday or tomorrow. It is appropriate—in fact, it's fine—to congratulate the patient who stays sober for several consecutive days or weeks. At the same time, it's important not to lose sight of the fact that a slip can happen at any time. Slips do not negate the period of sobriety that went before them; nor do they cast a shadow on the sobriety that can follow them. But it is dangerous for the facilitator or the patient to drift into perfectionism in regard to sobriety. What is ultimately most important is what the patient is doing today about his/her drinking. In this regard it is helpful to avoid discussions of giving up drinking or using "forever." If the patient raises this issue, respond by saying something like this: "AA and NA doesn't ask people to give up anything forever. People in AA and NA have only decided not to drink or use today. They make that decision one day at a time."

For the patient who has slipped, honesty is critical. The facilitator must encourage and value honesty over perfection. The patient who has slipped needs to make a decision: to drink (or use) again that day, or to not drink (or use) again that day. Comfort may be found in the one-day-at-a-time wisdom of AA and NA:

> There are two days in every week about which we would not worry, two days which should be kept from fear and apprehension. One of these days is yesterday, with its mistakes and cares, its faults and blunders, its aches and pains. Yesterday has passed forever beyond our control. All the money in the world cannot bring back yesterday. We cannot undo a single act we performed. We cannot erase a single word we said. Yesterday is gone beyond recall.
>
> The other day we should not worry about is tomorrow, with its possible adversities, its burdens, its large promise, and perhaps its poor performance. Tomorrow is also beyond our immediate control. Tomorrow's sun will rise, either in splendor or behind a mask of clouds, but it will rise. Until it does, we have no stake in tomorrow, for it is as yet unborn.
>
> This leaves only one day—today. Anyone can fight the battles of just one day. It is only when you and I add the burden of those two awful eternities, yesterday and tomorrow, that we break down. Let us therefore do our best to live but one day at a time.

> Just for today my thoughts will be on my recovery, living and enjoying life without the use of drugs. Just for today I will have faith in someone in N.A. who believes in me and wants to help me in my recovery. Just for today I will have a program. I will try to follow it to the best of my ability.[11]

Commitment to the Program

If this program is to succeed for any patient, the facilitator must personally believe in the conception of alcoholism and addiction that lie at the foundation of the twelve-step approach: that alcoholism or addiction is an illness affecting the body, the mind, and the spirit, and that it is characterized by compulsiveness, loss of control, and progressive unmanageability in living. The facilitator must believe that the only viable solution for this illness is total abstinence from all mood-altering substances. Because his/her individual willpower has been defeated, the alcoholic or addict needs to reach out for help. AA and NA are sources of group support and practical advice, as well as faith and hope. Recovery is based on complete honesty and on the patient's decision, renewed daily, to not drink or use drugs.

The facilitator must be prepared for patients to resist any or all of these ideas. As the Big Book and NA Big Book make amply clear, patients may criticize or demean the twelve steps, or they may attempt to draw the facilitator into a discussion (or argument or debate) about whether alcoholism or drug addiction "really is an illness," or about whether "controlled" drinking or using is possible. They may attempt to change the agenda of this facilitation program—for example, to make it into marital therapy or family therapy. The facilitator is advised not to enter into such debates, not to react defensively to criticism, and not to get off the agenda of the program. Keep the following in mind:

• The objective of this program is the facilitation of the patient's active involvement with AA and/or NA.

• The facilitator does not need to defend AA and NA—they do very well on their own and will continue to do so regardless of whether a particular patient chooses to "believe in" them.

• Believing in a Higher Power may be less important than simply going to meetings and following good advice, which should be the first goal in recovery.

• A patient may insist on doing things his/her way for now, rather than following the twelve steps. The facilitator must respect this right.

• Every sober day (and sometimes every sober hour) is important and should be recognized. Whenever the facilitator is confronted with a patient's slip, think about how many sober days (or hours) that patient has had since seeing you last.

Getting Active in AA or NA

A Program of Action

"Getting active," or Core Topic 4, refers to the idea that recovery comes only through "working the program"—through active involvement in a twelve-step program—and not from solitary "white-knuckle" determination not to drink or use, or even from passively attending AA/NA meetings. The AA publication *Living Sober* puts it this way:

> Just stopping drinking is not enough. Just not drinking is a negative, sterile thing. That is clearly demonstrated by our experience. To stay stopped, we've found we need to put in place of the drinking a positive program of action.[1]

Getting active, then, refers to the cognitive and behavioral changes that patients need to make in order to support their sobriety. (Some AA members have been known to say that the letters "AA" stand for "attitude adjustment.") The alcoholic or addict needs to stop and think, then to systematically and purposefully replace many old habits and ways of thinking with new ones. Considering the scope of change that sustained recovery requires, it is little wonder that many patients become highly resistant to the facilitation program at this stage. The facilitator should be prepared for this and by doing so will be at an advantage to the facilitator who is surprised—and perhaps dismayed—by it. Getting active means patients making a commitment to change. It is at this point in the program that the true implications of the twelve-step approach become apparent to many patients.

Presenting the Material

To begin Core Topic 4, the facilitator should present the following material, adjusting it as necessary to the individual patient so as to make it clearly understandable.

Addiction is an illness that affects, among other things, the individual's will. As alcoholism and addiction progress into an "illness of the mind"[2] whose essence is obsession, they become stronger and eventually overpower the will altogether. Some addicted individuals can stay sober when they are feeling good, but they will be vulnerable to a slip as soon as they find themselves in situations that evoke certain emotions, such as anger or loneliness, or that tire them—in other words, in any situation where willpower may be weakened. Each time the alcoholic's will is defeated, s/he becomes more hopeless and alienated. Not a few alcoholics have committed suicide while they were in such a state of despair.

Alcoholism and addiction also become associated over time with many habits and ways of thinking. The compulsiveness of alcoholism and addiction is usually extended to incorporate numerous rituals: drinking or using at a certain time and place, in certain ways, with particular people, and so on. As substance abuse gives way first to habitual use and then to compulsive use, the alcoholic's or addict's life "accommodates" to drinking or using.[3] The lifestyle of the alcoholic or addict literally revolves around drinking or using. All relationships become secondary to the "primary relationship" with alcohol or drugs, and all other commitments take a back seat to the "commitment" to staying drunk or high.

To the patient who feels good and "in control," as patients commonly do early on in the facilitation program, getting active in AA or NA by getting telephone numbers and making calls, making coffee, or finding a sponsor may seem pointless. But in the long run getting active can literally mean the difference between life and death, since slips are very likely. It is precisely when the patient slips that s/he needs to be connected to a fellowship—to a "power greater than themselves." Getting actively involved in AA or NA is like putting money away for a rainy day or purchasing a disability insurance policy. Moreover, the spiritual aspect of AA and NA provides comfort and support that is always available to the individual whose spirit has been eroded by alcoholism or drug addiction. Staying sober for a few days or weeks can lead to a false sense of security. Complacency is the enemy of the addict and can make the emotional impact of a slip much worse. Steps 2 and 3 invite the alienated and defeated individual to find faith; getting active invites the addict to make a commitment to personal change through involvement.

Defining "Getting Active"

After checking to see that the patient understands the gist of this material, the facilitator should move on to a discussion of what getting active actually entails.

Facilitator: "We need to discuss this matter of 'getting active.' The Big Book tells us 'Faith without works is dead.'[4] What that basically means is that it takes more than good intentions to stay sober. It takes action. It means getting involved. It means taking your commitment to recovery seriously enough to make it a priority in your life.

"Beyond merely attending AA or NA meetings—sitting there passively—getting active involves 'working the program' in each of three areas. Let's look at each one of them."

Participating in Meetings

The facilitator should explain that beginning to attend meetings marks the start of establishing a new network of friends who will be critical to the patient's recovery. But merely going to meetings without participating in them is not the same thing as "working the program." A history of passive attendance is not likely to help the patient when s/he has a strong urge to drink or use or after s/he has had a slip. At those times the patient needs to know what to do—who to call and where to go—and to feel comfortable doing so without hesitation. This is one reason why getting active is vital.

There are many different kinds of meetings: "speaker" meetings, "step" meetings, "discussion" meetings, women's and men's meetings, and others. Initially, the facilitator should work closely with the patient to select meetings that are most appropriate for him/her. Eventually, a sponsor and other AA/NA friends will provide further information about meetings. Some patients may be comfortable going to speaker and discussion meetings right away, whereas others may need to be eased into the twelve-step program by attending a beginner's meeting for a while.

We advise facilitators to be as concrete as possible with respect to helping the patient find the right meetings. Write down the times and places of meetings, and develop a list of things for the patient to do at meetings. The patient can take this list with him/her, and the facilitator can use it later for follow-up purposes.

Examples of "things to do" to get active in AA or NA include volunteering to make coffee or to clean up after meetings, attending AA/NA socials, and actively participating in discussions. We strongly encourage facilitators to become personally familiar with meetings in their area so as to be familiar and comfortable with local traditions. There are regional differences in meeting formats and protocol. In some areas for example, discussion meetings are much more common than step meetings. In some areas, a business meeting is held every month right after the regular meeting, at which time certain commitments (making coffee, passing the hat, and the like) are rotated.

Telephone Therapy

The facilitator can avoid problems ahead of time by telling the patient that s/he most likely will not like everyone s/he meets at the AA/NA meetings. On the other hand, the more meetings (and the greater the variety of meetings) the patient attends, the more likely it is that s/he will connect with at least a few people sooner or later. The chances of this happening are much greater if the patient gets active in meetings.

One goal of this facilitation program is to get patients to attend and participate in meetings. Another is to encourage them to get the telephone numbers of people that they can call, then do it. When should recovering people use the telephone? At any number of times.

- daily, simply to stay in touch with other recovering persons (especially important in early recovery);
- whenever they have an urge to drink or use;
- as soon as possible after they've had a slip;
- when they feel lonely, angry, or tired;
- when they feel overwhelmed by life's problems; and
- when they feel good (and perhaps complacent) about their sobriety.

There are other good reasons for the patient to call AA/NA friends as well:

- to see how they're doing;
- to talk about something good that happened to the patient;
- to ask them if they're going to a particular meeting;
- to invite them to go with the patient to an AA/NA social; and
- just to say hello.

The more people the patient meets and talks to and the more phone numbers s/he gets, the more people s/he will have to call at those critical times, not to speak of the times in between.

Telephone therapy has long been a tradition in AA and NA.[5] Like going to meetings and getting a sponsor, using the telephone is a cornerstone of recovery. The facilitator should assure the patient that AA/NA members expect to give out their telephone numbers, and they expect to get calls. Since this is part of the AA/NA tradition, the patient need not feel that s/he is imposing. Conversely, there is no reason for the patient to feel put off at a meeting when an AA/NA member offers his/her own phone number or asks for the patient's.

Patients who are only just integrating themselves into a twelve-step fellowship may feel uncomfortable about making the first calls. The facilitator should reassure the patient that an AA/NA member who gives out a phone number expects it to be used. Often, there is no need for an AA/NA member to even explain the reason for calling. It's okay just to call and say hello.

The facilitator should explore the patient's resistances or anxieties about asking for phone numbers or using them.

- "When do you hesitate to make calls: in the middle of the night? On a weekend? From work?"
- "Why do you hesitate to make calls: because you are feeling angry? Depressed? Lonely?"

Explain to the patient that all of the above are exactly the right times to call!

Work through the patient's resistances to using the telephone as much as possible, using role playing (practice) if necessary, and suggest telephoning as a recovery task for the next week.

Sponsors

The facilitator should explain to the patient that the use of sponsors is one of the oldest traditions in AA, predating even telephone therapy. Originally, sponsors had a much more limited role in recovery than they do today. They were people who took responsibility for visiting alcoholics in the hospital and for taking them to AA meetings when they were discharged. Sponsors were also used as resources for answering questions about material in the Big Book.

Today all twelve-step programs incorporate sponsorship into their traditions. Sponsors are obtained through meetings. But their role today is different from what it once was. They do not visit inpatients or take them to meetings, although to some extent sponsors still "explain" the Big Book to newcomers. But perhaps most important, sponsors today serve as sources of practical advice for people who are less experienced with recovery than they. The sponsor is someone the patient can call (in addition, hopefully, to other AA/NA friends), who provides basic information about AA and NA and their traditions, who helps answer questions about the steps, who steers the patient toward meetings that might be helpful, and who facilitates getting active. Even people who have been in recovery for many years are apt to have sponsors, though their sponsors may be peers in terms of recovery.

It is a privilege and a responsibility to be a sponsor. But there are some things a sponsor is not. A sponsor is not a therapist or a judge. A sponsor does not tell a patient what to do (although s/he may offer a suggestion or two if asked). A sponsor does not attempt to resolve personal or marital problems, offer moral judgments, or give a patient a job. Despite these limitations, there is plenty of room for sponsors to help. A sponsor understands from personal experience the agonies of addiction and the conflicts that face the newly recovering alcoholic or addict. The sponsor sincerely cares about the patient and is an ally—but not a best friend, an employer, or a surrogate parent. The difference lies in the caring detachment that good sponsorship requires.[6]

Characteristics of Sponsors. We recommend that the facilitator explain to the patient how to go about getting a sponsor. But first, explore any of the patient's resistances to getting a sponsor. What concerns or reservations does the patient have? What qualities would s/he like in a sponsor (age, background)? NA suggests these ground rules:

- Anyone who has the desire to stay clean and sober should have a sponsor.
- The patient should not have a sponsor with whom s/he might have a sexual relationship.
- A patient should have only one sponsor at a time.
- A sponsor should have at least several months of "clean time," though what is more important than the quantity of clean time is the quality of that time. A sponsor should be someone who has a good understanding of the twelve steps and who is actively involved in a twelve-step fellowship, including going to meetings, using the telephone, and having a sponsor of their own.[7]

How to Get a Sponsor. NA gives this advice about getting a sponsor:

> Listening is the key to finding a sponsor. The most obvious place to look for a sponsor is at NA meetings. Talk, share, and listen to members of the Program; get plenty of phone numbers and use them. When you find someone with whom you can talk openly and relate, simply ask them to be your sponsor. Chances are the answer will be "yes." Sometimes the person may be unable to sponsor you. Keep on trying! Remember that when one door closes, another will open. Continue to attend meetings, listen and soon you will find a sponsor.[8]

Temporary Sponsors. Sometimes newcomers to AA and NA feel an immediate need to have a sponsor, yet they know relatively little about the people they have met there. In such instances it's appropriate for them to seek out a "temporary" sponsor—someone who will act in this role until the newcomer has had a chance to learn more about the people at meetings by listening and thereby find someone to relate to who can become a permanent sponsor.

The process for getting a temporary sponsor is simple. The patient goes to a meeting, waits for the time for announcements, then announces that s/he needs a temporary sponsor. Usually there will be at least one volunteer. Alternatively, a shy patient can just go to a meeting, making sure to arrive early, and casually let people know that s/he is looking for a temporary sponsor.

The facilitator and the patient may decide to role play, or rehearse, the process of asking for a sponsor, in the session itself. Openly discussing what characteristics the patient should look for in a potential sponsor can also be very helpful. Finally, the patient may find it useful to discuss with the facilitator the likely candidates that s/he has met and spoken with. The book *Living Sober* contains much good material on sponsorship, as does the book *Things My Sponsors Taught Me*. The facilitator may want to refer the patient to both of these.

Recovery Tasks

Suggested recovery tasks for this facilitation session are as follows.

Meetings

The facilitator should review the number of meetings the patient is attending each week, and how close the patient is to making an honest commitment to "ninety and ninety" (ninety meetings in ninety days).

After clarifying the patient's commitment, the facilitator should help the patient to select specific meetings. Discuss any potential obstacles to keeping this commitment and how they can be overcome.

Reading

- *Living Sober*: "Getting Active," "Making Use of Telephone Therapy," and "Availing Yourself of a Sponsor." These parts of *Living Sober* reinforce the material presented by the facilitator in this session and provide more practical advice on how to get advice in the AA/NA fellowships.

- The Big Book. *"Alcoholic Anonymous Number Three."* This story illustrates several important points about the twelve-step philosophy, including the fundamental importance of sharing and peer support. It also shows how they tend to be "programs of attraction" that seek to gain members not through shame or guilt but through empathy and free choices. Here are excerpts:

  > She told me that these two drunks she had been talking to had a plan whereby they thought they could quit drinking, and part of that plan was

that they tell it to another drunk. This was going to help them to stay sober. . . .

They said to me, "Do you want to quit drinking? It's none of our business about your drinking. We're not up here trying to take any of your rights or privileges away from you, but we have a program whereby we think we can stay sober. Part of that program is that we take it to someone else who needs it and wants it. Now, if you don't want it, we'll not take up your time, and we'll be going and looking for someone else."

The next thing they wanted to know was if I thought I could quit of my own accord, without any help, if I could just walk out of the hospital and never take another drink. If I could, that was wonderful, that was just fine, and they would very much appreciate a person who had that kind of power, but they were looking for a man that knew he had a problem and knew he couldn't handle it himself and needed outside help.

- The NA Big Book. "I Kept Coming Back.", This story is a testament to the fact that recovery often begins in earnest only after many slips and falls. The common expression for this state is "bottoming out." In this story the victim of addiction takes many falls before finally catching on to the importance of getting active.

Then, one night at a meeting, it was like someone hit me over the head with a two by four. I realized what was happening. I realized where I was coming from and where I was trying to go. I started going to more meetings. I was attending an average of ten meetings per week. I became active by becoming a secretary of one group. I got a sponsor and a lot of phone numbers. I started writing down how I felt about given situations.[10]

This story neatly illustrates that recovery needs to become more than a sideline in the addict's life and that it must, in fact, become an organizing theme in the individual's lifestyle.

- Recommended: *Things My Sponsors Taught Me.*[11] This book is a compendium of helpful hints about sponsors and how to use them, as well as practical information about meetings and how to get active in a twelve-step fellowship. We suggest that the facilitator read it, then use it as an aid in the facilitation, suggest it as reading for the patient, or both.

Participating

Ask the patient to do two specific things that s/he will do in order to get active in AA or NA. Write these down, then give him/her a copy.

1. _____
2. _____

Getting a Sponsor

Remind the patient that one of the goals of the facilitation program is to get a sponsor. The patient needs to keep this goal in mind when talking to people at meetings. Help the patient identify three key things s/he will be looking for a sponsor.

1. _____
2. _____
3. _____

Telephone Therapy

Ask the patient to get three names and telephone numbers of people at the meetings s/he attends.

Ask the patient to call one person whose phone number s/he gets, just to establish contact, before the next meeting. This call can be as brief as two or three minutes. People with whom the patient may have a possible sexual relationship should be removed from the list of names.

Wrap-Up

End the session with a brief wrap-up by asking two questions:

- "How would you summarize this session? What were the most important points we covered for you?"
- "How do you feel about making a commitment to getting active?"

Facilitator Notes

Recovery Is Work: Resistance to Getting Active

Facilitators commonly describe the session on Core Topic 4 as the make-it-or-break-it point in the entire facilitation program. This is probably because by this session the "honeymoon" period of early sobriety is coming to an end and the idea of lifelong abstinence is becoming a reality. Moreover, it calls upon the patient to make a real commitment to many lifestyle changes (going to meetings regularly, developing a relationship with a sponsor, and calling other program members). It's at this point that some patients begin missing or rescheduling sessions, and some will drop out of the program. New obstacles to getting active appear or get worse: babysitting problems, work commitments, fear of driving, and agoraphobia are but a few of the obstacles that may arise at this point in the program.

We recommend a straightforward approach to dealing with resistances that appear to correlate with getting active. We recommend stating frankly to the patient that recovery involves making a commitment and that it takes a certain amount of time and effort. It requires making a decision about what is more important: going to a meeting or relaxing in the living room after a hard day's work; calling a program friend or taking a bath; reading the Big Book or watching television. The patient needs to cross this bridge of commitment sooner or later, and it is appropriate for the facilitator to press the issue in a respectful way at this time.

In discussing this issue of commitment to recovery, it can be helpful to keep in mind the old AA slogan, "First Things First." For the patient who is conflicted over what choice to make, "First Things First" refers to the need to make staying clean and sober the alcoholic's or addict's first priority, since nothing else will matter if s/he continues drinking or using. Life will soon enough become unmanageable again for the alcoholic or addict who chooses complacency over commitment, or expects sobriety to come without sacrifice. Modern life is fraught with many competing commitments, but recovery must be the alcoholic's or addict's first commitment. Getting active in a twelve-step fellowship can be taken as evidence of the breakdown of denial and acceptance of the solution for addiction; at the same time, getting active can be a vehicle for this process of surrender: "Bring the body and the mind will follow."

Part III
The Elective Program

The six topics that make up the elective part of the facilitation program are intended to support and strengthen patients' active involvement in Alcoholics Anonymous and/or Narcotics Anonymous as a long-term solution to their problems of alcohol and/or drug abuse. Living clean and sober requires a commitment and ongoing vigilance for those whose problems with alcohol or drugs have led to symptoms of dependency. The potential for relapse is ever present in these men and women; therefore, recovery demands their ongoing participation in a supportive fellowship like AA and NA, combined with significant changes in their lifestyle, including their habits and values.

It generally requires between four and six sessions to cover all four of the core topics. After that, facilitators can expect to find themselves still having to refer back to one or another core topic, to clarify it, to work through resistances to it, or to encourage and support changes related to it. Moreover, even as the program moves on to one or more elective topics, it will continue to focus primarily on three behavioral objectives:

- going to meetings;
- getting active in AA; and
- getting and using a sponsor.

When the agenda for a session is an elective topic, the facilitator should not lose sight of the importance of these three objectives. We encourage the facilitator to take whatever time is necessary to explore resistances, to make suggestions, and to elicit a commitment to reasonable progress in these areas.

The elective topics in this section should be incorporated into the individual patient's treatment plan as they are appropriate and as time permits. The primary factor that will influence which electives are pursued is the patient's overall progress in getting active. Again, for many if not most patients, the main work of this facilitation program is focused on the four core topics. Although these topics may be covered in four to six sessions, clinical experience suggests that any changes in the patient's life initiated during this time need to be consolidated. Ongoing support, reinforced by work in several elective areas, will help to insure that recovery continues. The elective topics are as follows:

- Elective Topic 1: Genograms
- Elective Topic 2: Enabling
- Elective Topic 3: People, Places, and Routines
- Elective Topic 4: Emotions
- Elective Topic 5: Moral Inventories
- Elective Topic 6: Relationships

Once the core program has been completed, it is possible for the facilitator to proceed with the elective program in a number of different ways. The simplest and most straightforward way is to continue meeting individually with the patient on a weekly basis. Alternatively, for the patient who is staying sober and getting progressively more active in AA or NA, sessions can be scheduled biweekly. In some cases (again, contingent on staying sober and getting active), small group sessions may be substituted for individual sessions for the elective program.

Review Format

We recommend that the facilitator begin each session with the following basic review, taking ten to fifteen minutes to do so.

- Meetings
  - "What meetings did you attend, and what reactions did you have to them?"
  - "What is your plan for attending future meetings?"
  - "What resistance do you have at this point to going to meetings?"
  - "What is your level of participation at the meetings?"
- Sober Days
  - "How many days were you sober?" (Recognize each day of sobriety, regardless of how many slips may have occurred in between.)
  - "How are you doing with living 'one day at a time'—making a decision each and every day not to drink or use?"

- Urges to Drink or Use
  - "When and where did you have urges to drink or use?"
  - "What did you do about those urges?"
  - "How could you use AA or NA when you experience urges in the future?"
- Slips
  - "What were the specific circumstances when you drank [or used]?"
  - "How did you 'justify' drinking [or using], or 'justify' letting your guard down about the need to abstain, in these situation(s)?"
  - "How are you doing at coming to terms with Step 1, accepting that alcohol or drug use has made your life unmanageable?"
  - "What did you do after the slip? Did you call an AA/NA friend or sponsor, or go to a meeting?"
  - "What AA/NA resources could you call upon if you have a slip in the future?"
- Readings
  - "What AA/NA literature have you been reading?"
  - "What are your reactions to the readings?"
  - "What questions do you have?"
- Sponsors
  - "What progress are you making in getting a sponsor?"
  - "What do you think is the basis of any resistance you have to this?"
  - "What commitments will you make toward getting at least a temporary sponsor?"
- Telephone Therapy
  - "How are you doing at telephone therapy?
  - "What commitments will you make in this area?"

Elective Topic 1: Genograms

Addiction as a Family Illness

Generally speaking, genograms combine elements of genealogical family trees with elements of social history to produce a visual, intergenerational representation of family relationships pertaining to a particular subject. Genograms can be used to highlight virtually any issue or dynamic within a family. They can be used to examine family patterns in marriage and career choices, for example, or in lifestyle, or in parenting. In family therapy, genograms have been used extensively to help patients and therapists alike gain a better understanding of the ways family dysfunction is perpetuated, and to raise the issue of choice—of the patient's choosing to break family patterns and build a different and hopefully healthier lifestyle than other family members have had.

In this facilitation program, the primary purpose of doing a genogram is to reinforce the concept of alcoholism as an illness—and to show how that illness can often be traced across generations. A graphic visual representation of patterns of alcohol and drug use in his/her family, as in a genogram, can help to motivate a patient to break an intergenerational family cycle of addiction and decide to actively work a twelve-step program.

A second and related purpose of the genogram is to highlight the concept of alcoholism and drug addiction as "family illnesses." The genogram is intended to serve as a catalyst for a discussion of how alcoholism and addiction have harmed not only the patient but others in his/her family, including previous generations.

Presenting the Material

Facilitators who are unfamiliar with genograms are advised to seek consultation prior to using this technique in a facilitation session. Preparation is essential—genograms have the potential to evoke intense emotional reactions from patients. Sometimes these reactions are immediate and powerful; but it is not uncommon for genograms to have their greatest emotional impact after a session is over. Moreover, it can be difficult for an inexperienced facilitator to keep the focus of the discussion of the genogram on the issue of alcoholism or addiction as a family illness. For the facilitator, practicing genograms by using role-playing techniques and by doing a personal genogram with a supervisor can be good preparation for using this technique with patients.

Constructing a Genogram

A blackboard or flipchart is helpful for doing a genogram. If neither is available, use as large a piece of paper as possible.

Ask the patient to name the members of his/her immediate family and indicate their relationship to him/her. Include at least three generations in the genogram, starting with the patient's own generation. Place each family member in the appropriate position on the genogram, to create a family tree. Use squares to symbolize males and circles for females. We suggest listing each person's current age beneath their name. If they are deceased, list their age (or their estimated age) at the time of their death, and place an X beside it, along with the cause (if known) of their death. Then, for each person listed, fill in the following information on the genogram itself about the persons' history of alcohol or drug abuse. To elicit this information, ask the patient,

- Do any of his/her siblings have what could be considered a drinking or drug problem. Are any of them known as big drinkers or drug users?
- Which one(s)?
- What do they use?
- What negative consequences have they experienced that may be related to their use of alcohol or drugs?
  - legal (such as DWI)
  - social (such as divorce)
  - occupational (such as losing jobs or poor reviews)
  - physical (health problems)
  - emotional/psychological (such as depression or suicide)
  - financial (such as chronic money problems or bankruptcy)

Next, fill in the genogram with information about alcohol and drug abuse for the previous generation (the patient's parents, uncles, and aunts). Collect the information as above.

Next, obtain as much information as possible about the generation twice removed, the patient's grandparents.

Finally, if the patient has children, obtain information about their alcohol or drug abuse, if any.

Example

This sample genogram outlines three generations of alcoholism for the patient Harry. Harry was suspended from his job as a result of being drunk on the job and driving while intoxicated, and he was referred for an evaluation. At forty-five, he'd been drinking more or less since he was a teenager. The progression of his alcoholism had been gradual and insidious. His job brought him into frequent contact with heavy drinkers, many of whom drank at lunch and even on the job. His own tolerance was formidable—even his wife reported that she rarely saw him visibly drunk. Still, when he was arrested his blood alcohol level was three times above the legal limit. He said this had been a typical evening for him in terms of how much he drank.

When he first came for the evaluation, Harry admitted that he had a drinking problem. At the same time he minimized its severity in comparison to that of other men he knew. He flatly rejected the idea that he was an alcoholic, despite the fact that he frequently drove under the influence, had a problem with high blood pressure, and "didn't feel normal" until he had that first drink after work.

The genogram that the facilitator and Harry created together is shown in figure 1. An asterisk beside a person's name denotes that s/he had a

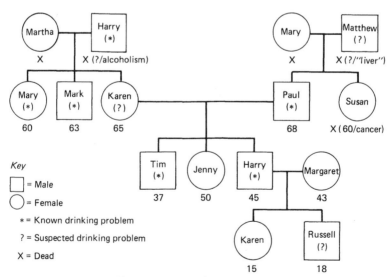

Figure 1: Sample Genogram

known drinking problem. A question mark denotes someone in whom a drinking problem was suspected on the basis of information Harry provided.

This genogram tells the following story. Harry's maternal grandfather (also named Harry); his maternal uncle Mark and maternal aunt Mary; his father and his younger brother Tim—all had acknowledged drinking problems. According to Harry, Tim had also been a regular user of marijuana for years. His uncle Mark had a history of losing jobs, had been through alcohol detoxification more than once, and had a heart condition that was most likely linked to his drinking. His aunt Mary had been married and divorced, was still a drinker, and lived with her son and his wife. His maternal grandfather Harry had been a notorious drunk whose temper his own mother as well as her siblings had feared. His mother had told him once that all three siblings would hide beneath their beds whenever their father came staggering in after a bender. He was universally hated and was widely known to have drunk himself to death.

On his father's side, Harry identified his own father, Paul, as a man who drank too much, although he justified this as a reaction to the stress from when Paul's wife, Karen, had been ill and Paul had had to work "endless" hours in their family business and even then had barely managed to support them. On reflection, he said that he was aware of his mother sometimes drinking, but he wasn't sure it had ever been a problem. He'd never thought to relate her drinking to her chronically poor health. Harry knew little about his paternal grandfather, Matthew, although he did know that Matthew had died at a relatively early age "of some kind of liver problem." And he had once overheard his mother tell someone else that her father-in-law "liked his liquor."

Finally, Harry and his wife, Margaret, had two children, Russell and Karen. Six months before Harry's arrest, Russell had also been arrested for driving while intoxicated and had had his license suspended. Though Harry and Margaret had spoken little about it, Harry was worried about Russell. He suspected that Margaret was angry at him over this incident, and he acknowledged that his own drinking hadn't presented a good model for his son to follow.

After completing his genogram, Harry was noticeably subdued. When he came in for a second session, he started out by saying that he had "reconsidered" things. "I guess booze has been making my life somewhat unmanageable, as you say. I think maybe I should think about giving it up. So you want me to go to AA? Do you have a schedule or something?"

Discussion

Discuss the genogram and its implications with the patient. Ask these questions.

- "How many people in your family, past and present, have been affected by alcohol or drugs?"
- "What consequences did they suffer? Did anyone die, or commit suicide, either wholly or partly as a result of alcoholism?"
- "How were the other family members affected by the person's alcoholism or addiction?"
- "Does any intergenerational pattern emerge from the genogram; in other words, is there any evidence here of addiction as a family illness?"
- "What choices do you want to make about your life, and that of your children? Where will the chain of addiction be broken?"

Wrap-Up

A genogram—any genogram—can give insight into many aspects of a family's history, and many of them would no doubt lead to fruitful discussions. But the focus in this elective topic is on substance abuse and its effects. The lure of other interesting subjects, combined with the patient's probable anxiety about talking in depth about alcohol or drugs, can easily lead the facilitator astray. Although that would be understandable, it would be counterproductive with respect to the specific goals of the facilitation program.

We recommend that the facilitator make every effort to stay on focus. One way of doing this is to sum up the discussion by making specific reference to alcohol and drug use. We suggest asking questions like:

- "What do you conclude about how alcohol [or drug] abuse has affected your own family?"
- "Do you see any evidence that alcoholism [or addiction] is a 'family illness' in your family?"
- "How do you think alcohol [or drugs] has affected the members of your family who abused them?"
- "How do you think others—the bystanders—may have been affected by these alcohol [or drug] problems?"
- "How do you fit into this picture of alcohol [or drug] problems?"
- "How has drinking [or using] affected you personally?"
- "How has your own drinking [or using] affected those close to you?"
- "How do you feel about your own drinking [or using] now that you've seen it in this perspective?"
- "Do you think you have a choice about taking alcohol or drugs? In other words, do you think it's possible for you to change the pattern, or for those who will come after you to do so?"

Recovery Tasks

Recovery tasks that the facilitator may suggest for following up the genogram session are:

- Meetings
  - Make a list of meetings for the patient to attend. Remember the goal of the patient committing to ninety meetings in ninety days. Ask how the patient feels about making this commitment in light of the genogram.

  - Suggest any other kinds of meetings that the patient might find it helpful to attend, beyond those s/he has already committed to attending.
- Telephone Therapy
  - Decide how many phone numbers the patient will obtain at meetings this week.

  - Decide how many phone calls the patient will make this week.
- Sponsor
  - If the patient does not yet have a sponsor, decide on the specific steps the patient will take between now and the next session to get one.

  - If the process of getting a sponsor needs to be facilitated, role playing could be useful here.
- Reading
  - Encourage the patient to continue reading the Big Book and/or the NA Big Book, the Twelve and Twelve, and *Living Sober*.

  - Suggest other readings that might be particularly relevant to the individual patient.
- Journal
  - Ask the patient to write down his/her reactions or thoughts about this session in his/her journal.

  - Encourage the patient to write his/her reactions to the genogram in the journal, to talk about it with AA friends or the sponsor, and to discuss it at a meeting if that seems appropriate.

Make a point of asking the patient to call (which is not normally encouraged in this program) in the event that s/he is experiencing distress as a result of the genogram exercise.

Facilitator Notes

Focus the Discussion

When extraneous issues arise as a result of constructing a genogram, we cannot emphasize enough the importance of the facilitator keeping the focus of the discussion on substance abuse and its consequences. The patient may be tempted to go off onto a discussion of any number of meaningful collateral issues. Keep in mind the possibility that such diversions represent denial—avoidance of facing the issue of alcoholism or addiction, and its consequences for the individual and the family.

If collateral issues are pursued in the genogram discussion, we recommend that the facilitator correlate them to substance abuse. A patient like Harry may want to discuss his relationship with his father. If the facilitator cannot shift the discussion back to substance abuse, allow the discussion but try to couch it in terms of substance abuse and its effects. Ask, for example, whether Harry noticed any changes in the way his father treated him when he was drinking as opposed to when he was not. Ask how his father acted after he sobered up, and so on.

Coping with Repercussions

Genogram exercises have the potential to stir up emotions that may have lain dormant for years in the depths of the patient's unconscious. Sudden and painful recollections of growing up in an alcoholic home, of abuse, of abandonment, or of neglect can evoke intense feelings of anger, anxiety, and shame. The facilitator may not be in a position to work through all such emotions with the patient, but s/he should nevertheless be sensitive to them and prepared to offer helpful guidance.

• Validate emotional reactions as they are appropriate to their context. Say, for example, "I can understand how you must have felt ashamed to bring friends home with your mother drunk most of the time"; or "I can understand that it must have been frightening not knowing when your father might get drunk and become violent"; or "It's understandable that recalling the sexual abuse you suffered when your father drank would make you depressed."

• Direct the patient to AA or NA as a sourse of comfort and support from people who have had similar experiences. Suggest that the patient speak to an AA/NA peer, or his/her sponsor, about this exercise and the patient's emotional reactions to it.

• Encourage the patient to write down his/her feelings and thoughts about the genogram itself and the thoughts and feelings that the genogram raised.

• Encourage the patient to "write a letter" to a family member whose drinking is associated with negative consequences for the patient (such as a father who was abusive when drunk). The letter need not be actually mailed to this person. But in it, the patient can express his/her past and present feelings about the person's drinking and its consequences.

• Encourage the patient to write a "letter of amends" to anyone whom s/he believes has been emotionally injured as a result of his/her alcohol or drug problem. This letter, too, may or may not be mailed. (It can be used, as well, as a prelude to doing Step 4 and Step 5 work—see "Moral Inventories.")

• Suggest that the patient might experience an urge to drink or use as a result of this exercise, and what s/he could do about it (such as go to a meeting or call an AA/NA peer or sponsor).

• Refer the patient to appropriate concurrent treatment, such as a group for survivors of sexual abuse.

If the patient shows signs of extreme distress or discomfort during the genogram exercise, it may be necessary to stop, to focus on those feelings, and to comfort the patient, then to discontinue the exercise for the time being.

We also advise the facilitator to strike a balance in the discussion of the patient's family so that the creative and positive aspects of family life are also acknowledged. For example, suggest that the patient give him/herself (or someone else) credit for accomplishments and successes. It is entirely reasonable to encourage the patient to honor him/herself and other family members for the positive things they've done, while still having the courage to acknowledge the harm done through alcohol or drug abuse. The point is that some of the people in the patient's family may have been basically "good" people who had an illness that led them to behave in ways that were hurtful to themselves and others. The simple act of casting a flash of brightness now and then on what might otherwise be a grim picture can help to offset a patient's tendency to fly into a rage or sink into shame and despair.

Elective Topic 2: Enabling*

The Other Side of Addiction

Enabling can be defined as any and all behaviors by others that have facilitated the patient's continued drinking or using, or that have helped the
patient to avoid or minimize the negative consequences related to drinking
or using. In other words, *enablers* provide the means, the excuses, and the
safety net that allows the alcoholic or addict to continue. Enabling is poign-
antly illustrated by a mother's response to her teenage daughter's drinking:

> The convulsions she had had at home were so thoroughly covered up by
> me that she could not remember them the next day. I massaged her, poured
> honey down her throat, soothed her and applied cold compresses. It proved
> futile to tell her what had occurred because, within a short time, the
> drinking began again. It is now clear to me that it is necessary for the
> alcoholic to feel the pain. But it was I who bore my daughter's pain. I
> deprived her of some of the incentive to take constructive action for the
> consequences of her drinking. In essence, I took on the responsibility and
> the consequences of her disease.[1]

Enabling can also be seen as indulgence or pampering. It can be motivated by caring and concern, as in the mother above, or it may reflect the
enabler's own personality and desire to deny reality, as it does for this wife
of an alcoholic who suggests:

> False pride helped me create a prison in which I lived for the next twenty
> years. I wanted to be proud of our marriage and our family (we had six
> sons), so I buried the resentment and began pretending. By the time our
> sons were in their twenties, one had gone through treatment for chemical
> dependency. I also realized that three of our other sons were chemical
> abusers. I didn't want to believe this was happening or that alcohol was

---

*For patients who are in a relationship with a partner who is willing to participate in treatment,
Conjoint Topic 1 may be substituted for this elective topic.

the problem. So I kept on pretending and I played the role of caretaker for the whole family. I assumed it was my job to control them, make them happy, keep them from hurting and out of trouble. The family seemed to agree. Their dependent personalities accepted such mothering and only occasionally did they rebel.[2]

Addiction and enabling may in fact be psychologically complementary. The addict, as a dependent person, needs the enabler, who in turn "needs to be needed."

However it is defined, enabling serves to mitigate the negative consequences of alcoholism or drug addiction and thereby has the (perhaps unintended) effect of prolonging the process. Many "unenabled" alcoholics and addicts might "bottom out" sooner than "enabled" alcoholics and therefore perhaps take the "constructive action" to which this woman refers sooner.

Presenting the Material

We recommend that the facilitator open this session by asking the patient if s/he has heard the term *enabling* and, if so, what it means to him/her. Check that the patient has a clear understanding of the concept. Reading the passages above aloud can be useful: so can paraphrasing the definition given above.

Finally, illustrate enabling by using a few examples. Enablers are:

- friends who give you drinks (or drugs) when you're already drunk or high;
- friends who make sure they have enough liquor or drugs around for you when you visit them;
- friends who joke and make light of the fact that you get drunk or high as often as you do;
- partners or friends who make "liquor runs" or "drug runs" for you;
- partners or friends who "lend" you money for alcohol or drugs;
- partners or friends who make excuses for you when you're intoxicated (such as by calling in sick for you when in truth you're hung over); and
- partners or friends who nurse you when you're hung over.

Constructing an Enabling Inventory

A blackboard or flipchart is helpful for this; if neither is available, use a large sheet of paper. When the inventory is completed, we recommend that the facilitator give the patient a copy, or else ask the patient to make a copy in his/her journal.

To make an enabling inventory, ask the patient to fill in the blanks, in the following series of questions. Persistence is the key here, since the patient may be reluctant to admit to how much his/her problem with alcohol or drugs has been actively facilitated by friends or loved ones.

Enabling Inventory

• List the significant others who have enabled the patient.

_____

_____

_____

• List specific ways in which these significant others have enabled the patient to:
  • gain access to alcohol or drugs.

_____

_____

_____

  • minimize or avoid the negative consequences of use.

_____

_____

_____

Discussion: The Dynamics of Enabling

Enabling behavior is fairly easy to discern, but the underlying motivations for enabling may be complex and less apparent. Before the facilitator asks the patient to examine his/her own role in the "dance" between him/herself and the enabler, it can be helpful to discuss the enabler's possible motivations.

As background for this discussion, the facilitator should know that most people enable not because they "want" the alcoholic or addict to continue drinking or using, but because they desire to "protect" the alcoholic or addict or because they have a sense of responsibility and duty. A person's motives for enabling are usually benign and loving, but they end up being mutually destructive to addict and enabler alike.

Enablers often feel guilty because they secretly fear that they have somehow caused or contributed to the substance abuse problem. Many alcoholics and addicts play on this hidden fear in their enablers in order to promote enabling. Many partners and family members of alcoholics and addicts report having deep self-doubts about their adequacy in the relationship.

Enablers are fearful and anxious because they don't know what could happen if they stopped enabling, or perhaps because, ironically, they are afraid that the alcoholic or addict will abandon them if they do.

Enablers also feel frustrated and angry that the alcoholic or addict won't change, won't listen to advice, and continues to use. They find themselves repeating scenes that have happened before and that they'd hoped would never happen again: calling in sick for the hung-over husband, making excuses to leave parties early, cleaning up messes, and so on. Many alcoholics in particular are aggressive and abusive when they are drunk, and their relationships tend to become progressively more scarred as their illness progresses. In time the enabler's feelings of anger and frustration give way to a deep and abiding resentment, combined with a good dose of self-pity. They feel sorry for themselves for having to carry the burden of alcoholism or addiction, and they resent the abuse, the lack of intimacy, the inconsideration, and so on.

Sooner or later, enablers come to feel hopeless and depressed as a result of the continued drinking and the progressive unmanageability not only of the addict's life but also of their own lives. Alienation sets in gradually and undermines the enabler's spirit and health and they may turn to alcohol or drugs, to food, or to work as a compensation for the desperation they feel. In the end they succumb to alienation, writing off both the alcoholic or addict and the relationship.

Promoting Enabling

The facilitator should explain to the patient that a vital part of recovery is acknowledging enabling and actively resisting it on a day-to-day basis. Every addict and alcoholic actively promotes and encourages enabling in those around them, since it is almost as important to their addiction as their source of liquor or drugs. Without his/her enablers, the alcoholic or addict would suffer many more negative consequences and hit bottom that much sooner.

The patient needs to learn to be honest about enabling and the role it has played in sustaining his/her addiction. S/he needs to acknowledge not only who his/her primary enablers are and how they enable, but also the specific ways in which s/he has actively promoted others' enabling. We suggest that the facilitator help the patient continue the personal inventory of enabling.

Facilitator: "Every addict needs to own up to his/her methods for encouraging enabling in others. Getting honest in this area will help you to sustain recovery. Typically, alcoholics and addicts learn to use the emotional vulnerabilities of others, such as their guilt or fear, to promote enabling. An alcoholic, for example, may attempt to blame a binge on an argument with his partner ('You made me do it!'); another may attempt to arouse anxiety through some form of threat ('If you don't cover up for me, I'll lose my job!').

"You might benefit from doing a personal inventory of who your enablers are and how you yourself encourage them to keep on enabling you."

Ask the patient to give several examples of how s/he has encouraged or coerced others into enabling, being as specific as possible:

1. _____
2. _____
3. _____
4. _____

Resisting Enabling

To begin to eliminate enabling from his/her life, the patient should make a practice of beginning and ending every day with a frank, personal acknowledgment that s/he is an alcoholic or addict. This acknowledgment is reinforced when the patient makes a commitment to daily attendance at AA/NA meetings. The acknowledgment should later be extended to all those people to whom the patient is close.

Along with a frank acknowledgment of alcoholism or addiction, the patient should be encouraged to make a daily affirmation to this effect: "I am responsible for my own recovery, which will come through active involvement in the twelve-step fellowship."

Honesty is the key to recovery, and being honest about enabling is probably just as important as being honest about using. The partners, friends, and relatives of recovering addicts need to learn to identify their own tendencies to enable, and how to resist them. The best resource for these individuals is Al-Anon and/or Al-Anon Family Group meetings. Enabling and its opposite—detaching with love—are central to these twelve-step fellowships. For further information, refer to the conjoint program material in this book.

Recovery Tasks

Recovery tasks that the facilitator can suggest for this session on enabling are:

- Meetings
  - Make a list of meetings the patient will attend before the next session.
  - Suggest other kinds of meetings the patient might attend.
  - Suggest how the patient could get more active in AA or NA.
- Telephone Therapy
  - Decide how many phone numbers the patient will get this week.
  - Decide how many phone calls the patient will make this week.
- Sponsor
  - If the patient has gotten a sponsor, suggest ways the patient can make constructive use of the sponsor.
  - If not, decide what specific steps the patient will take toward getting a sponsor before the next session.
- Reading
  - Encourage the patient to continue reading the Big Book, the NA Big Book, the Twelve and Twelve, and *Living Sober*, and to make note of his/her reactions in the journal.
  - Recommended: The facilitator may want to suggest that the patient purchase and use a daily meditation book such as *Twenty-Four Hours a Day* (published by Hazelden). The book *Al-Anon Faces Alcoholism*, which is available through Al-Anon Family Group Headquarters, contains much valuable information about enabling and its relationship to addiction.
- Enabling
  - Ask the patient to make firm commitments to do three specific things to resist enabling. These things should not include trying to "re-form" significant enablers. Instead, talking to a specific other about enabling, making a decision to avoid certain people, and the like would be useful.

Facilitator Notes

When discussing the concept of enabling, it is very important to discourage the patient from blaming others in any way for his/her drinking or using, and from pathologizing them at all for their enabling. Enablers are typically motivated by concern, anxiety, or confusion about what to do. Wives of alcoholics, for example, may fear loss of income or even spouse abuse if they don't somehow "help" their husbands. Husbands may fear humiliation if they don't "cover up" for their alcoholic wives, and so on.

Addicts and enablers engage each other in a dance of mutual destruction—but not necessarily because of psychopathology. Patients need to understand not only how enabling contributes to their drinking or using but also the role they've played, consciously or unconsciously, in encouraging that enabling. The key insight for the alcoholic or addict to gain here is how s/he helped to create the enabling system that supports his/her problem. The first way to break out of this is to embrace Step 1 and openly acknowledge unmanageability and loss of control—not just once but on a daily basis. Nor can enablers be "cured" by the alcoholics and addicts they support—rather, enablers can get support for themselves through Al-Anon or Nar-Anon. Alcoholism and addiction, as family illnesses, cause life to become unmanageable not only for the alcoholic or addict but for those who are closest to him/her as well.

The goal in discussing enabling is to help the patient make specific commitments to dismantling his/her enabling system. S/he can begin to do this by either avoiding enablers or by being honest with them about being an alcoholic or addict.

Elective Topic 3: People, Places, and Routines

> Recovery is easy—all you have to do is change your whole life.
>
> To avoid slipping, avoid slippery people, slippery places, and slippery things.
> —AA adages

Lifestyles and Recovery

Alcoholics Anonymous has a long history of being very pragmatic about what it takes to stay sober—whatever works for the individual is fine. Bill Wilson devoted much time over many years to answering practical questions from recovering alcoholics about how to stay sober in various problem situations. His strategy, which has become an integral part of the AA/NA tradition, was to share "suggestions" that others had found helpful in those same problem situations, but to make it clear that following the advice was strictly optional.[1]

AA describes the situation facing the newly recovering alcoholic in this way:

> Certain set times, familiar places, and regular activities have been woven closely into the fabric of our lives. Like fatigue, hunger, loneliness, anger, and overelation, these old routines can prove to be traps dangerous to our sobriety.[2]

The facilitation session devoted to Core Topic 3, "People, Places, and Routines," is intended to review and address some of the practicalities of staying sober: what the patient should do about spending time with friends who drink or use, about going to parties, about changing habits intimately associated with drinking or using, and the like. It is not realistic for the patient to expect the world to change in response to his/her efforts to stay sober; rather, the patient must change his/her lifestyle in order to stay sober. Moreover, any tendency to think that recovery can occur without fundamental changes in attitudes and behaviors is unrealistic. Following the model of Bill Wilson, the facilitator should be prepared to be pragmatic, flexible,

113

and nondogmatic. The objective is to brainstorm ideas with the patient for how s/he can stay sober in different problem situations.

Presenting the Material

We suggest that the facilitator begin the session by reading the two AA adages at the beginning of this chapter out loud, then asking the patient for his/her gut reaction to them. Does this view of recovery and what it takes seem overwhelming to the patient? It doesn't have to be. The patient needs to cross only one bridge at a time, to cope with only one situation at a time. The wisdom in these two slogans refers to the need to change many aspects of one's lifestyle in the interest of recovery, but AA also tells us, "Easy Does It."

The fact is that the alcoholic's or addict's lifestyle has accommodated to drinking or using: S/he has most likely drifted toward people and situations that facilitate and support his/her drinking or using and has given up relationships that don't support or enable it. S/he has probably also evolved a range of habits and rituals associated with drinking or using. Some of these rituals may have to do with daily routines, such as cooking meals, ironing, cleaning the house, coming home from work, and watching the six o'clock news on television. Other rituals may involve certain people, certain places, or even certain items or clothing. Consider this example:

> One patient who had been smoking marijuana daily for seventeen years had evolved a complex ritual surrounding his use. A middle-level manager by day, he would never smoke until after work. But as soon as he left the office and got to his car, the first thing he would do was to remove his tie. Then he'd put a tape in the cassette deck—music that he liked to listen to when he was high, but that he never played until he was ready to get high. No sooner was he out of the company parking lot than he had lit his first joint and hit the play button on the cassette. By the time he got home, which took about forty minutes, he'd have smoked two joints. As soon as he got home, before he lit his next joint, he'd change his clothes. He liked wearing the same clothes when he was high: old jeans and flannel shirts. Lighting his third joint, he'd carefully roll six more: three more for that day, two for the ride home tomorrow, and one for when he was rolling joints again the next afternoon.

If anything happened to disrupt this man's marijuana routine, he would immediately feel irritated. Being asked to work overtime, for example, as he occasionally was, was such a source of irritation. Another was having to stop to pick up something on the way home—he preferred to do all his shopping at other times.

The process of connecting drinking or using with particular people, places, things, and routines happens naturally as drinking or using becomes habitual. Although the alcoholic or addict is increasingly preoccupied with maintaining a certain level of a mood-altering substance in his/her body, using is also intimately connected with rituals. Engaging in the rituals themselves leads to feelings of eager anticipation; disrupting the rituals leads to anxiety and anger.

In a sense we are all creatures of habit. Changing old habits, no matter how mundane, is no easy matter. In order to stay clean and sober the alcoholic or addict needs to change many patterns associated with habitual use; otherwise, his/her willpower will be no match for the power of ritual and routine combined with his/her obsession with alcohol.

Inventorying Rituals and Routines

The purpose of inventorying the patient's rituals and routines is to help the patient recognize the people, places, and routines that s/he associates with drinking or using and that must therefore be changed. We suggest writing these things out on a blackboard, if possible, and having the patient copy them down into his/her personal journal. Build the inventory by covering these areas.

• "Can you identify any rituals associated with your drinking or using? Is there a certain sequence of events that you normally follow?" Most alcoholics and addicts readily own up to their ritualistic behavior around drinking or using, and the facilitator who has a feeling for this concept can usually elicit these patterns.

• "Can you identify certain routines that you associate with drinking?" For one woman, it was ironing—she ironed every day and got drunk in the process. A salesman drank every night as he went over his orders and receipts for the day. By the time he was tallied out, he'd tied one on.

• "Can you identify a list of slippery drinking or using partners? How much of your social life do these people make up?" "Who do you spend time with who doesn't abuse alcohol or drugs?"

• "What habits have you tried to change in the past? What was the experience like, and what were the results? Can you appreciate the power of habit—how powerful routines and rituals can be, and how they can actually be stronger than your willpower?"

• "Can you see how your preoccupation with drinking will be no match for your personal willpower in one of the slippery situations?"

Creating a Lifestyle Contract

The recovering alcoholic or addict needs to identify and then change the people, places, rituals and routines that s/he associates with drinking or using, if s/he hopes to stay clean and sober. To help the patient in this effort, this "Lifestyle Contract" exercise can be useful. We suggest that the facilitator make a copy of the contract and fill it out with the patient.

In general, it is easier to give up or change an old habit if we are able to settle on a new one to replace it. The purpose of the lifestyle contract is to help the patient do just that—develop a "blueprint" for change, or a list of what s/he needs to give up and what s/he needs to substitute for it. Without both parts of the contract in place, the patient is apt to fail. In other words, giving up old, drinking-associated habits will not work in the long run unless they are replaced with new, sobriety-associated habits.

Lifestyle Contract

Instructions: Complete all parts of this contract. It will be most helpful to you if you can be as specific as possible.

People

1. Who did you spend the most time drinking or using with in the past? What, in other words, are the "slippery" relationships you will need to avoid in order to stay clean and sober?

   _____

   _____

   _____

2. You will need to replace these slippery relationships with nonslippery ones. Who will be the members of this new group of clean and sober friends?

   _____

   _____

   _____

Places

1. Where did you spend most of your time drinking or using?

   _____

   _____

2. Where will you spend your time in the future? Include some specific ideas about places that you associate with supporting your sobriety.
   a. AA/NA meetings you enjoy:

   _____

   _____

   b. AA/NA-sponsored activities you enjoy:

   _____

   _____

   c. Activites you enjoy:

   _____

   _____

Places/Things

1. What specific things (clothing, television shows) or places (couches, rooms) were most associated with your drinking or using?

   _____

   _____

2. What will you do about these places or things so that they don't arouse an urge in you to drink or use?

   _____

   _____

Routines/Rituals

1. What day-to-day routines or rituals have been associated with your drinking or using?

   _____

   _____

   _____

2. What new routines or rituals will you establish to support your sobriety?

   _____

   _____

   _____

   _____

Recovery Tasks

Suggested recovery tasks for this session are as follows.

- Meetings
  - Make a list of meetings the patient will attend.
  - Suggest any other kind of meetings the patient could attend.
  - Suggest what the patient could do to get more active.
- Telephone Therapy
  - Decide how many phone numbers the patient will get this week.
  - Decide how many phone calls the patient will make this week.
- Sponsor
  - If the patient has gotten a sponsor, suggest new ways that s/he can make use of the sponsor.
  - If not, suggest steps the patient can take toward getting a sponsor.
- Reading
  - Encourage the patient to continue reading the Big Book, the NA Big Book, and the Twelve and Twelve. Particularly important for this elective topic are the following sections in *Living Sober*:
    - "Changing Old Routines"
    - "Being Wary of Drinking Occasions"
    - "Is It Necessary to Give Up Old Companions and Habits?"
  - Recommended are the following sections in *Things My Sponsors Taught Me:*[3]
    - "About the Old and the New You in Alcoholics Anonymous"
    - "About Cocktail Parties"
- Lifestyle Contract
  List the specific commitments ("first steps") that the patient is willing to make relative to his/her lifestyle contract.

1. _____
2. _____
3. _____

Facilitator Notes

In helping the patient to create a lifestyle contract, it is important to concentrate on the small but specific commitments to change that the patient can make, and to follow up on these commitments in later sessions. We suggest that the facilitator read the above passages in *Living Sober* and *Things My Sponsors Taught Me* prior to this session. Choose one or two points. Go over them with the patient, and "brainstorm" about how they might apply to his/her life and about what they imply for avoiding "slippery" people, places, and routines.

Change and Grief

The session on people, places, and routines often evokes a great deal of resistance from patients. No doubt this is because, like the session on getting active, it essentially presses the patient to commit him/herself to making concrete changes in behavior. In other words, talk may be cheap, but action costs. Action costs time, for one thing. It costs going out of one's way. It means not only developing new habits but giving up old ones. It means not only making new friends, but possibly giving up old ones. It may mean giving up or limiting old pastimes.

Though this elective topic is straightforward on the surface, the emotional impact of the lifestyle contract should not be minimized. Simply put, it challenges the patient to take a hard look at what s/he might have to sacrifice in the interest of recovery. Little wonder that patients may give more lip service than action to this work. To help overcome this resistance, we recommend that the facilitator do the following:

Allow the Patient to Grieve. Recognize the fact that the patient is being asked to give something up: old friends, old habits, perhaps old activities. It is natural for people to grieve over such losses. The patient who minimizes the impact of the loss of slippery people, places, and routines on his life may be in a state of denial about how this might feel. S/he may also be simply placating the facilitator with no real intention of following through.

A common exercise used in alcohol and drug rehabilitation programs is to have patients write "good-bye letters" to alcohol or drugs, expressing their grief over having to give up this "relationship". Such a "letter" can be written to many of the other things that the patient must "give up" for sobriety. The patient can write a good-bye letter to his/her best drinking or using friends, to music that s/he too closely associates with drinking or using to risk listening to anymore, or to places where s/he used to get high.

We recommend facilitating and validating as much as possible the patient's real experience of grief in session.

Emphasize Both Losing and Gaining. When a son marries, the saying goes, his parents gain a daughter. The wisdom in this simply remedy for grief is also appropriate for the man or woman in recovery. For the individual who truly embraces a twelve-step fellowship, in the long run there are easily as many gains as losses. Conscious living, new and trustworthy friends, spiritual renewal, self-esteem—these are only a few of the gains that can be realized through recovery. To achieve them does require giving something up, but those things that must be sacrificed are also things that are associated with the abyss of alcoholism or addiction.

While the facilitator should recognize and respect the legitimate feelings of grief that can be evoked by this session, we recommend trying to provide some balance for the patient's outlook as well. Being specific and practical, rather than general and abstract, can make this an even more effective strategy. Ask the patient to specifically balance losses with gains: What new relationships are emerging to replace old ones? What new interests may be developing to replace old ones? In this way the patient may experience grief without despair, and the anxiety of loss may be offset by the excitement of new opportunities.

Elective Topic 4: Emotions

Don't let yourself get too tired, too hungry, or too lonely.
—*Living Sober*

Illnesses of Emotion

The purpose of the facilitation session devoted to Elective Topic 4 is to help the patient identify emotions that, according to AA/NA lore, are commonly associated with his/her slips. These are the emotions that most often lead to taking "that first drink," which in turn sets off the alcoholic's craving and lead him/her back to compulsive drinking.

The twelve-step movement has long recognized the connection between emotions and substance use, as is evidence in some of the section titles of the AA publication *Living Sober*:

- "Fending Off Loneliness"
- "Watching Out for Anger and Resentments"
- "Looking Out for Overelation"
- "Being Grateful"
- "Eliminating Self-Pity"
- "What Can I Do When I Get Lonely?"
- "As Long As I'm Happy, Am I Safe?"

Within the section "Watching Out for Anger and Resentments," sixteen more emotional states, ranging from intolerance to jealousy, are delineated.[1] Clearly, AA/NA members have long recognized that substance abuse is triggered by certain emotions. Here are two examples of their thinking on this:

[Alcoholics] felt the power and freedom while drunk to express anger they could not comfortably display when sober.

Large numbers of us can see that we often drank in order to intensify an already jubilant mood.[2]

Of course, drug abusers report very similar experiences, and as in all cases of addiction, there is a strong link to emotions.

121

A Case Study

Not only does the newly sober patient need to understand the connection between emotions and substance abuse, s/he also needs to expect that emotions that s/he previously "drank or drugged away" are apt to surface in recovery. Here is an example of how this happens.

Although Rick was barely nineteen, he already had many symptoms of alcohol and drug dependency when he was admitted to a twelve-step treatment program. He reported drinking "at least" a case of beer (twenty-four cans) a day for nearly two years. He'd also smoked marijuana daily for nearly that long, and more recently he had taken up cocaine.

A simple alcohol/drug history was completed as soon as Rick was steady enough to talk coherently, and it revealed that he'd been smoking pot and drinking beer since he was twelve years old. But his problem use of both had begun only two years earlier, a few days after his girlfriend was killed in a car accident. She'd gone out drinking with a friend of his after they'd had a fight. He'd never seen or spoken with her again.

In treatment Rick did fine for the first week, but then he began to be a problem. His temper was short and he got into fights. At first these fights were verbal, but then he hit someone, then another. Confronted about his need to find a socially acceptable way of dealing with his anger, he flung a chair across the room and nearly injured still another person.

The case of Heather also shows how previously drunk-away emotions surface in recovery. Heather, age thirty, had been sober and attending both AA and NA regularly for six months when she sought personal therapy for depression. She had managed to stay clean and sober, but the price had been enormous. She lost more than twenty pounds over those six months; she had problems sleeping that included nightmares and persistent early waking; she had anxiety attacks that struck at work and that had no apparent cause; and she had guilt feelings that she could not connect to anything but that were intense enough to make her think about killing herself. She had resisted the urge to drink and use by attending meetings at least daily and often twice a day.

The cause of Heather's emotional ordeal turned out to be a history of sexual abuse that had spanned six years of her childhood, from the age of seven to thirteen. To complicate the trauma and shame associated with the abuse itself, Heather's mother had refused to accept the reality despite blatant evidence. At one point she had discovered her ten-year-old daughter in bed, naked, with her husband and had reacted by walking out of the room. Later on, when Heather had brought it up and asked for help, her mother flatly refused to talk about it.

Difficult Emotions

The cases of Rick and Heather show some of the emotions that commonly rise to the surface of consciousness once sobriety replaces a chronic state of altered consciousness. Some of the feelings that patients need to be prepared to encounter in recovery include:

- loneliness
- anxiety
- shame
- anger
- boredom
- guilt
- grief
- frustration
- resentment.

The alcoholic or user is most vulnerable to experiencing these emotions— and is therefore also most likely to be tempted to "drink or drug them away"—when s/he is either hungry or tired, as AA/NA lore shows. Depleting one's energy is dangerous to the recovering individual. Therefore, AA and NA strongly emphasize getting rest and eating well.

Coping in Recovery

To stay sober, then, the recovering person has to learn to manage emotions differently—that is, without drinking or drugging them away. AA/NA members talk a great deal about how obsessive-compulsive tendencies like perfectionism and impatience, for example, lead to frustration and in turn to alcohol or drug use. These tendencies need to be dealt with by learning to put "first things first," by learning to "let go and let God," and so on. AA's and NA's also speak of how alcohol in particular, but also drugs, can be used to cover up or avoid the grief over a loss or the shame and anger generated by abuse. Finally, AA and NA recognize the need for alcoholics and addicts to learn to experience "natural highs" and to give up efforts to experience or enhance elation through mood-altering substances.

Presenting the Material

We suggest that the facilitator go through the following material and present those aspects of it that are most relevant to the particular patient. To make this session truly meaningful, the facilitator should first thoroughly review the patient's alcohol/drug history. If necessary, delve into the patient's history further in order to ascertain the following:

- What personal experiences (such as abuse, loss, neglect, or trauma) may be connected to emotions that played a role in the patient's abuse of alcohol or drugs?
- To what extent did alcohol or drug abuse prevent the patient from developing "natural" ways of socializing, recreating, and having fun?
- What emotions appear to be surfacing in recovery?

Many AA/NA slogans—"Easy Does It," "Let Go and Let God," "One Day at a Time," "First Things First," "Turn It Over"—relate to one or more of these difficult emotions. They reveal common wisdom regarding ways to handle those emotions. The slogans may have their limitations, but their value lies in their simplicity. Through these slogans twelve-step fellowships like AA and NA teach alcoholics and addicts how they can cope with their emotions without resorting to alcohol or drugs. Teaching patients to identify their emotions, to understand the roots of those emotions, and to cope by drawing on particular slogans may not be sufficient, but it can be extremely helpful.

Hunger and Fatigue

The recovering alcoholic needs to develop a lifestyle that allows him/her to get adequate rest.[3] A state of exhaustion is an invitation to drink or use. Moreover, a body that is poorly exercised and that lacks adequate nutrition will be much more vulnerable to getting tired than a body that is being nurtured and taken care of. The facilitator can determine the patient's physical condition by asking:

- "How much sleep do you get, on average? Is this adequate for you? What changes, if any, could you make to get more rest?"
- "Have you ever experienced drinking [or using], or had a strong desire to drink [or use], when you were feeling especially fatigued?"
- "What is the overall state of your health? Are you capable of doing some form of regular exercise, in the interest of gaining stamina?"

AA and NA emphasize the need for recovering alcoholics and addicts to avoid not only exhaustion but excessive hunger.[4] Regular meals, well balanced, are encouraged, and beyond that the recovering person is encouraged to snack enough so as to avoid getting too hungry. In this regard AA even encourages the recovering person, and especially the novice, to use sweets as necessary.[5] Ask the following questions:

- "Do you sometimes experience cravings for sweets?"
- "How can you satisfy this need?" (Point out that whatever sweets a

recovering alcoholic eats may not contain as many calories as alcohol. On the other hand, some recovering alcoholics, like ex-smokers, experience a significant weight gain in early recovery. A referral to a nutritionist, or a sensible book on nutrition, may be helpful.)

Anxiety

Anxiety has many sources, but one of them has to do with anxiety about making decisions—about knowing the "right thing" to do and feeling right about doing it. Anxiety runs as a theme throughout the AA/NA writings. Indeed, the spirituality within AA and NA seems partly directed at relieving the anxiety associated with being alone, of having no trusted person (or faith) upon whom to rely, and consequently of having to make difficult choices in isolation.

The Serenity Prayer. The "serenity prayer" addresses such feelings of isolation and confusion:

> God grant me the serenity
> To accept the things I cannot change,
> Courage to change the things I can,
> And wisdom to know the difference.

We suggest that the facilitator read the serenity prayer aloud, then ask the patient for his/her initial reactions to it. Then follow up with a line of inquiry such as:

- "Do you experience feelings of isolation or loneliness—of having to face difficult decisions and choices but feeling totally alone in making them?"
- "Do you ever pray or otherwise turn to a 'Higher Power' in times of stress, despair, confusion, or anxiety?"
- "Do you sometimes have difficulty deciding what you cannot change versus what you can (and should try to) change?"
- "How would you feel about saying the serenity prayer at times of stress or confusion? About talking to AA/NA friends or to your sponsor about particular dilemmas you face?" (Some patients may not know how to apply the serenity prayer to their own lives. To teach them, ask for an example of a worrisome situation from the patient's life. Then "brainstorm" the serenity prayer: Say it aloud, line by line, and talk about how each line might apply to that situation.)

Other methods for dealing with anxiety are couched in several AA/NA slogans:

"First Things First." The first priority for the alcoholic or addict is to not take that first drink, or use that first time. At times, all recovering alcoholics and addicts find themselves in a position where they must choose between taking care of themselves and taking care of someone else, between tending to their own recovery and other responsibilities. At times, their choice may be between pleasing themselves and pleasing someone else; between making themselves happy and making someone else happy; between working the program and sacrificing it.

The facilitator should encourage the patient to make ongoing sobriety his/her first priority, even if that means frustrating or disappointing someone else. The facilitator might want to elicit the patient's experiences of situations in which s/he felt conflicted about taking care of themselves versus taking care of others, or of tending to their own recovery versus tending to some other responsibility. These questions can be useful food for thought and discussion:

- "What could be the price of pleasing or satisfying others at your own expense?"
- "What did you do in a situation where it was 'you or them'? Was that consistent with putting your sobriety first?"
- "What responsibilities compete with your responsibility to be active in AA and/or NA? What choices do you make? Do you ever put your program first?"

"Easy Does It." The pressures of deadlines and overcommitment create anxiety that invites drinking or using as a means of coping. The AA/NA slogan "Easy Does It" speaks to this particular kind of anxiety. Ask these questions:

- "Do you identify with the stresses of having to meet deadlines?"
- "Do you have a habit of taking on more commitments than you can reasonably satisfy?"

One strategy for dealing with this form of anxiety is to develop a system of prioritizing that is doable.[8] For example, patients can be encouraged to:

- make up a list of things to do today, then discard half of it;
- schedule things twice as far in advance as they usually would;

- sit quietly for ten minutes each day;
- take out five minutes in the middle of the day to read an affirmation and reflect on it;
- talk to someone else (preferably another recovering person) about feeling overextended and "stressed out";
- allow themselves a day off, to include no scheduled activities other than routine recovery maintenance (such as going to meetings or meditation or prayer).

Anger and Resentment

Anger seems to be a pivotal emotion for most recovering alcoholics and addicts. Many alcoholics can relate to the idea of drinking in order to find the "courage" to express anger that they ordinarily would suppress.[9] Resentment, which appears to grow out of the frustration that comes from unexpressed or unresolved anger, also presents a more-or-less constant threat to sobriety for the same reasons.[10]

We recommend that the facilitator engage the patient in a discussion about anger and resentment. Begin with getting some background information this way:

Facilitator: "Anger and resentment are two emotions that are closely connected to using alcohol and drugs. Many men and women who have trouble expressing their anger when they are sober use alcohol to help them find the courage to tell someone off. If the reasons for their anger are not resolved, these people develop resentments. They may continue to drink in order to be able to transform their resentment into anger, or they may turn to alcohol or drugs in an effort to help them 'drown out' what is bothering them. Of course this usually backfires, particularly in the case of alcohol.

"Resentment, then, usually represents unexpressed or unresolved anger. If issues go unresolved, resentment builds up. The recovering person cannot afford to live in the past, yet cannot afford to hold on to resentment either. The recovering person has to learn to express anger effectively and to either resolve issues or let them go. You have to let go of the past and learn to live in the present, one day at a time. AA and NA offer us much useful advice about resentment. Slogans like 'Live and Let Live' and 'Let Go and Let God' contain special wisdom on what to do about resentment."

After giving this background information, the facilitator should explore the following areas relative to the patient's resentment:

- "Over what experiences do you harbor resentment?"
- "How did you handle these situations when they occurred?"
- "Did you feel injured, either emotionally or in terms of your self-esteem, as a result of these experiences? How and why?"
- "Can you realistically resolve these issues now, or do you need to let go of them?"
- "Do you feel that you need to learn how to express your anger more effectively, so as to resolve issues and avoid building up stores of resentment?"

We suggest that the facilitator use the following guidelines when working on issues of anger and resentment:

- Be specific. Identify specific incidents over which the patient feels resentment.
- Use cognitive reenactment and role-playing techniques. What did the patient actually do in those situations, and what could s/he do in such circumstances in the future?
- Help the patient make the connection between unexpressed anger and resentment that results from holding on to anger.
- Help the patient understand what stops him/her from expressing anger in the first place, if that seems to be an issue. Role playing the expression or anger can help desensitize an anger-phobic patient, and help all patients practice effective anger expression and anticipate possible reactions from others, especially counteraggression.
- For the patient who feels guilt over anger, suggest that s/he try to turn the anger over to his/her "Higher Power." Encourage the patient to have faith that expressing anger honestly and straightforwardly will prove to be the "right thing to do" in the long run. Remind the patient that s/he is responsible for making the effort—for expressing anger appropriately but effectively—but not for the outcome, the other person's reaction.

Grief

Grief is another powerful emotion that is often relevant in addiction. The personal histories of many alcoholics and addicts are marked by losses that went ungrieved. As a child, Bill Wilson, the co-founder of AA, experienced abandonment by both his parents and subsequently when his first girlfriend, with whom he had fallen deeply in love, died.[11] One can only wonder what these losses contributed to the chronic sense of loneliness that seems to have haunted Wilson throughout his life, and that appeared to play a role in his early drinking career.[12] Another young man started, in his own words, "drinking himself to death" soon after the death of his girlfriend.

As preparation for discussing grief, the facilitator should be familiar with the following ways in which people commonly respond to the loss of an attachment object or person.

- *Anxiety.* The immediate response to loss, anxiety can promote substance abuse if more effective means of coping are not available.

- *Denial.* Denial involves minimizing or denying the importance of what was lost in an effort to minimize or avoid anxiety.

- *Bargaining.* Bargaining attempts to replace the lost thing with something else, thereby not completely acknowledging its loss.

- *Anger.* Anger involves getting mad at the lost object or person, or venting aggression toward a substitute object or person.

- *Sadness.* The truest emotional expression of loss, sadness is usually experienced only if anxiety is not overwhelming.

Those who specialize in understanding and treating grief say that true acceptance of loss comes slowly and usually only as denial breaks down and the individual can come to terms, without panic, with the reality of the loss.[13] Moreover, it is only when some level of acceptance is reached that the individual is truly emotionally free. So long as loss is denied, substance abuse as a means of coping with it remains a possibility.

Presenting the Material

We recommend that the facilitator first talk with the patient about the above ideas. Describe the various reactions to loss in ways that the patient can understand them. Then ask the patient to choose one significant loss from his/her past, preferably one that s/he feels that s/he has accepted relatively well. Explore his/her initial and subsequent reactions to this loss, and ask the patient to explain how "acceptance" was reached. (Note: As a "test" of acceptance, see if the patient can experience some sadness when talking about this loss. To the extent that s/he cannot, chances are that his/her acceptance of the loss is still limited.)

Next, ask the patient to think about another loss, one that s/he believes s/he has not yet worked through, that s/he may still be in denial about. Explore this loss, including the patient's past and present reactions to it. Help the patient to identify where s/he is with respect to accepting this loss. (Note: The facilitator must be prepared to encounter any of the emotional reactions noted above in this session. Intense anxiety and anger are common, as are efforts to deny the true significance of the loss.)

Finally, the facilitator should encourage the patient to share this discussion with AA/NA fellowship friends and/or his/her sponsor. It is very important to reassure the patient of two things: that all of the above emotional reactions are "normal," and that s/he can successfully grieve even the worst losses and ultimately achieve some degree of acceptance, as long as s/he is willing to reach out for the support of friends, and as long as s/he does not try to bury the grief in alcohol or drugs.

Recovery Tasks

- Meetings
  - Make a list of meetings the patient will attend before the next session.
  - Suggest other kinds of meetings the patient might attend.
  - Suggest activities the patient can do to get more active.
- Telephone Therapy
  - Decide how many phone numbers the patient will get this week.
  - Decide how many phone calls the patient will make this week.
- Sponsor
  - If the patient has gotten a sponsor, suggest ways that the patient can make use of his/her sponsor.
  - If not, suggest specific steps is that s/he can take to get one before the next session.
- Reading
  - Encourage the patient to continue reading the Big Book (especially Chapter 6) and/or the NA Big Book, the Twelve and Twelve, and *Living Sober* (especially those sections mentioned at the beginning of this chapter).
- Recommended
  - *Releasing Anger* (Center City, MN: Hazelden, 1985).
  - *Grieving: A Healing Process* (Center City, MN: Hazelden, 1985).

Facilitator Notes

The importance of the patient's going to meetings, getting involved in them, and developing relationships with other recovering alcoholics and addicts cannot be overstated. The patient can use the AA/NA fellowships as a source of support, advice, and comfort. By now, going to meetings should be a part of the patient's lifestyle. If it isn't, the facilitator should spend more time uncovering and working through the patient's resistance to this. A "contracting" approach can be a useful technique: here, the facilitator and patient agree that the patient will try out a certain number of AA/NA meetings, or experiment with some form of participation. The patient's experiences at meetings, like his/her reactions to the Big Book or the NA Big Book need to be processed in the review at the beginning of each session.

Role playing can be a very effective technique for helping the shy or reticent patient overcome internal barriers to going to meetings. Have the patient practice, for example, saying his/her name out loud, "as if" s/he were doing so at a meeting. Assure the patient that at meetings s/he will not be pressured to say more than s/he feels comfortable saying. Have the patient imagine going to a new meeting, being greeted by others, and introducing him/herself. Of course, to do this effectively, the facilitator must be familiar with meetings.

Once the patient has become regular in attending meetings, the next step is to encourage him/her to talk at the meetings. Meetings and subsequent telephone contacts with fellow AA/NA members can be used as opportunities to talk about issues like resentment and grief. Patients who merely attend AA/NA meetings but do not participate and develop communicative relationships with other recovering men and women are at risk for slipping into alcohol or drug use as a means of coping with unpleasant emotions.

The patient also needs to come to terms with the loss of alcohol or drugs as a means of coping and as a "friend" of sorts. Along these lines, a possible additional recovery task for this session is to ask the patient to write a good-bye letter to a lover or a best friend. Dependency on alcohol or drug needs to be conceptualized in just this way—as a "relationship" that must be ended (and grieved) in the interest of the patient's recovery. This requires sensitivity and respect on the part of the facilitator, along with an appreciation for the grief process itself and an ability to work sympathetically with the patient through his/her grief over the loss of alcohol or drugs.

Elective Topic 5: Moral Inventories

Most of us find that we were neither as terrible, nor as wonderful, as we supposed.
—*Narcotics Anonymous*

Spiritual Malaise

Alcoholism and addiction are often described as not only physical, psychological, and social illnesses but as spiritual illnesses.[1] They are illnesses of the spirit in part because alcoholics and addicts are driven by their disease to behave in ways that compromise their personal ethics and values. Moreover, addiction tends to undermine any sense of faith that an alcoholic or addict may once have had. Alcoholics and addicts commit crimes and misdeeds of commission and omission in order to satisfy their "master"—alcohol or drugs—and as a result of the imparied judgment that handicaps them when they are under the influence. Their moral and ethical lapses undermine their self-esteem and promote isolation. They generate alienation, and they make finding hope in a Higher Power and trust in others more and more difficult.

Steps 4 and 5 of Alcoholics Anonymous address the fact that alcoholics and addicts suffer feelings of guilt and shame related to their behavior. Implicit within them is the acknowledgment that sharing these feelings has healing value.

The goals of the session devoted to Elective Topic 5 are:

- to continue to work through the patient's resistance to Step 1 (acceptance) by asking him/her to think and talk about some of the wrongs or errors s/he has committed as a result of alcohol or drug abuse;
- to explore the extent to which the patient experiences guilt and shame that have not been shared and that can therefore threaten his/her recovery;
- to balance the patient's recognition of wrongs s/he has committed and harm s/he has done with recognition of some "positives" in the patient's behavior and relationships; and
- to prepare the patient for further work in the twelve-step program.

132

From its inception, AA—and, later on, other twelve-step programs—regarded itself as not only a means of achieving the pragmatic goal of staying sober a day at a time but as a program for personal spiritual renewal. In fact, the majority of the twelve steps address the issue of identifying and overcoming character defects and personal shortcomings. In part, this may reflect an acknowledgment that addiction leads individuals to make many moral compromises, but it may also embody a philosophical position: that alcoholism and addiction have their psychological roots in qualities of character such as self-centeredness and arrogance, and that moving away from these qualities, toward qualities like humility and altruism, is essential to "recovery." In this regard, it is of interest to note that the ultimate result of following the twelve steps is described as a spiritual awakening. The process of spiritual renewal within the context of the twelve steps begins in earnest with the fourth and fifth steps, which have to do with taking an "inventory" or one's moral failings and then sharing this inventory with another person.

We would like to emphasize that this session is not intended to conduct a thorough and complete—in other words, a "searching and fearless"[3]—moral inventory, in the truest sense of AA Steps 4 and 5. In general, that kind of moral inventory is best attempted by an individual who has been clean and sober and actively working a twelve-step program for six months to a year, and who has a sponsor. Constructing and working with such a moral inventory needs to be shared with a trusted person such as a sponsor or member of the clergy. It is more often a process than an event. In this facilitation program, the purpose of taking a moral inventory is more limited: to help the patient accept responsibility for some of the negative consequences of alcohol or drug abuse, to release some guilt or shame, and to seek a balance in the patient's view of his/her own moral character. The facilitator needs to keep these limited goals in mind while at the same time recognizing that the patient will need to do more work on AA Steps 4 and 5 at some point in the future in order to continue the process of spiritual rebirth that is part of twelve-step recovery.

The facilitator should be thoroughly familiar with pages 42 through 62 of *Twelve Steps and Twelve Traditions*, as well as pages 26 through 32 of the NA Big Book. Additionally, facilitators who have not attempted to do a moral inventory of themselves are advised to do so and to share it with an appropriate, trusted other person prior to attempting to conduct a session on Elective Topic 5 with patients. What the facilitator needs to communicate to the patient is a message of hope—that it is possible to get through these steps and experience a sense of healing as a result.

Presenting the Material

> The purpose of a searching and fearless moral inventory is to sort through the confusion and the contradiction of our lives, so that we can find out who we really are.
>
> Sharing the exact nature of our wrongs sets us free to live.

These statements from the NA Big Book are as good a summary of the purpose of the moral inventory as any, and reading them aloud can be a good starting point for a dialogue with the patient. There are two key issues that the facilitator should keep in mind when talking with a patient about his/her "moral history": honesty and balance. These issues need to be communicated to the patient in a way that is understandable to him/her.

Honesty

To be of real value, a patient's moral inventory must be honest. The facilitator must carefully guide the patient, without judging or censuring, to own up to ways in which s/he has hurt other people, either willfully or accidentally, or has compromised his/her ethics as a result of alcohol or drug abuse. The patient needs to be encouraged to admit his/her contributions to strained marriages or friendships, problems with children, and the like. Obviously, this is sensitive work. The practiced facilitator who sincerely believes that alcoholism and addiction are not the products of flawed character, but are illnesses that are ultimately stronger than individual willpower, will be most successful in guiding the patient through these treacherous waters and in encouraging frankness without promoting needless guilt. A successful moral inventory leads not to guilt or shame but to commitment to recovery.

Balance

A moral inventory should also be balanced, meaning that it should also include the patient's positive moral qualities, right choices, and heroic efforts. Even the most severe alcoholics and addicts "do things right" now and then. It will not jeopardize this work if the facilitator encourages the patient to think about and share positive things about his/her character and actions. On the contrary, discussing the positives can help minimize excessive guilt and shame and form the basis for renewed self-esteem in recovery.

Taking the Moral Inventory

Exploring Liabilities

We suggest that the facilitator read AA Steps 4 and 5 aloud:

Step 4: Made a searching and fearless moral inventory of ourselves.

Step 5: Admitted to God, to ourselves, and to another human being the exact nature of our wrongs.

Explore the meaning of these ideas with the patient. Explain that they refer to "character defects": those negative qualities and tendencies that each and every person, not only alcoholics and addicts, possess. Indeed, one could argue that everyone has character defects but that alcoholism and addiction have the effect of worsening them. It is the compulsion of addiction, which overcomes the will and the conscience, that leads the addict to make ethical and moral compromises.

Character defects are reflected in behavior that suggests personal qualities such as:

- jealousy
- exploitiveness
- self-pity
- greed
- grandiosity
- meanness
- selfishness
- arrogance
- callousness

Alcoholics and addicts often commit errors of judgment that hurt others. They neglect or abuse their relationships, betray trust, and so on. That the effects of alcohol and drug abuse on personality and moral conduct are so predictable is further evidence that they are indeed illnesses. By serving the "master," alcohol or drugs, alcoholics and addicts serve others (as well as themselves) poorly. AA, NA, and other twelve-step programs have long recognized this reality, as well as the alcoholic's or addict's need to be honest about these wrongs and errors in order to be able to experience a spiritual renewal.

Moral Inventory

- Which of the character defects listed above (or others) have emerged in this patient as a result of alcohol abuse?

_____

_____

_____

• List specific examples of these character defects and how others have been hurt by them. Take time to explore one or two key incidents in which the patient, under the influence of alcohol or drugs, has done something that hurt someone else, and which s/he now regrets.

_____

_____

_____

Exploring Assets

After exploring the patient's character defects, it is important for the facilitator to balance the moral inventory by taking an equal amount of time to explore the patient's better qualities, supported by specific examples of behavior that reflect them. Look for specific examples of qualities such as:

• generosity
• altruism
• love
• herosim
• kindness
• helpfulness
• charity
• humility
• compassion

List several examples of these qualities:

1. _____
2. _____
3. _____

Recovery Tasks

Recovery tasks that the facilitator may suggest for this session include:

• Meetings
  • Make a list of meetings the patient will attend.
  • Suggest other kinds of meetings the patient could attend.
  • Suggest other ways the patient could get active.
• Telephone therapy
  • Decide how many phone numbers the patient will get this week.
  • Decide how many phone calls the patient will make this week.

- Sponsor
  - If the patient has not gotten a sponsor, decide what specific steps the patient will take between now and the next session to get one.
- Reading
  - Encourage the patient to continue reading the Big Book (Chapter 6 in particular) and/or the NA Big Book, the Twelve and Twelve (the sections on Steps 5 and 6), and *Living Sober.*
- Recommended additional reading:
  - *Shame Faced* (Center City, MN: Hazelden, 1986)

Facilitator Notes

Coping with Shame and Guilt

Patients may occasionally experience periods of intense guilt or shame as a result of work on the moral inventory. These feelings may occur during the course of the session, but they are even more likely to arise after the session, when the patient has had time to reflect on this material. It can be helpful for the facilitator to prepare the patient for this eventuality and to give him/her specific suggestions for what to do if this happens. Here are some key points to keep in mind.

Making Amends. Built into the Twelve Steps are the ideas that alcoholics and addicts who find the courage to face their moral mistakes can humbly seek forgiveness from a Higher Power, and in some cases do something to make up for them. This concept of making amends gives patients a decided advantage over those who refuse to admit their defects. Making amends in appropriate situations and in appropriate ways can heal much guilt and shame. The question is, when is making amends appropriate, and what constitutes appropriate amends? This task is best approached only after a period of sustained sobriety. The recovering person is well advised to consult several others about the appropriateness of making amends before venturing down that path.

An Ongoing Moral Inventory. Alcoholics and addicts should not be led to believe that nonalcoholics and nonaddicts do not make moral mistakes. In fact, recovering persons who keep an ongoing moral inventory (as in AA Step 10) may very well lead lives more spiritual than those of many of their nonrecovering peers.

Using Affirmations. The patient should be encouraged to keep his/her positive qualities in mind without avoiding or minimizing character defects. The facilitator can help the patient design one or more personal "affirmations"—statements that assert positive qualities and that the patient can be encouraged to repeat several times a day—to help counter unreasonable guilt and shame.

Other Sources of Support. Sponsors and AA/NA friends, as well as clergy, can be key sources of support for patients during items of intense guilt and shame. Patients should be encouraged to identify their specific sources of support—people they could talk to, and who they think could understand their feelings.

Avoiding Minimization. The facilitator should not minimize, rationalize, or avoid addressing the patient's feelings of guilt and shame, for to do so can make the patient feel all the more isolated with his/her feelings. Remind the patient that s/he is not responsible for his/her illness, although s/he is responsible for recovery. Reinforcing this idea can be especially helpful in this session, since it offers hope at the same time that it acknowledges responsibility for harm done.

Grieving the Loss of Self-Esteem. The facilitator should be prepared to talk about the patient's need to grieve the loss of self-esteem associated with the mistakes s/he made under the influence of alcohol or drugs.

Contact Outside the Session. Advise the patient that it would be appropriate in this case to contact you between sessions if s/he is experiencing an intense emotional reaction to the moral inventory work. An emergency session could be appropriate here, as it could be after a session on genograms.

Elective Topic 6: Relationships

> Almost without exception, alcoholics are tortured by loneliness. Even before our drinking got bad and people began to cut us off, nearly all of us suffered the feeling that we didn't quite belong.
> —*As Bill Sees It*

On Love Betrayed

Throughout his adult life, Bill Wilson struggled with a tendency to regress into self-centeredness and grandiosity—to give in to a needy and infantile aspect of the self that his psychotherapist labeled "his majesty the baby."[1] As the above quotation suggests, Wilson was also prone to chronic feelings of loneliness and isolation. The sense of emptiness and the social isolation that appears to have characterized most of Wilson's life may have had its roots in the relationships he lost early on.[2] Whatever the causes, however, these same themes—isolation and of infantile regression—repeat themselves in the stories of many alcoholics and addicts. Consider the following comments quoted in the AA/NA literature:

> I was thirty-five years old and had a very responsible job as office manager of a small firm. I was a workaholic and spent long hours and weekends at my job. I was always tired and did not have a social life, other than sporadic one-night stands that never developed into any deeper relationships.

> I continued to do my chores and felt more resentful. I wondered how I could have an intimate relationship with a husband I treated like a son. I wanted to be a wife.[3]

Clinical experience suggests that prior to turning to alcohol or drugs many addicts and alcoholics suffered from a lack of satisfying social relationships, from loneliness, and from problems of intimacy. Many struggled with the same neediness that Bill Wilson acknowledged. Invariably, substance abuse exacerbates these problems. Active addicts are nothing if not infantile. They are grandiose and self-centered, as arrogant and demanding as any infant, as self-absorbed and self-pitying as the most pampered child. The addict's primary, in fact only, "relationship" is with a mood-altering substance. As the lament goes, "He loves his bottle more than he loves me."

Sometimes the paraphernalia associated with substance abuse become an "attachment object." The fact that alcoholics and addicts "love" alcohol or drugs more than anything else causes stores of resentment to build up in their loved ones and poisons their relationships.

In sobriety, recovering alcoholics and addicts are freed from the obsession that became the primary relationship in their lives. No longer preoccupied solely with alcohol or drugs, the eyes of the newly recovering person open. Possibilities for new relationships, as well as for healing existing ones, present themselves. But how can the recovering person do this? AA advises against "emotional entanglements" in early recovery.[4] This is probably good advice for the alcoholic or addict who is not already emotionally "entangled," but many recovering persons are already in relationships. Most of these relationships have been badly damaged by addiction. They may actually be founded on dependency and codependency more than on love and mutuality.[5] A great many end in divorce. Despite this grim picture, the question remains—and usually arises in the facilitation program—as to how to proceed with healing relationships in recovery.

Presenting the Material

Intimacy and sexuality are major concerns for recovering persons and their partners. Much of this relational work is probably best done after the patient has established some good recovery habits, altered his/her lifestyle, and formed a firm connection to a twelve-step program. Meanwhile, the partners of recovering persons can help extricate themselves from the bonds of codependency through active involvement in Al-Anon or Nar-Anon. Contrary to what many people think, these programs exist less for the benefit of the alcoholic or addict than for the benefit of those who are in relationships with them.

As desirable as it is to postpone intensive relationship counseling until recovery has established itself, the facilitator in this program may be pressed to offer at least some initial guidance.

The first order of business for the recovering person may be to make amends to others who have been injured as a consequence of his/her addiction, and to heal injuries to self-esteem. The latter will be discussed later on; first, we recommend that the facilitator talk with the patient about making amends and opening communication in his/her relationship.

The Relationship Inventory

The most obvious source of injury to relationships caused by addiction is the patient's "abandonment" of a spouse or significant other for alcohol and/or drugs. There is no way that the alcoholic or addict can escape taking responsibility for this abandonment. No matter how stressed a relationship may have been before the patient's addiction, it is invariably worse as a consequence of that addiction.

In addition to abandoning partners for alcohol or drugs, addicts may have been abusive and exploitative during their active addiction. As preparation for making amends, we suggest that the facilitator work with the patient to make a list of relational errors of commission and omission that were associated with addiction in a relationship inventory. This can be used as a basis for discussion.

The Relationshp Inventory

- Can the patient relate to the idea of having *abandoned* a significant other for alcohol or drugs? Have the patient express this in his/her own words.

- In what if any ways did the patient *exploit* a significant other in the interests of addiction? Did s/he steal money, lie, or otherwise take advantage of the other's trust and commitment? Make a specific list of several such incidents.

- Did the patient ever *abuse* a partner, either physically or verbally, while actively addicted? Make a list of specific incidents that the patient needs to acknowledge.

The process of taking the relationship inventory can easily evoke intense feelings of guilt or shame in the patient. Negotiating these treacherous emotional waters by helping the patient separate responsibility for harm done from responsibility for addiction can test the facilitator's skill. The facilitator should emphasize that the patient is not responsible for having an illness, although s/he is responsible for the harm done as a consequence of addiction, and for his/her ongoing recovery. Addiction, in other words, is no excuse for the emotional injuries caused by abandonment or exploitation. The patient who harbors any desire to "get off the hook" for these abuses by pleading addiction is apt to be sorely disappointed. At the same time, recovery presents the patient with an opportunity for healing and renewal in his/her relationships.

Making Amends

Once the patient has prepared the relationship inventory, s/he needs to decide whether amends are appropriate, and if so, how to go about making those amends. Relationships that have already ended as a result of addiction may best be left alone. The patient's acceptance of responsibility for his/her actions in those relationships may constitute sufficient work—attempting to contact a divorced spouse or former partner may be unwelcome.

For relationships that are more amenable to healing, the facilitator might approach making amends in the context of a conjoint session. We recommend that this work not be attempted until after the conjoint program has been completed. Alternatively, it may be helpful for the facilitator to have the patient write a "letter" to the person who s/he abandoned or exploited, expressing recognition of this fact and accepting responsibility for it. This letter may or may not be sent as part of the amends process. After discussing the relationship with the patient, the facilitator needs to exercise judgment as to whether to recommend actually sending the letter. (We do not recommend sending such letters until the patient and his/her partner have completed the conjoint program.) The patient may choose to break the ice by sending the letter, by communicating the gist of the relationship inventory personally, or both. However it is done, we advise that the facilitator caution the patient not to expect any particular reaction. Sometimes amends are accepted gratefully; at other times they are rejected, at least initially. Making amends may set off tears or bring to light anger and resentments that have been stored unexpressed for years. The patient needs to accept the partner's right to have these feelings. The best course of action, in our experience, is for the patient to make amends and accept whatever reactions are forthcoming. That is the best the patient can do—the rest is up to the other person. (In preparation for making amends, it might be helpful for the facilitator to once again review the serenity prayer and its meaning with the patient).

Discussion: Opening Communication

Addiction usually has devastating effects on communication. In addictive relationships stores of resentment build up, the list of unsettled issues gets longer, and alienation replaces intimacy. Addictive relationships are notoriously alienated. Resentment often stands as an impenetrable barrier between partners whose relationship has been dominated by the patient's alcoholism or addiction and the partner's codependency. The openness and communicative intimacy may have once contributed to a couple's coming together may be nothing more than a vague memory by the time recovery begins.

Recovering alcoholics and addicts need to learn how to begin to build relationships. In a sense they have "related" to little else besides alcohol or drugs for some time, maybe for years. The younger the addict, the greater the developmental lag that s/he is likely to have suffered in terms of basic relationship skills.[6] Even mature adults are apt to start recovery with impoverished communication skills. Their relationships, to a great extent, have been marred by chronic dishonesty, and whatever communication has gone on has been compromised by clouded consciousness. Moreover, not all alcoholics and addicts ever possessed effective communication skills in the first place. Many recovering persons report that they were shy or unassertive, or had difficulty being direct, well before their substance abuse began.

Honest and sober communication can begin when the patient creates and absorbs the meaning of the relationship inventory and takes responsibility for some of the effects that addiction has had on his/her relationship. Beyond that, the patient may need help in learning how to communicate effectively. In particular, s/he may benefit from some simple instruction and role-playing practice in being direct, clear, and assertive. Recovery brings the clarity of thought and freedom from obsession that make communication possible.

Discussion: Assertiveness

Assertiveness means being able to communicate clearly one's real feelings, thoughts, desires, and opinions. Unassertive people, by contrast, don't communicate these things very often, or very clearly.[7]

For patients who have difficulty with assertiveness, the facilitator can help them see that being assertive means being able to communicate positive feelings just as much as negative ones. Explain to the patient that learning to be positively assertive means learning to be able to say things like:

- "I want _____."
- "I liked it when you _____."
- "I appreciate _____."
- "You look nice."
- "Thanks for _____."

On the other hand, learning to be negatively assertive means being able to say things like:

- "Please stop that."
- "I don't like _____."
- "No."

- "That makes me mad."
- "I can't _____."

Point out to the patient that effective, assertive communication plays a vital role in relationships. Relationships in which partners lack assertiveness tend to get bogged down in avoidance. Issues don't get settled, honesty is absent, and the sense of intimacy and connectedness wanes. Many alcoholics and addicts lacked good assertiveness skills even before they got involved with alcohol or drugs. Practicing basic assertiveness can help. We recommend role laying both positive and negative assertive statements in this session. Help the patient identify two or three actual situations in which s/he was not positively assertive, as well as two or three in which s/he was not negatively assertive. Identify appropriate—positive and negative—assertive statements for these situations and practice them with the patient.

Discussion: Conflict Management

Since alcoholics and addicts often flee from life into alcohol or drugs, in sobriety they may feel anxious about conflict and confrontation. Indeed, in addition to learning basic communication and assertiveness skills, the recovering person may benefit from some guidance in conflict management. S/he may need some help in dealing with disagreements or in negotiating for what s/he wants in the relationship. Again, we recommend that the facilitator role-play effective confrontation with the patient, based on one or two actual situations from the patient's life. Selecting current issues can be most effective. Encourage the patient to try out his/her new skills in the actual relationship between sessions.

Here are some simple guidelines for effective confrontation and conflict management in relationships[8]:

- Guideline 1: Know what you want. Suggest that the patient think about what it is s/he wants from the partner, or what is bothering him/her, so that thoughts will have the best chance of being stated clearly.
- Guideline 2: Communicate what you want. As obvious as it may seem, many resentments build up over issues that never get stated. Help the patient to role-play making clear statements.
- Guideline 3: Persist until you feel heard. In role playing a confrontation with a patient, the facilitator should "play difficult" so that the patient has to persist. For example, question the patient's right to want whatever it is s/he wants; or try to deflect the conversation onto some other issue. Encourage the patient to "stick to his/her guns" and repeat his/her position until s/he feels heard.

- Guideline 4: Be a good listener. One can only guess how many mountains of resentment in relationships have arisen from chronic miscommunication. To avoid this, clear communication skills much be matched by good listening skills. We suggest that the facilitator coach the patient, through role playing, to paraphrase what the other person has just said prior to responding to it. Teach the patient to pause, take a moment to "say back" what s/he thinks s/he heard, to verify his/her perceptions.
- Guideline 5: Compromise. Compromise is the middle ground between giving in and getting everything one's own way. Role-play with the patient a negotiation process for compromising in disputes. Show the patient how to give and take so that both partners come out of a confrontation feeling like winners.

Discussion: Sexuality

Sexuality is an area that is of great concern to many recovering persons but that is too little discussed. Many alcoholics and addicts, especially women, report being sexually victimized or exploited while they are actively drinking or using.[9] Women are especially likely to drink or use drugs in order to overcome sexual inhibitions whose origins may lie in incest or sexual trauma.[10] Although alcohol and some drugs have transient disinhibiting effects, in the long run alcohol use is associated with lowered sexual arousal in both men and women, and chronic use is associated with sexual dysfunction in both sexes.[11]

A Case Study

Judy and her husband Tom are a typical example. They went for sex therapy at his insistence. In fact, it was only under Tom's threat of divorce that Judy reluctantly agreed to go. The sexual problem between them was her lack of sexual desire. Whereas she rarely wanted to make love, he wanted to almost every night. It had been that way throughout their marriage, although, as both agreed, before they married, Judy had been much more interested in sex. Tom was angry and frustrated, while Judy was filled with guilt and resentment.

Not only did Tom like to make love often, it turned out that he also liked to play sexual "games." Mostly these involved Judy dressing up in lingerie he'd bought, then playing games like pool or poker together. Tom's favorite games, in fact, were strip pool and strip poker. Sometimes Tom liked them to watch pornographic movies together as a way of getting "turned on."

Judy's personal sexual history included a sexually repressive and shame-oriented family. This was compounded by the fact that she had gotten pregnant and had an abortion at the age of sixteen. That had made her, in her words, the "black sheep" in the family. She admitted in therapy that she had felt shame ever since and had been "uptight" about sex. Then at age seventeen, she discovered that a couple of glasses of wine, or a couple of beers, "loosened her up" so that she was able to make love and enjoy it. Afterward, when she sobered up, the idea of making love would make her tense all over again. So she came to rely on alcohol to overcome her anxiety and make love.

Later on, Judy discovered that a combination of alcohol and marijuana was even more effective than alcohol alone in lessening her anxieties and lowering her inhibitions. She found that she orgasmed less and less often, and sometimes intercourse was uncomfortable, but she minimized the importance of her loss of pleasure.

For nearly twelve years, three or four times a week, Judy and Tom made love with Judy drunk and stoned. Not surprisingly, she eventually found herself drinking every day and using pot almost as often. Tom started getting on her case about it, and she'd get angry and defensive in response. Then, about a year before they came for therapy, the combination of alcohol and marijuana lost its ability to facilitate their sexual relationship. By that time, she was clearly dependent on both substances.

Treatment had to begin with Judy's recovery from her addictions. It was agreed that Judy would work on that for at least six months, and that the matter of sexuality would be dealt with then. Fortunately, Judy was willing to look at her addictions and do something about them. Tom said that as long as she was willing to do that, he was willing to postpone sex therapy until his wife could establish some recovery.

Happily, the long-term outcome for Tom and Judy was positive. Judy, in recovery, was able to work through the sexual shame that had its roots in her childhood and adolescence, and to build a sense of sexual pride and power. The nature of her and Tom's sexual relationship changed: They stopped the sexual "games" that Tom had liked, and they got rid of his pornography collection. He was actually more willing to do these things than the therapist had expected him to be, but it turned out that he'd done them in a misdirected effort to "turn on" his wife. He was reinforced by seeing her gradually become a sexual person in her own right. The last step in the sexual healing process was to desensitize Judy to her anxiety about making love, which she had "associated" through years of experience with being drunk and stoned. Initially, the idea of making love brought on her cravings to drink and use, as well as feelings of shame. Through patient but persistent work with a sex therapist sensitive to the sexual issues of men and women in recovery, this anxiety too was eventually conquered.

Taking a Sex History

Realistically, the facilitator in this program cannot expect to heal longstanding sexual wounds or to help patients overcome sexual dysfunctions in a few sessions. Rather than attempting to achieve such an unrealistic expectation, a better course of action at the early stage of recovery would be for the facilitator to help the patient assess his/her own sexuality and to identify problems that need to be worked on and how the patient could go about doing that.

Taking a sex history is a standard practice in sex therapy. It allows the therapist to identify the patient's issues and prioritize problems that need attention. The following sex history differs from those typically found in texts on sex therapy[12] in its greater emphasis on determining the relationship between alcohol, drugs, and sexuality. It takes about forty-five minutes to administer.

When taking a sex history, we suggest that the facilitator adopt a conversational attitude. Introduce the subject by explaining that people rarely have an opportunity to look at their own sexual development or to talk about the influence that alcohol or drug abuse, in themselves or in others, had on their own sexuality. After helping the patient take an "inventory" of his/her own sexuality, the facilitator should discuss it with the patient and, if appropriate, set some goals for growth and healing in this important area.

Sex History

Childhood

- How did your family's background influence your early attitudes about sex? What is your cultural background, and what attitudes does that culture tend to have about the sexuality of people of your own sex? How closely did your own family of origin adhere to these cultural attitudes?

- What role, if any, did religion play in shaping your early attitudes about sex? What did you perceive to be the "position" of your religion relative to sexuality?

- What attitudes did your parents have about your sexuality? What are your earliest memories about your parents' reactions to your own (or a sibling's) sexuality? Do you recall any experiences that caused you to feel anxiety or shame about being sexual?

- Were you able to ask questions about sex as a child? Who were you able to talk to?

- What are your earliest memories about your own sexuality? Did you feel good or bad about your body and the sexual feelings you got from it?

- Were you the object of any unwanted sexual interests from others? How did this make you feel?

- Do you believe that you were sexually abused or exploited as a child? By whom? Do you have any reason to believe that anyone who abused you was a substance abuser?

- What influence did your siblings and friends have on your sexual attitudes and beliefs as a child?

- When did you first learn "the facts of life"? What did you learn? How accurate was the information? What were your reactions to it?

- Overall, how would you summarize your childhood feelings about sex and about your own sexuality? Do you see any reason why your early experiences might lead to feelings of anxiety or shame about sex?

Adolescence

- Were you either an "early bloomer" or a "late bloomer" with respect to puberty? How did your early or late development make you feel about yourself? Did you have any negative experiences associated with your physical development? (For example, girls who develop early often feel self-conscious and uncomfortable if they're stared at.)

- Were you either exceptionally tall or short, fat or skinny, as a teen? How did that affect your self-image?

- Who were the objects of your first crushes? Did you experience any anxiety about your sexual orientation? What is your current sexual orientation?

- When, if ever, did you first masturbate to orgasm? What kinds of sexual fantasies did you have as a teenager? How did you masturbate? Did you feel guilty or ashamed about masturbation?

- Can you remember going through puberty? How did you feel about the sexual changes in your body?

- Did you ever experience a loss of control over eating—such as eating too much (binging), or not being able to eat (anorexia)? Did you ever have a problem with eating, then feeling guilty and vomiting (bulimia)?

- When did you first become sexually active? What were your first voluntary sexual experiences? Who were they with, and how did you feel while they were happening and afterward?

- Did you have any negative (frightening, traumatic) sexual experiences during your adolescent years?

- Were any of these experiences related to alcohol or drug abuse on your part, or the part of the person who abused you?

- Did you ever have sex for money or drugs as an adolescent? If so, how did that make you feel about yourself?

- What did you think were your most attractive features as an adolescent? What did you think were your least attractive features?

- Overall, as an adolescent, how did you feel about yourself as a sexual person?

Adulthood

- What do you think are your most attractive features today? What do you think are your least attractive features?

- Are you sexually active now? Who are your sexual partners? How satisfied are you with your sexual relationship(s)? What, if anything, would make it (them) better? Do you and your partner(s) have conflicts over sex? What are these about?

- How do you deal with the issue of contraception? Do you feel responsible for it?

- How do you deal with the issue of "safe sex," or protecting yourself from sexually transmitted diseases?

- Were you ever exposed to, or did you contract, any sexually transmitted diseases when you were actively abusing alcohol or drugs? Do you have any concerns today about sexually transmitted diseases?

- How often did you have sex as an adult while under the influence of alcohol or drugs? How closely associated are alcohol, drugs, and sex in your mind?

- Do you masturbate? How often? Do you reach orgasm? How do you masturbate? What, if any, sexual fantasies do you use?

- Are you concerned or anxious about your sexual performance? Are you or your partner concerned about a lack of interest in sex? Do you experience problems of sexual arousal (impotence, painful penetration, painful intercourse)? Were these problems associated with drinking or using? What specific problems did you have? Do you ever experience problems reaching orgasm?

- Have you experienced any frightening or traumatic sexual experiences as an adult? Were you drinking or using at the time? What happened?

- Were you ever sexually exploited when you were actively drinking or using? In what way? Have you ever "worked this through" in counseling?
- Did you ever do anything sexually that you are ashamed of now, when you were abusing alcohol or drugs?
- Have you ever used alcohol or drugs in an effort to overcome a sexual inhibition, or to "enhance" lovemaking? When and how? What happened? Did this become a habit?
- If you could change two things about your sexual history, two things about your sexuality, and two things about your sexual relationship, what would they be?

The above sexual history is not exhaustive—sex therapists would likely conduct a much more extensive history before formulating treatment goals and beginning sex therapy. But in this facilitation program, this abbreviated history can achieve several goals. It conveys to the patient the important message—that the facilitator believes sexuality is important and expects that the patient could have some concerns in this area that have not been previously addressed. It gives the patient "permission" to express sexual concerns. And many of the questions explore the connection between substance abuse and sexuality.

The sex history can also help identify factors within the patient's sexuality and sexual relationship(s) that could become risk factors for relapse. In the case of Judy and Tom, Judy's sexual anxieties could well have undermined her recovery from substance abuse. Her history of reliance on alcohol and marijuana to overcome her inhibitions and facilitate her sexual relationship with her husband needed to be addressed.

Sex therapy lies beyond the scope of this facilitation program, but in the discussion that evolves from taking a sex history, the facilitator can make specific suggestions to the patient as to how best to proceed to overcome sexual problems such as the effects of abuse and trauma or dysfunction. After completion of the facilitation program, self-help resources or professional therapy may be recommended.

Recovery Tasks

Recovery tasks that the facilitator may suggest for this session include:

- Meetings
  - Make a list of meetings the patient will attend.
  - Suggest other meetings that could be attended.
  - Suggest other things the patient could do to get active.

- Telephone therapy
  - Decide how many phone numbers the patient will get this week.
  - Decide how many phone calls the patient will make this week.
- Sponsor
  - If the patient has not yet gotten a sponsor, decide what specific steps s/he will take between now and the next session to get one.
- Reading
  - Encourage the patient to continue reading the Big Book or the NA Big Book, the Twelve and Twelve, and *Living Sober*. Make suggestions as to readings that might be particularly relevant to the individual patient.
- Recommended
  The following self-help books may be useful to patients concerned with various issues related to sexuality and relationships.
    - Readings on relational communication, intimacy, and sexuality
      - *A Lifelong Love Affair*, by Joseph Nowinski, W. W. Norton (1988).
      - *Getting The Love You Want*, by Harville Hendrix, Henry Holt (1989).
    - Readings on female sexuality
      - *For Yourself*, by Lonnie Barbach, Signet (1976).
      - *Becoming Orgasmic* by Julia Heiman and Joseph LoPiccolo, revised ed. Prentice-Hall (1988).
    - Readings on male sexuality
      - *Men, Love, and Sex*, by Joseph Nowinski, Thorsons/ HarperCollins (1990).
      - *Male Sexuality*, by Bernie Zilbergeld, Bantam (1978)

Facilitator Notes

The issue of relationships in recovery is the last topic in the elective program because its subject matter takes the facilitator and patient into territory best approached only after the patient has had some chance to establish sobriety through active participation and involvement in a twelve-step fellowship. The material discussed in this session can be emotionally charged, to say the least. It can easily lead the discussion astray from the primary goal of this program, which is the integration of the patient into AA and/or NA. For these reasons we suggest leaving it until last (including after the conjoint program).

As with the genogram, we do not recommend that a facilitator attempt to use any of the techniques presented here, least of all the sexual history, without prior training and personal experience. We advise the facilitator, at a minimum, to both give and take a personal sex history with a peer before trying to do one with a patient. This will help the facilitator be able to ask questions of a sexual nature, and at the same time sensitize the facilitator to what it is like to be asked such questions.

We suggest that the facilitator be cautious when setting treatment goals based on this session. For the patient, it can be very important to identify issues that need further work, but unresolved sexual and relationship issues can pose decided obstacles to recovery. Yet, a single session, or even two, is not likely to be sufficient to resolve many of these issues. Referral to self-help groups such as Incest Survivors Anonymous, Overeaters Anonymous, or Sex and Love Addicts Anonymous can be a starting point for "recovery" from sexual or relational malaise. Self-help may need to be supplemented by intensive individual or group therapy, and/or marital or sex therapy.

The most useful outcome of this session for the facilitation program would be the identification of significant issues relevant to recovery, prioritizing those issues, and the development of a reasonable plan for working on them.

Self-Help Books

The recovery tasks for this elective topic include reading several self-help books that deal with relationship and sexual issues. We suggest that the facilitator be personally familiar with any book prior to recommending it to a patient. Self-help books do have their limitations, most notably the fact that they cannot be individualized the way actual therapy (or this facilitation program) can be. Clinical experience suggests that it is advisable to refer patients to specific sections of books and to prepare them in advance for what they will read. The books on female sexuality, for example, contain exercises in self-exploration and masturbation. The patient who reports a sexually repressive childhood and who experienced much shame associated with early self-stimulation experiences, or who has an aversion to her own genitalia, is best forewarned about this material. This patient could be told that what she will read could evoke some discomfort, and then assured that that would not be an uncommon reaction. She could be assured that some anorgasmic women become orgasmic by following self-help books, while others do not. She could be encouraged to write down her responses and perhaps to discuss them with a professional sex therapist if they prove to be intense.

Despite the limitations of self-help materials, many patients report feeling "validated" as well as comforted to discover that their own struggles and concerns are not unique and that others before them have found remedies. We therefore encourage twelve-step facilitators to make use of these materials, just as we encourage them to suggest to the patient who has worked this facilitation program well that s/he "try out" other relevant twelve-step fellowships.

Part IV
The Conjoint Program

P art of this twelve-step facilitation program is a conjoint program, consisting of two sessions for patients who are in relationships and whose partners are willing to participate in them. Any individual whom the patient considers his/her partner, regardless of their relationship status or how long they've been together, is eligible to participate in these sessions.

The objectives of the conjoint program are:

- to determine the level of partner involvement in the patient's alcohol or drug abuse,
- to describe the twelve-step facilitation program to the partner, and
- to encourage the partner to attend Al-Anon Family Groups or Nar-Anon, as appropriate.

Partners who themselves have no harmful involvement with alcohol or drugs will be educated regarding:

- the facilitation program,
- the concept of enabling,
- the concept of detaching, and
- Al-Anon and Nar-Anon.

Partners who are suspected of themselves being harmfully involved with alcohol or drugs will be informed about the facilitation program and the concept of enabling, but they will also be encouraged to seek an independent assessment of their own use and possible need for treatment.

In order to be maximally effective, we recommend that facilitators read the book *Al-Anon Faces Alcoholism* prior to using this program with patients and their partners.[1] Finally, the facilitator is advised to have current Al-Anon and Nar-Anon meeting schedules handy.

Conjoint Topic 1: Enabling

This first conjoint session may run as long as one and a half hours. We suggest that at the outset of the facilitation program (the first session) the facilitator advise the patient who is in a relationship that the program includes two conjoint sessions and strongly encourage the patient's partner to attend these. The facilitator should take responsibility for contacting the partner directly by phone in order to invite the partner to the first conjoint session and confirm the date and time.

Although this session may be substituted for the session on Elective Topic 2, enabling, in the elective program, it is perfectly permissible to incorporate both sessions into the facilitation program. Facilitators have reported that this "redundancy" is often very worthwhile because of the added reinforcement it provides.

After introductions, begin the first conjoint session by explaining that its main goals are to outline the twelve-step facilitation program in which the patient is involved, to answer the partner's questions, and to explain the concepts of enabling and detaching.

Outlining the Facilitation Program

We suggest that the facilitator spend five minutes outlining the facilitation program itself. Try to cover these essential points before fielding questions from the partner.

The program is grounded in the principles of Alcoholics Anonymous and Narcotics Anonymous. This means that it assumes that:

- Alcoholism and addiction are an illness of the body, mind, and spirit that is characterized by loss of control and obsession with drinking or using. Alcoholism and addiction have predictable symptoms and a predictable course that, if untreated, may lead to premature death or insanity.
- While there is no "cure" at present for alcoholism or drug addiction,

156

they can be arrested. The best method for this, in our opinion, is active involvement in AA and/or NA.

- Alcoholics and addicts resist the idea that they are actually addicted to alcohol or drugs—they cannot reliably control or limit their use or the effects of that use. This is called denial. There are many forms of denial, but its essence is that alcoholics and addicts attempt to convince themselves and others that it is somehow "safe" for them to have a drink or to use drugs—that what happened last time won't happen again.

- Recovering alcoholics and addicts need to resist taking the first drink or drug, and they need to do this one day at a time.

- Having a "slip" means drinking or using after a period of sobriety. Slips are unfortunate but understandable, given the fact that alcoholism and addiction are "cunning, powerful, and baffling" illnesses that "tell their victims that they aren't really sick." What is most important is how the recovering alcoholic or addict responds to a slip—it is not to be seen as an excuse to drink or use more. Going to meetings, calling an AA/NA friend or sponsor, or calling the AA/NA Hotline are the best ways to deal with urges to drink as well as with slips.

- Alcoholics and addicts are responsible for their own recovery. While many factors lead people to use alcohol as a way of coping, addiction is ultimately a personal problem, and recovery is ultimately the personal challenge and responsibility of the alcoholic or addict. Neither alcoholism nor addiction can be blamed on anyone else; nor can anyone else take blame for the alcoholic's or addict's slips or credit for his/her sober days. Al-Anon advises its members, "You didn't Cause the illness, you can't Control the illness, and you can't Cure the illness either."

Follow up this presentation of the ideas underlying the program by soliciting questions about it. We recommend limiting this discussion to approximately ten minutes. If necessary, cut the question-and-answer period short by explaining that there is important material still to be covered.

Sometimes the partner will have many questions or will appear to have a long list of grievances to air. It can be helpful even at this point to refer such a partner to Al-Anon or Nar-Anon for further information, advice and support. Many facilitators have found it very useful to have Al-Anon and Nar-Anon meeting schedules on hand and available for partners to use or take home.

Determining Partner Substance Use

It is important for the facilitator to ask the partner briefly about his/her own use of alcohol or drugs. Of course, the partner should be assured that this information is confidential. Since time is limited, general questions such as these may be most useful:

- "Do you drink at all? How often do you drink?"
- "Have you ever used marijuana? When was the last time? How often do you use it now?"
- "Have you used any other mood-altering substances, such as cocaine or amphetamines, hallucinogens such as LSD, or narcotics? If so, when was the last time? How often do you use _____ now?"
- "Do you use any prescription drugs such as tranquilizers, sleeping pills, or antidepressants? If so, what? Who gave _____ to you, and for what reason? How often do you use _____?"
- "Have you ever felt that you had a problem related to your own use of alcohol or drugs?"
- "Has anyone ever told you that they thought you drank or used drugs too much? If so, who, and when? What, if anything, did you do about it?"
- "Do you know where you could go if you ever wanted to get an honest evaluation of your alcohol or drug use?"
- "Are you concerned about the alcohol or drug use of anyone else who is close to you? If so, who, and why?"

Finish this part of the discussion by asking the partner if s/he has any questions about alcohol or drugs, their effects, or addiction. Assure the partner that you will be happy to answer questions if they arise and can be reached by telephone.

This discussion may cause the facilitator to have concerns about the partner's alcohol or drug use, or either the patient or the partner may express such a concern. It is best to be prepared to respond to these concerns by making a referral for a more thorough evaluation. It is not uncommon for facilitators to make such referrals, and they should not be shy to do so.

Discussion: Enabling

Enabling represents a dysfunctional response to addiction, while detaching represents a functional response. Explain to both the patient and the partner that this first session will focus on enabling, while the subject of detaching will be covered in the second conjoint session.

We suggest that the facilitator present an overview of enabling to both the patient and the partner together. This presentation may run like this:

Facilitator: "As people become addicted, the people around them are also inevitably affected. The closer you are to an addict—the more you love and care about them—the more you're likely to be affected. Out of concern, we often tend to take too much responsibility for the alcoholic or addict we care about. Al-Anon and Nar-Anon recognize these simple truths, which is why they were formed as fellowships for persons who are in relationships with alcoholics or addicts, respectively. The following passage from *Al-Anon Faces Alcoholism* reflects this awareness:

As their lives become compulsively centered on trying to get the alcoholic to stop drinking through unsuccessful attempts to manipulate and control, most of their actions only enable the alcoholic to continue the drinking. Family members are caught in a cycle of repetitive non-helpful behavior that leaves them frustrated, angry and alone. They feel helpless and hopeless.[1]

Facilitator: "The concept of *codependency* refers to this 'obsession' that partners can develop with the alcoholic or addict and his/her behavior. In trying to help, control, or limit the alcoholic's or addict's use, the partner can become as obsessed with them as they are with alcohol or drugs. Can you see how this can happen? Can you relate this concept of codependency to your own relationship?

"*Enabling* refers to another aspect of people who are in relationships with alcoholics or addicts. It means that they often do things that have the unintended effect of 'helping' the alcoholic or addict) keep drinking or using. Any behavior that serves to help the alcoholic or addict minimize or avoid the negative consequences of alcohol or drug abuse could be called enabling behavior. Similarly, behavior that supports drinking or using is also a form of enabling.

"People don't enable because they want the alcoholic or addict to keep on drinking or using. On the contrary, enabling usually has its origins in and is motivated by an interest in controlling the person's use. It often has the effect, though, of allowing the substance abuse to continue or even get worse by cushioning the person instead of letting him/her suffer the negative consequences of drinking or using. Those negative consequences could include being arrested for driving while intoxicated, being arrested for drug possession, getting into trouble at work, or having to answer to others for being irresponsible.

"Examples of enabling include:

- making excuses to cover up for the individual when he/she is drunk and would otherwise get into trouble;
- giving an alcoholic a little alcohol in the hope that s/he won't want any more;
- giving in to the nagging drug addict's demands to borrow money for drugs;
- calling in sick for the person who in truth is hung over;
- excusing or justifying hostility or abuse that results from drinking or drug use;
- accepting guilt-ridden apologies after the fact for harm done while under the influence;
- making beer runs to liquor stores in order to keep an alcoholic off the street (to avoid a DWI arrest, an accident, or an injury), or making drug runs for the addict who is too strung out to do it him/herself;
- defending an alcoholic or addict to his/her accusers for inappropriate or irresponsible behavior; and
- giving a spouse liquor in order to calm or quiet him/her down.

"The common theme in all these examples is that enabling in any form has the effect of helping the alcoholic or addict avoid the real issue, which is alcohol or drug abuse, by helping to minimizing the negative consequences that would otherwise result from it."

This presentation and the kinds of enabling it describes should provide a springboard for a discussion of how the partner has enabled the patient. To be certain that both the partner and the patient clearly understand the concept of enabling, elicit from them several examples of it in their own relationship by an enabling inventory.

Enabling Inventory

- The partner enables the alcoholic or addict in this relationship by:

1. _____

2. _____

3. _____

4. _____

5. _____

6. _____

If there appears to be any doubt about the partner's understanding of the concept of enabling, review it briefly and try once again to elicit some examples from the patient-partner relationship. If necessary, prompt the patient to give examples. (The partner's capacity to understand detachment will in part depend on understanding enabling and how it has been operative in this relationship.)

Motives For Enabling

The concept of enabling may evoke guilt in the partner. This is especially likely if s/he somehow misconstrues what the facilitator says about the motivations that underlie enabling. For this reason, it is important to take some extra time to be certain that there is no misunderstanding. Again, we suggest presenting an overview:

> *Facilitator:* "Enabling has the effect of making the problem worse, but people do not enable because, consciously or unconsciously, they 'want' their alcoholic or addict partner to continue drinking or using. This program, like Al-Anon and Nar-Anon, believes that people's motivations for enabling are actually benign: caring, concern, and commitment. Sometimes their motivation is fear—fear of being abused or abandoned, for instance."

Ask the partner what motivated his/her enabling. Typical responses include the following:

* "I did it because I didn't want her to get into trouble."
* "I was afraid that I'd lose him."
* "When we got married I said it would be for better or worse. I didn't like it, but I was just trying to keep my marriage together as best I could."
* "I was scared and didn't know what else to do."
* "Not helping her seemed like a cruel thing to do."
* "I was afraid he'd hit me or the kids if I didn't help him."
* "If he lost his job, what would happen to us then?"

The facilitator should acknowledge any or all of these motivations for enabling and the fundamentally benign intent behind them. This will help to reduce any stigma the partner associates with enabling, which in turn will enhance the partner's motivation for detaching. If the partner has trouble discerning any motivation at all for his/her enabling, the facilitator might simply suggest some of the motives listed above and ask the partner to think about them.

The Addict's Role in Enabling

Substance abuse and enabling, like addiction and codependency, represent complementary processes. The facilitator should make the point to both partners that alcoholics and addicts usually actively encourage enabling in their partners since it helps them continue drinking or using. Engage the couple in a discussion of how the patient has either encouraged or coerced the partner's enabling. The most common forms of this are appeals to anxiety or guilt, or plays on sympathy:

- *Anxiety:* "If you don't help out [or cover up], something terrible will happen to me, you, or both of us."
- *Guilt:* "It's your fault that I have this problem, so you owe it to me to cover up for me." Or: "You should cover up for me out of loyalty."
- *Sympathy:* "I know I've got a problem, but I'm feeling really strung out and I really need some _____. Won't you help me out?"

Help the couple to make a list of ways the patient actively promotes the partner's enabling:

1. _____
2. _____
3. _____
4. _____
5. _____
6. _____

Wrap-Up

We suggest that at this point the facilitator take a few minutes to summarize the major points that were covered in this session and encourage the partner to try out Al-Anon or Nar-Anon to find other partners of alcoholics and addicts to talk to. Emphasize that "giving it a try" does not mean making a long-term commitment to attending Al-Anon/Nar-Anon meetings. The partner is free to stop going at any time. Still, a single meeting might not be enough to give the partner a true sense of these fellowships. We suggest that the partner attend meetings of at least two different Al-Anon/Nar-Anon groups, three times each. The facilitator can help the partner to locate convenient Al-Anon/Nar-Anon meetings. It can also be helpful to enlist the patient's support for the partner to "try out" Al-Anon or Nar-Anon.

Finally, the facilitator may wish to recommend one or more of the following books to the partner:

* *Al-Anon Faces Alcoholism* (Al-Anon Family Groups, 1985).
* *Facing Shame: Families in Recovery*, by Merle Fosum and Marilyn Mason (New York: W. W. Norton, 1989).

Facilitator Notes

Resistance

The partner's resistance to involvement in Al-Anon or Nar-Anon parallels the patient's resistance to involvement in AA or NA. Resistance to Al-Anon or Nar-Anon can also come from both. It is not uncommon, for example, for patients to protest the facilitator's interest in meeting conjointly. One patient expressed the often-voiced feeling that the conjoint program could make his partner feel guilty, or at least partly responsible, for his addiction. "This is my problem," he asserted. "She's been through enough with me. I don't want her to have to come in here and hear about how she enabled my use. I think that would be unfair."

This patient's reticence to "involve" his wife in the program, while understandable, is based on the assumption that it is possible to be in a relationship with an addict yet be unaffected by the overall dynamic process of addiction, codependency, and enabling. This assumption is questionable to say the least. Confronting the patient with this unrealistic assumption can help to allay anxieties and facilitate conjoint involvement.

Some patients may resist getting their partners involved out of less noble motives. Some may feel guilty themselves and fear blame and possible retribution from their partner. Their relationship may be strained or alienated, even teetering on the brink of divorce. Still others may seek to persist in trying to control their partners through their addiction. One man displayed a very patriarchal attitude. "My wife couldn't handle this," he explained. "Take my word for it."

Resistance can also come from the partners themselves. The partner who flatly (and perhaps angrily) refuses to attend, who agrees in order to placate the facilitator but then fails to show up, or who offers weak excuses for having to cancel should be contacted by telephone at least once. The facilitator should make a reasonable effort to get the partner to commit to coming in at least for the first conjoint session. Explain that there are only two sessions in all, that they are designed to benefit the partner, and that they are not intended as relationship counseling. Assure the partner that s/he will be welcome to express his/her honest feelings and opinions. Reassure the partner that s/he is entirely free to decide to attend or not attend the second session. Finally, assure the angry or anxious partner that the conjoint sessions are not intended to "diagnose" him/her. If the partner still refuses, there is nothing more the facilitator can do.

Relationship Conflict

Given the full agenda for each session, there is little time for meaningful relationship counseling in this conjoint program. That is not to say that relational conflicts will not arise. Typically, codependency, not unlike addiction, follows a predictable course. Most enablers react initially to a substance abuse problem with concern and a desire to help. As time goes on, however, and the problem gets worse instead of better, their concern and anxiety usually give way to frustration and anger, then resentment and finally alienation.

The facilitator should not be surprised to encounter anger, frustration, depression, or longstanding resentment in the partner. Partners may be skeptical or even cynical. They may resent not only the patient, but the facilitator and the program that purports to be able to do what they could not—get the patient to stop drinking or using. They may see it as, as one partner put it, "just another ride on the merry-go-round" of addiction.

We recommend that the facilitator validate the partner's feelings of frustration and resentment, even alienation. We do not recommend that the facilitator attempt to dissuade a partner from an implied or stated intention to divorce a patient who fails to stay sober, or even from considering divorce. In some cases divorce is an inevitable negative consequence of a patient's alcoholism or addiction, and the facilitator should not enable any more than the partner should.

We strongly advise against any attempt to resolve long-standing relationship conflicts, or to explore sources of resentment in any detail, in the conjoint program. Instead, if any of these situations arise, and if the couple is amenable, the facilitator should refer the couple to an appropriate resource for relationship counseling. But the facilitator may suggest that the couple wait to do so until the patient has completed this facilitation program, and the partner has attended at least six Al-Anon/Nar-Anon meetings.

Emergency Calls

Partners are most likely to call the facilitator if the patient has a slip or if a conjoint session evokes strong reactions (such as anger or depression). Consistent with what is done with the patient in the core and elective programs, the strategy to pursue here is to encourage the partner to contact Al-Anon or Nar-Anon and possibly to seek individual counseling as well (for example, if the depression appears to be severe).

If an emergency session seems essential, we advise that it be held with the patient and the partner conjointly, if possible. This may mean waiting a day—for example, to give the patient who has had a slip time to sober up. The therapeutic goal in responding to any emergency is to give advice consistent with Al-Anon and Nar-Anon. Discourage the partner from bringing a drunk or high patient to an AA/NA meeting or from calling the patient's sponsor—these actions would only foster the patient's continued dependence on the partner instead of taking responsibility for his/her own recovery. For similar reasons the facilitator should discourage a partner from arguing with (or trying to "reason with") a drunk or high patient. Help the partner see to it that the patient who has slipped is physically and medically safe, then "detach" from taking further responsibility.

"Secondary Gain"

Some therapists argue that partners of alcoholics and addicts can in fact derive some form of "secondary gain" from enabling—usually some "control" over the relationship. In our experience, enablers gain not control or satisfaction but helplessness and frustration, combined at times with anger and resentment. In other words, experience teaches us that addiction leads to powerlessness for all concerned, not "gain."

Concurrent Substance Abuse

Substance abuse in both partners is a delicate issue, but it needs to be addressed. If the facilitator has reason to believe that the partner of a patient is also abusing alcohol or drugs, it would be appropriate as a first intervention to refer the partner for an evaluation. At the same time, we recommend completing the conjoint program for the patient who is in the facilitation program. Our experience suggests that the same facilitator should not attempt to work with both partners of a couple, but should refer one partner to another facilitator.

Competition between two partners, both of whom are in the facilitation program, is a potential issue that best brought out in the open by the facilitator before it erupts. Two partners may not progress in the programs at comparable paces, and they should not expect to. Nor should their facilitators expect them to. Differences in background, in the particulars of their abuse, and in their attitudes toward addiction and recovery are only some of the factors that account for variability in progress. Similarly, one partner's slips should not be used as a yardstick of the other partner's success, much less personal worth; nor should they be used as justifications for slips by the other partner. The issue of what a patient should do if his/her partner slips, or if one partner continues to drink or use while the other tries to recover, can be brought to Al-Anon or Nar-Anon. Patients should be assured that these are actually common concerns that are routinely dealt with through the support of the twelve-step fellowships.

Conjoint Topic 2: Detaching

> For Al-Anon members, detachment is the culmination of applying themselves to all the steps and slogans of the Al-Anon program, especially the first step. This necessitates accepting a concept of powerlessness over another human being and over alcoholism.
> —*Al-Anon Faces Alcoholism*

The goals of this second conjoint session are:

- to define and illustrate "detaching" versus "enabling" using examples drawn from the couple's own experience together;
- to help the partner identify specific ways that s/he can learn to "detach with love"; and
- to encourage partners to attend six Al-Anon/Nar-Anon meetings of their choice.

Review

Briefly inquire about any questions the partner may have about the material covered in the first conjoint session. We recommend limiting this discussion to approximately fifteen minutes in the interest of time. Questions that seem directed at wanting to know "what to do" can be postponed, with the explanation that the new material presented in this session may help to answer that question and provide the partner with some direction.

Discussion: Al-Anon and Nar-Anon

As in the first conjoint session, we suggest that the facilitator give an overview. Read the quotation that opens this chapter aloud, and ask the partner to share his/her initial reactions to it. Explain that addiction is an illness characterized by obsession (with drinking or using), and that living with an addict can lead partners to become obsessed themselves over time. For the alcoholic or addict, the obsession is with drinking or using; for the codependent partner, the obsession is with controlling or changing the other person.

167

Enabling is the "help" that partners give to the alcoholic or addict. So we have seen, it is meant to control or contain a situation, but it has the inadvertent effect of allowing use to continue. Its basis may be fear or guilt, but regardless of the motivation behind it, enabling rests on the conscious or unconscious assumption that the drinking or using can somehow be "controlled." It is not until the partner accepts the reality of addiction—that it cannot be controlled—that detaching becomes a viable alternative to enabling. So long as the partner holds on to the belief that s/he can somehow control the situation, s/he is likely to continue the pattern of enabling and codependency.

The facilitator should explain that Al-Anon and Nar-Anon are twelve-step fellowships of men and women who find themselves in relationships with alcoholics and addicts, who have been affected by the illness of alcoholism or addiction, and who gather together in order to take care of themselves and seek support for their own growth process. Going to an Al-Anon/Nar-Anon meeting does not imply that the partner is in any way to blame for the alcoholic's or addict's problem. On the contrary, Al-Anon was originally formed by spouses of alcoholics in an effort to help one another learn to "detach" from any feelings of shame or guilt associated with their partners' illness, and to "detach" from the idea that they can somehow control their partners. Meetings are anonymous, there are no fees, and the only "condition" for membership is to be in a relationshp with an alcoholic or addict.

Ask the partner if s/he has ever attended either Al-Anon or Nar-Anon. If the partner went to a meeting as a result of the first conjoint session, ask about it. Ask the partner if s/he has gone to more than one group, more than once each. If not, s/he may not be getting a good overview of these fellowships. If s/he has, ask for his/her reaction. If the reaction is negative, try to determine if this could be interpreted as resistance to Step 1, to acceptance that one cannot control either addiction or an addict.

If the partner has gone to no meetings, ask if s/he would be willing to do so now. Specifically, ask if s/he would be willing to attend six Al-Anon/Nar-Anon meetings. If the answer is yes, provide him/her with an Al-Anon Family Group or an Nar-Anon meeting schedule. Take a minute to identify two or three meetings that might be convenient to where s/he lives or works.

If the partner expresses reservations about Al-Anon or Nar-Anon, explore these reservations by asking what questions s/he has or what concerns are stopping him/her from trying it out. Typical concerns are:

• *"What kind of people will I find there?"* Answer: "All kinds of people—some like you and some not like you. What you'll all have in common, though, is being in a relationship with an alcoholic or addict, and with being affected by that."

• *"What will I be expected to do?"* Answer: "You aren't required to do anything. You can just go and listen, and see if listening to others who are in or have been in the same boat with you is helpful to you in any way. If you want to, you can talk to some of the other people there after the meeting is over."

• *"What's the benefit of Al-Anon and Nar-Anon?"* Answer: "The alcoholic or addict is not the only one whose life is out of control. Over time, the lives of those who live with them get out of control too. Partners often experience stress or depression, not to mention frustration. They often don't know what's the right thing to do. They usually try to control or contain the situation. Sometimes they feel like failures themselves. The best source of help for these people is through fellowship with others who have had to deal with similar situations. Al-Anon and Nar-Anon offer such a fellowship: a place to get support for starting to take care of yourself, instead of trying to control someone else."

• *"What will I be committing myself to?"* Answer: "Nothing. We're asking you only to try out Al-Anon or Nar-Anon, not to commit to it. At the same time, we ask that you give one or both of them a fair try, meaning going to six meetings. If you don't think it's helpful after six meetings, just stop going."

Presenting the Material

"Detach!" we are told in Al-Anon. This does not mean detaching ourselves, and our love and compassion, from the alcoholic. Detachment, in the Al-Anon sense, means to realize we are individuals. We are not bound morally to shoulder the alcoholic's responsibilities.[1]

Explain to the patient and the partner that *detachment* is the opposite of *enabling*. Whereas enabling protects or cushions the alcoholic and is based on codependency, detachment allows the alcoholic to deal with the negative consequences of his/her substance abuse. Detachment is based on each partner taking responsibility for him/herself, while still feeling love and concern for the other. Another way to think of it is as allowing the alcoholic or addict to have "the dignity of his or her disease," without someone else taking it on.

Barriers to Detaching

Detaching makes intuitive sense to most people, yet on a practical level they often find it hard to adopt a detached attitude and to allow the alcoholic or addict to experience and deal with whatever consequences come his/her way. Why is this so?

The most common barriers to detaching are guilt and misplaced love, both of which usually have one or more sources, including:

- confusing love for someone else with responsibility for their actions;
- believing that allowing the alcoholic or addict to "suffer" negative consequences is somehow unloving or cruel; and
- believing that it is possible, through love or plain willpower, to control or change another person's obsession.

Guilt from feelings of disloyalty or cruelty can be worked through by acknowledging the partner's positive motivations for enabling while also pointing out how enabling is self-defeating in the long run, and how it unwittingly allows a drinking or drug problem to get worse instead of better. Consider the following:

> Learning to detach is a great kindness to ourselves and to the chemically dependent person, and well worth overcoming the obstacles in the beginning. One reward of detachment is that it frees us to grow, to "live and let live."[2]

Confusing love with responsibility is easy to do, but it is dangerous to the growth of both partners in a relationship. The facilitator can approach this issue through a role-reversal technique. Ask the partner if s/he believes that the reverse is true—that someone else should take responsibility for what s/he does or for problems that s/he has. Ask if that is a good attitude for parents to take toward their children, or for friends to take toward each other. Typically, the partner will see the fallacy of this idea, but will still need support in learning to "let go." That's where Al-Anon and Nar-Anon come in.

Holding on to (sometimes unconscious) beliefs that "love can cure all" and that one person's willpower can substitute for another's may be the most tenacious form of resistance to detaching. A frank and respectful dialogue around this issue may be necessary to help a reluctant partner put his/her own beliefs in perspective and set the stage for learning to "live and let live."

Distinguishing Enabling and Detaching

Ask the partner and the patient to think of two specific situations that might arise, and to identify enabling versus detached responses in each one. For example, take a situation in which an alcoholic husband wakes up hung over and leaves for work over an hour late. This is the third time he has done this in as many weeks. The enabling response would be for his wife to call in with an excuse. The detached response would be for her to let her alcoholic husband deal with his employer and to refuse to act as a "middle-woman."

Situation 1:_____

Enabling Response:_____

Detached Response:_____

Situation 2:_____

Enabling Response:_____

Detached Response:_____

Wrap-Up

Wrap up this session by encouraging the partner once again to avail him/ herself of any or all of the following resources:

- Al-Anon or Nar-Anon (including sponsors and friends);
- individual counseling (preferably with a professional trained in addiction treatment and comfortable with twelve-step fellowships); and
- marital counseling (preferably after the patient completes the facilitation program and the partner has given Al-Anon or Nar-Anon a try).

Facilitator Notes

A common complication of this session is when the patient resists the partner becoming involved in Al-Alon or Nar-Anon. Our experience teaches us that the potential loss of a prime enabler can arouse a great deal of anxiety in an alcoholic or addict. This anxiety is expressed through resistance to the partner's involvement in one of these fellowships. This resistance may be either obvious or subtle. One patient tried to undermine her husband's involvement in Al-Anon by assuring him that he "was okay and didn't need anyone else's help," thereby appealing to his masculine sense of self-sufficiency to get her way. A male patient "supported" his wife's hesitation by telling her that he agreed that she was "too busy" to go to Nar-Anon.

Spend some time discussing how enabling is a reciprocal process—how it is motivated by feelings within the enabler but also actively promoted by the alcoholic or addict—and how both partners can therefore have an "investment" in it. This discussion can provide a useful context for the discussion of any resistance that crops up in the patient when the partner starts going to Al-Anon or Nar-Anon. On the other hand, we also find it helpful to conceptualize detaching as a reciprocal process. Not only must the partner detach from the alcoholic or addict and allow him/her to be responsible for his/her own recovery, but the alcoholic or addict must also allow the partner to take care of his/her own needs and issues, including how alcoholism or addiction has affected him/her and how s/he should act in the future.

We suggest that the facilitator try to advocate both partners' right to take responsibility for their own issues and growth, and encourage them to seek the support and guidance of their peers through involvement in twelve-step fellowships. These, after all, share a common philosophy and outlook on alcoholism and addiction.

A second possible complication for this session can arise from the strong emotions that will emerge, especially anger and resentment on the part of the partner. The facilitator must once again avoid being drawn into marital counseling. With only two conjoint sessions, there is little chance of healing long-standing resentments. It may be necessary to frankly acknowledge not only that problems exist but that the future of the relationship may be in doubt. We do not recommend that the facilitator challenge resentment or cynicism in any way but merely encourage the couple to take some construction action in their own interest.

Part V
Termination

Termination Session

The termination session, like the introductory session, has a unique format. The main goal of this session is to allow the facilitator and patient together to process the patient's experiences in the twelve-step facilitation program. A second goal is to encourage the patient's continuing involvement in AA or NA through a cognitive enactment of a hypothetical slip.

Assessment

In helping the patient evaluate his/her experience in this program, the facilitator needs to encourage honesty. Different patients are likely to have found different parts of the program more or less helpful. Encouraging honest feedback will help to bring about honesty in the patient in making meaningful commitments to attend AA or NA meetings afterward.

Regardless of the patient's objective degree of success in the program (sober days versus slips), the program should end on a respectful note. Keep in mind that even patients with many slips and even those who are intensely in denial may someday see the light. Perhaps it will come after the next negative consequence, or maybe it will not come until many more negative consequences have taken their toll. The information this program provides a patient could be what makes the difference at some point down the road, when s/he may be ready to absorb and act on it.

Making an Evaluation

The following guideline can help the patient evaluate his/her experience in this program. We suggest taking about half an hour to do this.

Evaluation

- What was the patient's view of alcoholism and/or addiction prior to treatment, and what is it now?
  - Does the patient view it as a character defect or as an illness? What kind of illness? What are its major symptoms?

  - Does the patient now believe that addicts can control their use of alcohol or drugs, or are they powerless over their use?

  - How does the patient understand denial? What role did denial play in his/her addiction?

  - How did the patient promote enabling in others?

- What was the patient's view of AA and NA prior to treatment, and what is it now?
  - What has been his/her experience with:
  - going to meetings?
  - getting a sponsor?
  - getting active?
  - telephoning AA/NA friends?

- Would the patient recommend AA or NA to a friend who confided that they had an alcohol or drug problem? If so, why? If not, why not?

- What parts of this treatment program were the most useful to the patient?

- What parts of this program were the least useful to the patient?

- What information was most useful to the patient, and why?

- What are the patient's plans regarding AA and NA for the next ninety days?

The Relapse Scenario

> Recovery from alcoholism [or addiction] is much like walking up a down escalator. There is no such thing as standing still. When the recovering person attempts to stand still he finds himself moving backwards. Both recovery and relapse are ongoing processes rather than events.

The above passage summarizes the AA/NA view that there is no room for complacency in recovery. Simply put, although recovery starts with *getting* active, it is maintained by *staying* active. It is safe to say that, from the AA/NA perspective, relapse begins not when the first drink is taken or the first drug used, but when the sober person begins to feel complacent and becomes passive in his/her recovery. Relapse, like addiction itself, begins in the mind—in this case, with a false sense of security.

Hopefully, by this time the patient has become more or less active in AA and/or NA. Hopefully, the patient is attending meetings regularly and participating in the fellowship, has a sponsor with whom s/he has an active relationship, and has established an initial network of fellow recovering persons as friends. With this support in place, the patient's chances of staying sober, or getting sober again quickly after a slip, are greatly enhanced. Conversely, the chances of relapse (including long and damaging relapse) increase as soon as any of these conditions begin to change.

We suggest that the facilitator reinforce the idea of staying active through the following cognitive exercise:

Facilitator: "Hopefully, you will not have a relapse back into alcohol or drug abuse. But the collective experience of many persons in recovery tells us that it is probably wise to consider the possibility that you might. Slips can happen, and what is most important for you to understand is how one might happen to you and what you might do to prevent it.

"I'd like you to spend a few minutes with me, making up a fantasy or scenario of how you might relapse, if you were to.

"I'd like you to answer these questions as best you can:

- "What situations do you think are riskiest for you, in terms of tempting you to drink [or use]?"
- "Imagine yourself, just for a moment, being in one of those situations."
- "Can you describe what it would be like—how it would happen—if you were to relapse? Can you make up a story about your own relapse? Make it as realistic as you can. Would the slip just pop out of thin air, or can you foresee some changes in your own attitudes and behavior that would set the stage for relapse? What would those changes be?"

After going through this relapse scenario exercise, ask the patient to summarize what s/he learned from it. Specifically, ask what the patient could do to minimize the chances that this scenario will become a reality. Emphasize the AA/NA view that active involvement is the best insurance against relapse, or, if a relapse happens, against damage from it.

Ending

We suggest ending this termination session with whatever form of farewell is most comfortable. A handshake is fine, although a hug would not be inconsistent with the spirit of fellowship. If the facilitator wishes, giving the patient a simple AA or NA medallion might also be appropriate, or saying the serenity prayer together. Finally, we suggest a friendly reminder that AA and NA are always there, twenty-four hours a day, 365 days a year.

Appendix A
Jellinek Charts: Stages of Addiction in Men and Women

Symptoms and Phases of Alcoholism in Men[1]

I. Prodromal Phase
    Have you ever experienced: YES
    1. Increased tolerance (need to drink more to get the same effect)?   ——
    2. Temporary loss of memory (blackouts, times you couldn't remember what you did)?   ——
    3. Sneaking a drink when no one was looking?   ——
    4. Preoccupation with drinking (thinking about drinking while working, etc.)?   ——
    5. Hurried drinking ("chasing a high")?   ——
    6. Avoiding talking about your drinking because it made you uncomfortable?   ——
    7. Loss of memory (can't remember things you said, what you were supposed to do, etc.)?   ——

II. Crucial (Basic) Phase
    Have you ever experienced:
    8. Loss of control (inability to predict how much you'll drink)?   ——
    9. Justifying (making excuses for drinking)?   ——
    10. Disapproval from others about your drinking?   ——
    11. Being extravagant with money?   ——
    12. Aggression (verbal or physical)?   ——
    13. Remorse (or guilt or depression about drinking)?   ——
    14. Periods of abstinence (times when you tried to stop drinking)?   ——
    15. Changes in your pattern of use (switching types or brands of alcohol)?   ——
    16. Losing friends (or having fights with them) on account of your drinking?   ——

179

17. Losing a job or getting into trouble at work on account of your drinking? ——
18. Giving up old hobbies or activities in order to spend time drinking? ——
19. Having to get treatment of some form for your drinking? ——
20. Feeling resentful a lot toward others? ——
21. Escaping (moving or changing friends in an effort to get a "fresh start")? ——
22. Protecting your supply (hiding a stash of alcohol)? ——
23. Drinking in the morning (or before work)? ——

III. Chronic Phase
Have you ever experienced:
24. Drinking more or less continuously for at least eighteen hours (a "binge")? ——
25. Doing things that violate your own ethical or moral standards? ——
26. Inappropriate (or confused) thinking, such as hearing voices or not knowing where you are? ——
27. Decreased tolerance (feeling and acting drunk after just one drink)? ——
28. Vague fears or anxiety? ——
29. Tremors (shaky hands)? ——
30. Feeling hopeless or suicidal? ——

Symptoms and Phases of Alcoholism in Women[2]

I. Prodromal Phase
Have you ever experienced: YES
1. Increased tolerance (need to drink more to get the same effect)? ——
2. Unwillingness to discuss drinking? ——
3. Feelings that women who drink excessively are worse than men? ——
4. Personality changes when drinking? ——
5. Drinking more just before your menstrual period? ——
6. Feeling more intelligent and capable when drinking? ——
7. Being "supersensitive"? ——

II. Early Stage
Have you ever experienced:

8. Periods of abstinence (times when you've tried to stop drinking)? ____
9. Disapproval from others about your drinking? ____
10. Rationalizing (making excuses for) drinking? ____
11. Temporary losses of memory (blackouts, times you couldn't remember what you did) when drinking? ____
12. Unexplained bruises or injuries? ____
13. Drinking before facing a new situation? ____

III. Middle Stage

Have you ever experienced:

14. Neglecting eating? ____
15. Protecting your supply (hiding a "stash" of alcohol)? ____
16. Self-pity (feeling sorry for yourself)? ____
17. Feeling resentful toward others? ____
18. Being permissive or lax with your children because of guilt feelings about drinking? ____
19. Drinking to feel happier but finding yourself feeling more depressed? ____
20. Being told by others that you "couldn't be an alcoholic"? ____
21. "Predrinking"—drinking before a drinking occasion; or "postdrinking"—continuing to drink after a drinking occasion? ____
22. Feeling guilty about drinking? ____
23. Drinking more or less continuously for a period of at least eighteen hours? ____

IV. Late Stage

Have you ever experienced:

24. Starting the day with a drink? ____
25. Tremors (shaky hands)? ____
26. Decreased tolerance (feeling and acting drunk after just one drink)? ____
27. Sneaking drinks? ____
28. Gulping drinks? ____
29. Persistent remorse? ____
30. Devaluing personal relationships? ____
31. Carrying liquor in your purse? ____

Appendix B
The Twelve Steps of Alcoholics Anonymous[1]

1. We admitted we were powerless over alcohol—that our lives had become unmanageable.
2. Came to believe that a Power greater than ourselves could restore us to sanity.
3. Made a decision to turn our will and our lives over to the care of God *as we understood Him.*
4. Made a searching and fearless moral inventory of ourselves.
5. Admitted to God, to ourselves, and to another human being the exact nature of our wrongs.
6. We were entirely ready to have God remove all these defects of character.
7. Humbly asked Him to remove our shortcomings.
8. Made a list of all persons we had harmed, and became willing to make amends to them all.
9. Made direct amends to such people wherever possible, except when to do so would injure them or others.
10. Continued to take personal inventory and when we were wrong promptly admitted it.
11. Sought through prayer and meditation to improve our conscious contact with God *as we understood Him,* praying only for knowledge of His will for us and the power to carry that out.
12. Having had a spiritual awakening as the result of these steps, we tried to carry this message to alcoholics, and to practice these principles in all our affairs.

Appendix C
Case Study: Carol

This is a story of one woman's struggle to break the chains of addiction. Carol was one of the earliest patients to be treated in the program on which this book is based. Her story shows how this approach can help a person stay focused on recovery in spite of tremendous life stress. Outwardly, Carol coped with all the challenges a single mother faces who lives in a tenement, surrounded by drug dealers and violence. But inwardly, she was burdened by the scars of a childhood marked by severe neglect and abuse. By putting her sobriety first, Carol was able to tackle her other problems with living more effectively. The principles of twelve-step programs gave her tools she need to begin healing the emotional pain she had carried for much of her adult life. During her course of treatment, Carol moved from simply acknowledging that her use of mood-altering chemicals was out of control to beginning to surrender to a recovery process, one day at a time.

Session 1: Assessment

Carol was a twenty-eight-year-old African-American woman who came to the program for help with her addictions to alcohol and cocaine. She had recently given birth to a son and was fearful that if she didn't voluntarily seek help, she would lose him. The medical staff at the hospital had been aware of Carol's struggle with cocaine prior to her baby's birth. Carol was a single parent, as the baby's father had deserted her before his birth. Faced with these pressures, Carol decided that it was time to pull her life together. In her words, "I knew I had a drinking problem. I was having too many blackouts last month." She continued, "When I base, I can't breathe."

Carol reported that she'd undergone treatment for alcohol dependence when she was sixteen years old. At that time she was placed in a residential treatment program for nine months. While she was there, she was exposed to AA. She related that her experiences with the twelve-step recovery program had been good. Following her discharge from the residential treatment program, she did not attend any twelve-step support groups and quickly returned to her previous pattern of drinking and using.

Now Carol was looking for help and support to stay sober. As she spoke in this session, there was a sense of urgency in her voice. She did not want to repeat the mistakes that her own mother had made.

The session moved into an examination of Carol's alcohol/drug history. As she shared events from her past, the facilitator took careful notes as to her age of first use, the amounts she had used, how frequent the use was, any positive or negative effects, and significant events at relevant times of her life.

Carol's first use of mood-altering substances had been at age nine, when she began experimenting with marijuana once a month. She reported that using this drug helped her to escape from the turmoil of her family life. At this time her mother was divorcing her stepfather, who had been physically abusive toward both her and Carol. Additionally, Carol had responsibility for caring for her two-year-old brother, who had Down's syndrome and cerebral palsy. Carol continued periodic marijuana use throughout her early teens.

When Carol reached the eleventh grade, she began to drink. She escalated rapidly to daily drinking whatever alcoholic beverages were available. Typically, she drank to get drunk and reported having blackouts several times a week. Her home life continued to deteriorate as her mother's drinking also increased. Carol was arrested for shoplifting, and the local youth services agency placed her in a treatment program. She spoke fondly of this period of her life, saying that it was a relief for her to be in a safe place.

After leaving treatment, she entered the Job Corps, where she obtained a GED and a certificate as a nurse's aide. Even there, she continued to binge drink periodically.

During her late teens Carol continued to use both alcohol and marijuana routinely. She also experimented with methamphetamine and phencyclidine (PCP). She was able to obtain positions as a waitress, cashier, and nurse's aide, but she lost these due to her drug use. Carol turned to prostitution to raise money for food and drugs. At age seventeen she was arrested for prostitution and spent nine months in jail.

In her early twenties Carol decided to get her life back on track. She enrolled in a local community college to begin work on a nursing degree. She continued to periodically use both alcohol and marijuana to excess. At this point in her life she also began to use cocaine. She rapidly progressed from periodic intranasal use to daily smoking or freebasing. Her grades in school took a rapid decline. She began to write bad checks because she had spent her paycheck on cocaine. Her mother was also using alcohol and cocaine at this time. Her mother's boyfriend, who also was actively using alcohol and cocaine, sexually abused Carol with her mother's knowledge.

Carol dropped out of school, returned to prostitution, and resumed daily alcohol and cocaine use.

This pattern continued until the birth of her son. She had obtained a job at a local college and was attempting to control her use of cocaine, marijuana, and alcohol on her own. Unable to do so, she contacted the college's EAP office and was referred to the facilitator's agency for treatment.

Carol easily saw the negative consequences associated with her use of mood-altering substances. *Physically*, she had experienced blacking out and passing out from alcohol. Crack cocaine use has left her short of breath. Because of sexual relationships while under the influence, she was fearful of exposure to the HIV virus. *Legally*, her alcohol and drug use had led her to prostitution and writing bad checks. *Socially*, she'd lost clean friends and now associated exclusively with drug-involved peers. Her relationships with men centered on drug and alcohol use. *Sexually*, she'd prostituted herself for drugs. *Psychologically*, she carried around years of hurt and rage. She had violent mood swings. When she was drunk, she commonly flew into rages. *Financially*, she was in debt. She'd lost several jobs and was unable to pay bills. As a result she'd lost her driver's license and her automobile and was receiving partial public assistance.

Carol could also easily identify her progressive loss of control over her use of alcohol and cocaine. But she had more difficulty seeing the difficulty that marijuana had caused her. She did identify the progressive increase in the amount of alcohol she drank and the increase in the frequency of her alcohol and cocaine use. She readily diagnosed herself as an addict.

Carol saw treatment as an opportunity to get her life together. She had long-range goals of returning to school and providing a better life for her child. She was very open to using the twelve-step program to help her stay sober. She agreed to abstain from all mood-altering substances, one day at a time, and to attend AA meetings. She was given a journal to record her reactions to meetings, as well as schedules of AA, NA, and Cocaine Anonymous meetings. She reviewed these and picked two meetings to attend between sessions. She was also given a copy of *Living Sober* and agreed to begin reading this book. Her next session was scheduled for four days later.

Session 2: Acceptance

Carol returned for her second session and reported with pride in her journal that she had abstained from all cocaine use. She did drink a beer on one occasion. The facilitator explored the circumstances of this slip, and it turned out that she drank the beer after an argument with her mother. The facilitator suggested that she look at her anger as a possible trigger emotion for her disease. Furthermore, he suggested that she become involved in AA so that she could have a safe place to vent her feelings. Carol reported that she hadn't attended any meetings yet. She had wanted to, but she didn't have a baby-sitter. She said that she would get a sitter so that she could go to meetings. At this point the facilitator expressed concern and support for her circumstances and encouraged her to not drink or use and to go to meetings.

The facilitator used Carol's slip to show her her own powerlessness over mood-altering drugs. She readily identified with this. Her life had become unmanageable—financially, socially, emotionally, and mentally. She was especially concerned about financial problems and spent much time in the session discussing her need for a full-time, better-paying job.

Carol readily understood the concept of denial. She identified her main method of denial as isolating herself from others. Trusting others appeared to be very difficult for her. Carol easily fell into blaming others for her drug use. Her prime target for blame was her mother. Carol also relied on bargaining, such as "I'll only drink a little, and I'll feel better."

Her recovery tasks between sessions were to attend two AA meetings and to continue keeping her journal. She also was to begin reading *Living Sober*. Her next scheduled session would be the end of the week.

Session 3: Surrender

That Friday Carol came for her third session. She'd kept a journal, but before the facilitator could read it, she reported that she'd used cocaine for two days previously. She'd been clean so far that day and intended to remain clean for the remainder of the day. She had picked up the cocaine after a blood test at the clinic had shown positive for syphilis. This news had overwhelmed her emotionally. She had missed one day from work because she was recovering from the effects of the drug.

Carol had not yet been to an AA/NA meeting. Again, the facilitator stressed the importance of going to meetings and encouraged her to do whatever she had to do to get there. Carol responded that she didn't have time to attend meetings because she had to find another job that would pay her more money. Carol eventually agreed to go to meetings over the coming weekend.

Carol's resistance to attending meetings was an opportunity for the facilitator to discuss the process of surrender and Steps 2 and 3.

After reading Steps 2 and 3 aloud, Carol talked about her strong belief in a Higher Power. One of her strongest supporters in her neighborhood was a woman who was a minister at a local church. Carol had attended this church and was considering joining the congregation. Seeing herself as a survivor of emotional and physical abuse, Carol firmly believed that somehow her Higher Power had been watching over her. As she spoke, her manner appeared much less agitated and her face looked calm.

As time was running short, the facilitator chose to continue this topic in the next session.

Carol's recovery tasks were to attend AA meetings that she had identified in the schedule; to read Step 2 in *Twelve Steps and Twelve Traditions*; to continue reading *Living Sober*; and to keep her journal.

Carol scheduled a session for the following Monday. She later canceled that appointment with the clinic secretary and rescheduled for Friday of the same week.

Session 4: More Surrender

When Carol arrived for her fourth session, one week had since passed since the third session. She arrived thirty minutes late and brought her infant son with her. She'd been keeping a journal and had been reading *Living Sober*. She had been clean and sober for the entire week. The facilitator congratulated her for each of those days.

Carol said that being drug free was stressful for her. She experienced angry feelings often. Laughing, she said that she knew from the reading that she was avoiding dealing with her disease by working long hours.

Carol had gone to one meeting and met an old using friend there. Her friend advised her to go to ninety meetings in ninety days. Carol's resistance again came up, and she said, "I do plan to go, but right now I have too many financial debts. . . . Now I'm too tired to go to meetings."

The facilitator underscored the physical and emotional changes that Carol was going through as she abstained from cocaine and alcohol. He asked how she had felt after the AA meeting and emphasized that as she got to more twelve-step meetings, her edginess and mood swings would pass. Listening carefully, Carol requested a Cocaine Anonymous schedule, but then stated that she couldn't go to a meeting that night.

Carol then began talking about the stresses in her life—working two jobs, taking care of her son, and her concern over her mother's failing health. The facilitator acknowledged the pressure she felt and encouraged her to go to meetings to get support. He congratulated her again on having five clean and sober days and acknowledged the struggle. He pointed out that her denial system told her she had to handle all her stresses alone. He encouraged her to reach out for help. They reviewed the meeting schedule to find meetings that she could fit into her weekend schedule.

Carol's recovery tasks were to attend two meetings over the weekend and to keep writing in her journal. She set her next appointment for the coming Monday.

Carol failed to appear for this session; nor did she call to schedule another appointment. A week later she called to apologize for missing her appointment, but her facilitator was away on vacation at that time. Carol was instructed to call again at the end of the week to schedule another session. She did appear at the clinic and was scheduled to be seen.

Session 5: Getting Active

Twenty-five days had passed since Carol's last session. She arrived with her infant son. In reviewing the events of the previous three and a half weeks, she reported alternating periods of drinking alcohol and using cocaine with periods of abstinence. She had continued to write in her journal and had attended more meetings. On the days when she had gone to a meeting, she had been able to stay clean and sober. Carol saw the connection.

Carol had purchased the AA Big Book and had begun to read "Bill's Story." *Living Sober*, she stated, talked about going to meetings, getting a sponsor, and avoiding "hiding out" at meetings.

Carol connected her most recent slip with her disappointment that a fellow AA group member had failed to pick her up for a meeting as he had promised. Angrily, she stated that she wasn't going to depend on him in the future.

The topic shifted to Carol's getting active in the AA program. When the facilitator asked which meetings she'd attended, she listed six different groups. The facilitator encouraged her to attend ninety meetings in ninety days. "You need that kind of support," he advised her. "You need to be doing something every day for your recovery. There's support for you at meetings. Is it easier for you to stay straight after a meeting?"

"Yes, definitely," she replied.

"Have you gotten telephone numbers from women?" Carol had gotten an old friend's number and some others but had misplaced her phone number book. She stated that she would get more phone numbers so that she could call people when she got the "tremendous urge." The facilitator encouraged her to call people when she was doing well, too, and not to wait until she was in trouble. He asked her to obtain three phone numbers from AA friends and to call at least one of them for a five-minute conversation. She was advised not to be surprised if someone asked her for her number. Carol said that if somebody did, she would have to say she couldn't be reached. Then, after some thought, she said that she could give a work number, her mother's number, and a friend's number. Furthermore, she decided to have her telephone service restored before she bought a car.

"I'm in desperate need of a sponsor and I'm going to say so at a meeting tonight," she said. She had seen a woman at meetings who had seventeen years sobriety. Carol felt attracted to this woman's enthusiasm and energy, but she didn't feel that she had much in common with her. Carol didn't know what a sponsor was supposed to do. The facilitator reviewed the traditions of sponsorship with her:

- A sponsor has been sober at least one year.
- A sponsor is of the same sex as the sponsoree and the same age or a little older.
- A sponsor answers questions about the program; introduces the sponsoree to other people in the program who may have similar interests or backgrounds; suggests meetings that the sponsoree might like or find helpful; shares their experience of what has worked for them in maintaining their sobriety; and helps the sponsoree work through the steps.

Carol said that she would go to a women's meeting that night and look for a sponsor there.

Lastly, Carol was encouraged to attend meetings regularly and to help out by taking on a coffee commitment, setting up, or cleaning up.

The next session was set for three days later, in order for Carol to complete some of the clinic forms. She kept that appointment.

Session 6: The Genogram: A Family Disease

Two days later Carol returned for her scheduled session. Over the weekend she had gone to her first NA dance. She shared her amazement at having had an enjoyable time with "no drink to boost me up."

In her journal she reported going to three meetings on Saturday and to church on Sunday. One of the meetings she attended was a "step" meeting, and two were "open discussion" meetings. At one of these meetings she met Betty, whom she chose as a temporary sponsor. Betty had seven years sobriety and was the mother of twins. Carol said that she could relate easily to Betty and that she had already been calling her daily.

Carol had experienced cravings for marijuana after seeing her former drug cronies on the street. The facilitator reminded her of the power of slippery people, places, and things. Carol had been reading *Living Sober* and was examining how she might better structure her time. She expressed a desire to buy a copy of the NA Big Book.

The new material for this session focused on the effects that the disease of substance abuse had had on her family. Carol volunteered information readily. The genogram was completed, and she was able to see that she had been "set up" for the disease by her family history (see figure 2). She saw that the women in her family tended to become involved with chemically dependent men. She grasped the idea that she had an opportunity to make different choices in her life, to break the chain of addictions.

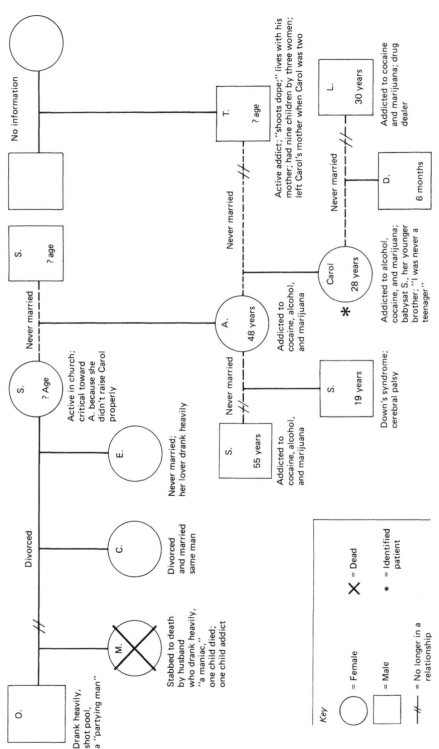

Figure 2: Carol's Genogram

O.

Drank heavily,
shot pool,
a "partying man"

Divorced

M.

Stabbed to death
by husband
who drank heavily,
"a maniac,"
one child died;
one child addict

C.

Divorced
and married
same man

E.

Never married;
her lover drank heavily

S.

? Age

Active in church;
critical toward
A. because she
didn't raise Carol
properly

Never married

S.

? age

No information

S.

? age

T.

? age

Active addict; "shoots dope;" lives with his
mother; had nine children by three women;
left Carol's mother when Carol was two

Never married

A.

48 years

Addicted to
cocaine, alcohol,
and marijuana

Never married

S.

55 years

Addicted to
cocaine, alcohol,
and marijuana

S.

19 years

Down's syndrome;
cerebral palsy

Carol

28 years

*

Addicted to alcohol,
cocaine, and marijuana;
babysat S., her younger
brother; "I was never a
teenager"

Never married

L.

30 years

Addicted to cocaine
and marijuana; drug
dealer

D.

6 months

Key

◯ = Female

▢ = Male

╱╱ = No longer in a
relationship

✕ = Dead

* = Identified
patient

Carol expressed concern for her son's future. She stated clearly, with conviction, "He'll grow up in AA and NA!" Her family history tapped into her feelings of low self-worth. Her hope was that by being involved in NA and AA, those feelings would begin to change.

The facilitator advised her to focus on staying clean and sober for one year before she attempted to tackle her issues with her family. Her recovery tasks were to write about the genogram in her journal and to talk to her sponsor about it. She committed to attend daily AA/NA meetings that week.

Session 7: Processing the Genogram

Eight days later, Carol appeared for her seventh scheduled session. She had had a slip, having taken two drags from a marijuana cigarette. She had gone to one of her old hangouts, an empty lot that was populated by older alcoholic men from the neighborhood. "I was in an area I had no business being in and got a ride with the wrong guy," she explained. "He had a joint." She said she felt guilty and disappointed in herself. The slip had taught her not to count the number of days she was clean and sober but to focus on "just for today." She had stopped herself and called her sponsor, who had directed her to go to a meeting and share. Carol went to an NA meeting and told the group of her slip. Their reaction, she related, had been negative, and she felt shunned by the group. After the meeting, she went to the house of a neighbor who was in AA and who was nine months sober. She spent three hours there talking out her feelings.

When the facilitator asked her what led to the slip, she said that she'd had a rough time the night before. She had allowed her mother to baby-sit for her son while she went to another NA dance. When she returned from the dance, around midnight, she found her son still awake. An argument ensued between Carol and her mother. She woke up the next day tired and still angry.

The focus of the session was to be enabling. When asked who made it easy for her to continue using alcohol and drugs, Carol immediately replied, "My mother!" Carol continued to elaborate on the anger, pain, and loneliness she had felt while she was growing up. She detailed episodes of sexual, physical, and emotional abuse. At age sixteen she began running away from home, using drugs and prostituting herself. As Carol portrayed it, she would get angry with her mother, then use alcohol or drugs. The feelings she shared in this session seemed to be left over from her work on the genogram.

The facilitator directed Carol to make use of her sponsor and other women in the program to get the nurturing and support that she couldn't get from her mother. She admitted that she had mixed feelings about her mother, but she said she couldn't allow those feelings to interfere with her moving forward in her life.

The facilitator responded by telling her that although her mother could hurt her deeply, it was not her mother who had the power to take her sobriety away from her. It was Carol's own disease that could do that. It was Carol's own disease that had taken her to the empty lot with the bottle gang that had eventually led to her slip.

Carol was given support for doing many things correctly. She had reached out for help and had stopped herself. She hadn't given up on herself.

Part of Carol's getting sober—not just dry—was coming to terms with all the losses in her life. She had never had the nurturing from her own mother that she needed and deserved. The disappointment was still fresh and renewed itself with each contact that she had with her mother.

Carol summed up the session by saying that she was breaking the chain by getting sober. "I'm changing me first so I can help my baby. So I can be there for him, because my mom wasn't there for me."

For her recovery tasks, she would read from the book *Thing My Sponsor Taught Me*, attend AA/NA meetings daily, call her sponsor and one other program friend, and keep her journal.

Session 8: People, Places, and Routines

Carol's next session was held, as scheduled, six days later. She had continued her daily attendance at AA/NA meetings. She had continued to abstain from alcohol, cocaine, and marijuana. Her journal was filled with details of her experiences at meetings. She had come across several old using friends at meetings.

Carol didn't agree with all the advice that she'd heard at the meetings. In particular, she did not agree with the advice to avoid beginning any new intimate relationships for a year. She was already involved with a new boyfriend now, and she stated adamantly that she knew her sobriety came first. She summed up her work on twelve-step recovery by saying, "I just deal with the first three steps." She used a shorthand version of these steps that she had heard at a meeting to describe what she meant. Her shorthand version went as follows:

- "I can't"; she admitted that she was powerless over alcohol and drugs.
- "He can": she had come to believe that her Higher Power could restore her to sanity.
- "I'll let him": she made the decision to turn her will and her life over to her Higher Power.

At one of the meetings, she strongly identified with a woman who spoke. The topic at this discussion meeting was "emotions." Carol had related that she was working on being less "nasty and defensive" with people. The woman at the meeting had shared similar feelings and experiences. She and Carol spoke after the meeting about this.

During the past week Carol had been able to pay off her telephone bill and restore service. She was extremely proud of herself.

The topic for this session was "people, places, and routines." Working with the facilitator, Carol generated a list of people, places, and routines that were dangerous to her sobriety, as well as a list of those new people, places, and routines that supported her sobriety. Her new relationships with clean and sober people were extremely important to her. She found herself staying home or going to meetings when she was not at work. As she talked about AA/NA–related activities such as dances, socials, and retreats, she commented that she had more to do now than she had when she was using.

Carol had changed the route she took to walk to her mother's house, so as to avoid the street corners and empty lots where she used to drink and obtain cocaine. She expressed a strong desire to move away from her roach-infested apartment, which was located next to a rooming house where crack cocaine was sold. She had begun to make concrete plans to make this move.

As an aside, she stated that she was going to get new eyeglasses and have her hair done this coming week. The facilitator took this as an outward sign of increasing self-esteem.

Carol's recovery tasks for the week were to maintain her journal, attend AA/NA meetings daily, call her sponsor and one other program person daily, and begin reading the NA Big Book.

Session 9: HALT (Hungry, Angry, Lonely, Tired)

Ten days later, Carol appeared for her ninth session. She had now abstained for more than twenty days from alcohol, cocaine, and marijuana. In her journal she reported that at an NA meeting she had told the group how hurt she'd felt by them three weeks before, when she had told them of her slip. Her daily routine now included saying a prayer based on the first three steps every morning. It resembled the shorthand version of these steps that she had described in the previous session. Her simple prayer went, "I can't, you can, I'll let you."

Carol reported feeling frustration toward her sponsor, who had become busy with her own life. This woman "just didn't understand me," according to Carol. The sponsor was a white woman who lived in the suburbs, and Carol was convinced that she could not understand what her life in the inner city was like.

Carol's anger toward her sponsor quickly converged with resentments and anger toward other people in twelve-step programs. She felt offended that people only spoke in what she saw as platitudes at meetings. She felt that other people weren't there to help when she needed them. Then she stopped herself midstream and noted that in the past when she had felt offended by something, she'd use drugs or drink. Now, when she had these feelings, she vented them. She said that she was determined to find another sponsor.

Carol's anger served as a vehicle by which she began to address the issues around emotions and slips. Meetings were clearly times and places that Carol identified as being for herself. She felt safe there to vent whatever feelings she needed to vent. During this session, she admitted, she had vented with the facilitator.

Fatigue and hunger were the topics for the rest of the session. Carol often found herself extremely stressed by the demands of single parenthood. Now she was beginning to take care of herself first, relating this to the AA slogan, "First Things First." After this session she planned to go home, take a hot bath, rest, and take her son with her to a meeting.

She found herself eating more sweets since she had been abstaining from alcohol and cocaine. Despite a small weight gain, she felt better. "I feel clean," she said, "and I think I sound less hostile."

Her recovery tasks for the week were to prepare to discuss anger and resentment further in the next session. She would read the sections in *Living Sober* about dealing with anger and would continue to write in her journal daily. She would continue to attend meetings daily and would consider asking her Higher Power for guidance in locating another sponsor.

Carol missed two scheduled appointments the following week. Fourteen days later, she appeared for the tenth session.

Session 10: Anger

Carol explained that her difficulty in getting to the last week's sessions had been caused by working a second job at a local retailer in order to raise the money to be able to move into a new apartment. The second job was during the evening, so she had cut back on the number of meetings she had been attending. But even though her attendance at meetings was down, she was maintaining daily contact with her sponsor and other program friends in the neighborhood. She acknowledged that having a telephone now made it easier for her to maintain contact with other recovering people. She revealed that her grandmother had sent her the money to get her phone service reconnected. Carol expressed tremendous gratitude for this help. She related that she had had no contact with her grandmother for many years because of her own and her mother's active addictions. Now that Carol was beginning her recovery, she was reaching out to her.

The cravings Carol had experienced over the previous two weeks had been minimal, she said. On one occasion she had had a "taste for beer," but she knew that this craving would pass, so she waited it out.

Carol related that at one NA meeting she had gotten into an argument with the caretaker of the building where the group met. But she had followed the slogan and "let it go," even though the caretaker hadn't.

The rest of the session focused on the tools twelve-step recovery programs offer for dealing with anger and resentment. This was an issue that Carol wanted help with. She acknowledged her short temper and her habit of provoking others verbally. She realized that since she had become involved with AA and NA, it took her less time to vent her feelings and calm herself down. She had been applying the principles of the serenity prayer—to accept that some things cannot change.

To cope with her low self-esteem, she applied the slogan, "Fake It Til You Make It." She saw that it would take time before she felt better about herself. Telling herself, "Easy Does It," and "Keep It Simple," also helped her cope with her frustrations at home and at work. Even though she was aware of the recovery principles, she found that her old "stinking thinking" kept creeping back. What helped her was to talk to other people in the program about how she felt.

Carol shared that her roommate had gone "back out"—he had returned to using crack cocaine and had left the apartment owing her rent money. She didn't know what to do with her anger at him. After verbally venting much anger in the session, a solution appeared for her: She could write two letters. One she would fill with her feelings of hurt and betrayal with no holds barred. Then she would write a second letter, copied from the first, which she would mail. After she mailed this letter, she could "turn it over to her Higher Power and let it go." With the facilitator's help, she reviewed the serenity prayer and applied it to this situation.

As the session ended, Carol said that she had talked to her sponsor about her resentment toward her for being too busy and too different to be able to understand her. Carol still saw differences between them, but as she listened to her sponsor's side of things, she discovered that they were very much alike after all. Both women had shared feelings of loneliness because they had viewed themselves as outsiders when they were younger. Her sponsor had given her a book of meditations for women, *Each Day a New Beginning*.

Carol's recovery tasks for this session were to read *Each Day a New Beginning* twice daily, in the morning and at night; to maintain her journal; to continue reading stories in the NA Big Book; and to read the sections on anger in *Living Sober*.

Carol's parting words for this session were ones that she'd heard at a meeting: "I am *powerless* over my disease. I am *powerful* over what I do."

Session 11: Moral Inventory

Six days later, Carol appeared for her eleventh session. She had remained abstinent and had attended four AA meetings during the week. She reported having had no episodes of cravings during the week.

Carol had reached several decisions during this week. First, she had decided to stop using her mother as a day-care provider and baby-sitter because of her mother's continued active drug involvement. She had also decided to travel south to visit her grandmother on a vacation in the near future. She was very excited by this, as it would be her first sober visit with her grandmother as an adult.

Carol was now maintaining almost daily contact with her sponsor. She did voice concern over what she saw as her sponsor's discomfort with her being African-American. The facilitator encouraged Carol to be honest with her sponsor about this.

The focus of the new material was on Steps 4 and 5 and the moral inventory. After reading the steps aloud, the facilitator explained the need for balance expressed in Step 4. A moral inventory is to include everything that is on the shelf, both the good and the bad. The facilitator initiated the exercise to take a moral inventory, to look at both character defects and character assets. Carol expressed regrets at having hurt her son and her brother because of her disease. She wanted very much to care for her brother when she could. She identified her assets as being a sharing and compassionate person. She even told of her generosity toward other, older addicts when she had been actively using.

Her recovery tasks included discussing Steps 4 and 5 with her sponsor; maintaining her journal; and attending a minimum of four AA/NA meetings that week.

Session 12: A Quick Check

Carol arrived thirty minutes late for this session, having been unexpectedly delayed by her job. There was no time to cover any new material, so the facilitator only reviewed the past week with her.

Carol had continued to be clean and sober. She had attended five AA/NA meetings over the past ten days, and she had gone to an NA-sponsored dance.

Carol had obtained a new full-time job in the health care field. The job was slated to begin in a week. She was excited by this, since it meant not only that she could give up her evening job but that she was taking a step toward nursing school. She expressed concern that her old "attitude" and mood swings could creep in and interfere at her new job. The facilitator encouraged her to use her program tools—the people, the meetings, the slogans.

Carol spoke briefly about her relationship with her boyfriend. She had defiantly defended this relationship in a session several weeks earlier, but now she acknowledged that since he wasn't in a twelve-step program, he wasn't growing as she was growing. She felt very sad about this.

The session ended with plans for termination. Carol wanted to continue in treatment with a woman therapist. The facilitator agreed to make a referral. The termination session was scheduled.

Session 13: Termination

Carol's final session was brief, lasting only one half-hour. She had continued to be clean and sober and to attend AA/NA meetings regularly. At her new job she'd been applying her program tools, the serenity prayer, and the slogans, to help her cope with stressful situations. Although she had maintained contact with her sponsor, she continued to look for a new one. Carol was still uncomfortable with the cultural and racial differences between them.

During the termination session Carol shared her deep belief that chemical dependency is a disease. The only way that had worked for her had been to stay abstinent one day at a time. She connected her mistrustfulness and her problems with anger and resentment to her disease as well. Her biggest traps in her denial system were using anger, resentment, and self-pity as excuses to drink or use. The twelve-step recovery programs of AA and NA had clearly saved her life. She planned to remain actively involved for the next ninety days. Carol's biggest fear about returning to using alcohol or drugs was that she would lose custody of her son.

Carol may have made her most telling statement when she said that the most useful aspect of the facilitation program had been that her facilitator kept pushing her to go to meetings.

The facilitator acknowledged Carol's hard work and honesty in working the program. He then gave her the referral she had requested the previous session. The session ended with Carol and the facilitator saying the serenity prayer aloud.

Postscript

Carol remained in therapy with a woman therapist for more than a year. Her work centered on issues of early abuse and family relationships. At this writing, Carol has celebrated her first-year anniversary in NA and has remained active in twelve-step recovery.

Notes

Preface

1. *Comments on A.A.'s Triennial Surveys* (New York: Alcoholics Anonymous General Services, 1990).
2. Project MATCH Research Group. "Matching Alcoholism Treatments to Client Heterogeneity: Project MATCH Posttreatment Drinking Outcomes," *Journal of Studies on Alcoholism* 58 (1997), pp. 7-29.

Introduction

1. "Models of Addiction." *Journal of Abnormal Psychology* 97 (May 1988).
2. *Diagnostic and Statistical Manual of Mental Disorders*, 3rd ed. rev. (Washington, D.C.: American Psychiatric Association, 1987).
3. *Narcotics Anonymous*, 5th ed. (Van Nuys, Calif: Narcotics Anonymous World Services, 1988), p. 8.
4. *Alcoholics Anonymous*, 4th ed. (New York: Alcoholics Anonymous World Services, 2001), p. 33.
5. *Alcoholics Anonymous.*
6. *Twelve Steps and Twelve Traditions* (New York: Alcoholics Anonymous World Services, 1952).
7. *Alcoholics Anonymous*, p. 58.
8. *Alcoholics Anonymous*, p.30.
9. *Narcotics Anonymous*, p. 7.
10. *Narcotics Anonymous*, p. 14.
11. *Alcoholics Anonymous*, p. 30; *Twelve Steps and Twelve Traditions*, p.21; *Narcotics Anonymous*, p. 7-8.
12. *Alcoholics Anonymous*, p. 22; *Narcotics Anonymous*, p. 14.
13. E. Kurtz, *AA: The Story* (San Francisco: Harper/Hazelden, 1988).
14. *Twelve Steps and Twelve Traditions*, p.40; *Alcoholics Anonymous*, p. 25; *Narcotics Anonymous*, p. 116; *Twelve Steps and Twelve Traditions*, p. 27.
15. *Living Sober* (New York: Alcoholics Anonymous World Services, 1975), pp. 21, 3.
16. *Twelve Steps and Twelve Traditions*, p. 139.
17. *Do You Think You're Different?* (New York: Alcoholics Anonymous World Services, 1977).
18. *Twelve Steps and Twelve Traditions*, p. 130.
19. *Twelve Steps and Twelve Traditions*, p. 134.
20. *Twelve Steps and Twelve Traditions*, p. 146-47.
21. *Twelve Steps and Twelve Traditions*, p. 160; *Narcotics Anonymous*, p. 64.
22. *Twelve Steps and Twelve Traditions*, p. 132.

23. J.O. Prochaska and C.C. DiClemente, "Towards a Comprehensive Model of Change," in *Treating Addictive Behaviors: Processes of Change.* ed. W.R. Miller and N. Heather (New York: Plenum, 1986).

24. Project MATCH Research Group, "Matching Alcoholism Treatments to Client Heterogeneity: Project MATCH Drinking Outcomes," *Journal of Studies on Alcohol* 58 (1997).

25. A. Bell and S. Rollnick "Motivational Interviewing in Practice: A Structured Approach," in *Treating Substance Abuse: Theory and Technique,* ed. F. Rotgers, D.S. Keller, and J. Morgenstern (New York: Guilford Press, 1996).

26. H.M. Tiebout, "Surrender Versus Compliance in Therapy," *Quarterly Journal of Studies on Alcohol* 14 (1953).

27. *Twelve Steps and Twelve Traditions,* p. 106–7.

28. W.R. Miller and S. Rollnick, "Motivational Interviewing: Preparing People to Change Addictive Behavior," (New York: Guilford Press).

29. C.D. Emrick, J.S. Tonigan, et al., "Alcoholics Anonymous: What Is Currently Known?" in *Research on Alcoholics Anonymous: Opportunities and Alternatives,* ed. B.S. McCrady and W.R. Miller (New Brunswick, NJ: Rutgers University Press, 1993).

30. L.A. Kaskutas, J. Bond, and K. Humphreys, "Social Networks as Mediators of the Effect of Alcoholics Anonymous," *Addiction* 97 (2000):7.

31. G.J. Connors, J.S. Tonigan, and W.R. Miller, "A Longitudinal Model of Intake Symptomatology, AA Participation and Outcome: Retrospective Study of the Project MATCH Outpatient and Aftercare Samples," *Journal of Studies on Alcohol* 62 (2001):6.

32. D.J. Anderson. *Perspectives on Treatment: The Minnesota Experience* (Center City, Minn.: Hazelden, 1981).

33. J. Spicer. *The Minnesota Model* (Center City, Minn.: Hazelden: 1993).

34. Project MATCH Research Groups, "Matching Alcoholism Treatments to Client Heterogeneity: Project MATCH Three Year Drinking Outcomes," *Alcoholism: Clinical and Experimental Research* 22 (1998):6.

35. N. Cooney, et al., "Matching Clients to Alcoholism Treatment Based on Psychopathology," in *Project MATCH Hypotheses: Results and Causal Chain Analysis,* ed. R. Longabaugh and P.W. Wirtz, (Bethesda, Md: National Institute on Alcohol Abuse and Alcoholism, 2001).

36. M.P. Millhouse, and R. Fiorentine, "12-Step Program Participation and Effectiveness: Do Gender and Ethnic Differences Exist?" *Journal of Drug Issues,* 31 (2001):3.

37. J.C. Longabaugh, et al., "Network Support for Drinking: Alcoholics Anonymous and Long-Term Matching Effects," *Addiction,* 93 (1998):9.

38. R. Fiorentine and M.P. Hillhouse, "Exploring the Additive Effects of Drug Misuse Treatment and Twelve-Step Involvement: Does Twelve-Step Ideology Matter?" *Substance Use and Misuse* 35 (2000):3.

39. P. Owen, *Milestones of Recovery: Review and Recommendations* (Center City Minn: Hazelden, 2003).

Program Overview

1. *Twelve Steps and Twelve Traditions,* p. 139.

Facilitator Guidelines

1. *Al-Anon Faces Alcoholism*, 2nd ed. (New York: Al-Anon Family Group Headquarters, 1985).
2. J. Nowinski, *Substance Abuse in Adolescents and Young Adults: A Guide to Treatment* (New York: W. W. Norton, 1990).

Core Topic 1: Assessment

1. *Alcoholics Anonymous*, p. 24.
2. *Alcoholics Anonymous*, p. 31; *Narcotics Anonymous*, p. 108.
3. Nowinski, *Substance Abuse in Adolescents and Young Adults*, p. 47.
4. H.M. Tiebout, "Surrender Versus Compliance in Therapy." *Quarterly Journal of Studies on Alcohol* 14 (1953), pp. 58-68; H.M. Tiebout, The Act of Surrender in the Therapeutic Process (New York: National Council on Alcoholism); and Nowinski, *Substance Abuse in Adolescents and Young Adults*, p. 135.
5. D. Anderson, *Perspectives on Treatment: The Minnesota Experience* (Center City, MN: Hazelden, 1981).

Core Topic 2: Acceptance

1. *Alcoholics Anonymous*, p. 59; *Narcotics Anonymous*, p. 17.
2. E. Kübler-Ross, *On Death and Dying* (New York: Macmillan, 1970), and G.E. Westberg, *Good Grief* (Philadelphia: Fortress Press, 1971).
3. See *Alcoholics Anonymous*, pp. 37-38, for the actual text.
4. Nowinski, *Substance Abuse in Adolescents and Young Adults*, p. 47.
5. *Twelve Steps and Twelve Traditions*, p.21.
6. P.C. McDonald, "Grieving: A Healing Process." (Center City, MN: Hazelden Educational Materials, 1985). Pamphlet.
7. E.M. Jellinek, "Phases in the Drinking History of Alcoholics: Analysis of a Survey Conducted by the *Grapevine*, Official Organ of Alcoholics Anonymous." *Quarterly Journal of Studies in Alcoholism* 7 (June 1946).
8. *Alcoholics Anonymous*, p. 41.
9. *Alcoholics Anonymous*, p. 46.
10. *Alcoholics Anonymous*, pp. 22-23.
11. M. Beattie, *Denial* (Center City, MN: Hazelden Educational Materials, 1986), p. 5.
12. Beattie, *Denial*, p. 5.
13. McDonald, "Grieving: A Healing Process," p. 9.

Core Topic 3: Surrender

1. *Alcoholics Anonymous*, p. 59; *Narcotics Anonymous*, p. 17.
2. *Twelve Steps and Twelve Traditions*, p.26.
3. *Alcoholics Anonymous*, p.45.
4. *Narcotics Anonymous*, p. 23-24.

5. *Alcoholics Anonymous*, p. 181.
6. *Twelve Steps and Twelve Traditions*, p. 31.
7. *Alcoholics Anonymous Comes of Age* (New York: Alcoholics Anonymous World Services, 1957); *Narcotics Anonymous*, p. 45.
8. *Twelve Steps and Twelve Traditions*, p. 29.
9. *Twelve Steps and Twelve Traditions*, p. 25.
10. *Alcoholics Anonymous*, p. 60.
11. *Twenty-Four Hours a Day* (Center City, MN: Hazelden, 1975); *Narcotics Anonymous*, p. 90.

Core Topic 4: Getting Active in AA or NA

1. *Living Sober*, p. 13.
2. *Alcoholics Anonymous*, pp. 22-23.
3. Nowinski, *Substance Abuse in Adolescents and Young Adults*, pp. 47-48.
4. *Alcoholics Anonymous*, p. 76.
5. *Living Sober*, p. 24.
6 AA publishes an excellent pamphlet on sponsorship. It is available, along with other AA literature, through AA World Service Headquarters, Box 459, Grand Central Station, New York NY 10163.
7. *Sponsorship* (Van Nuys, CA: Narcotics Anonymous World Services, 1983).
8. *Sponsorship*.
9. *Alcoholics Anonymous*, pp. 185, 186.
10. *Narcotics Anonymous*, p. 241.
11. Paul H., *Things My Sponsors Taught Me* (Center City, MN: Hazelden, 1987).

Elective Topic 1: Genograms

1. *Al-Anon Faces Alcoholism*, p. 3; S. Wegscheider-Cruse, *The Family Trap* (Rapid City, SD: Nurturing Networks, 1976); and *Family Denial* (Center City, MN: Hazelden, 1985).

Elective Topic 2: Enabling

1. *Al-Anon Faces Alcoholism*, p.182.
2. *Detaching With Love* (Center City, MN: Hazelden, 1984).

Elective Topic 3: People, Places, and Routines

1. Kurtz, *AA: The Story*, pp. 103-104.
2. *Living Sober*, p. 19.
3. *Things My Sponsors Taught Me*.

Elective Topic 4: Emotions

1. *Living Sober*, p. 39.
2. *Living Sober*, pp. 37, 43.
3. *Living Sober*, pp. 30-32.
4. *Living Sober*, pp. 22-24.
5. *Living Sober*, p.23.
6. *Living Sober*, pp. 18, 32, 41, 44.
7. *Twelve Steps and Twelve Traditions*, p. 41.
8. *Living Sober*, p. 45.
9. *Living Sober*, p. 37.
10. *Living Sober*, p. 39.
11. Kurtz, *AA: The Story*, pp. 10-12.
12. Kurtz, *AA: The Story*, pp. 13-14.
13. B.E. Kübler-Ross, *Questions and Answers on Death and Dying* (New York: Macmillan, 1974); G. Lerner, *A Death of One's Own* (New York: Harper and Row, 1980).

Elective Topic 5: Moral Inventories

1. J. Wallace, *Alcoholism: New Light on the Disease* (Newport, RI: Edgehill Publications, 1985).
2. *Alcoholics Anonymous*, p. 59.
3. *Narcotics Anonymous*, p. 27.

Elective Topic 6: Relationships

1. Kurtz, *AA: The Story*, p. 127.
2. Kurtz, *AA: The Story*, p. 11.
3. *Narcotics Anonymous*, p. 121; *Detaching With Love*, p. 7.
4. *Living Sober*, pp. 61-63.
5. M. Beattie, *Codependent No More* (New York: Harper and Row, 1988).
6. Nowinski, *Substance Abuse in Adolescents and Young Adults*, p. 179.
7. J. Nowinski, *A Lifelong Love Affair: Keeping Sexual Desire Alive in Your Relationship* (New York: W. W. Norton, 1988), p. 186.
8. Nowinski, *A Lifelong Love Affair*, pp. 91-92, 98-101.
9. W.D. Murphy, E. Coleman, E. Hoon, and C. Scott, "Sexual Dysfunction and Treatment in Alcoholic Women," *Sexuality and Disability* 3 (1980), pp. 240-55.
10. S.R. Leiblum and R.C. Rosen, "Alcohol and Human Sexual Response." In *Alcoholism and Sexual Dysfunction*, D. J. Powell, ed. (New York: Haworth, 1984).
11. G.G. Forrest, *Alcoholism and Human Sexuality* (Springfield, IL: Charles C. Thomas, 1983); G.T. Wilson and D.M. Lawson, "Expectancies, Alcohol, and Sexual Arousal in Male Social Drinkers," *Journal of Abnormal Psychology* 85 (1976), pp. 587-94; and G.T. Wilson and D.M. Lawson, "Expectancies, Alcohol, and Sexual Arousal in Women," *Journal of Abnormal Psychology* 87 (1978), pp. 358-67.

12. W. Masters and V. Johnson, *Human Sexual Inadequacy* (Boston: Little, Brown, 1970).

Part IV: The Conjoint Program

1. *Al-Anon Faces Alcoholism*, 2nd ed. (Al-Anon Family Group Headquarters, 1985), available by writing to the publisher at One Park Ave., New York NY 10159-0182.

Enabling

1. *Al-Anon Faces Alcoholism*, p. 28.

Detaching

1. *One Day at a Time in Al-Anon*. (New York: Al-Anon Family Group Headquarters, 1986), p. 54.
2. *Detaching with Love*, p. 5.

Termination

1. T. Gorski and M. Miller, *Counseling for Relapse Prevention* (Independence, MO: Herald House—Independence Press, 1982), p. 43.

Appendix A: Jellinek Charts

1. E.M. Jellinek, "A Chart of Alcohol Addiction and Recovery," *Journal of Iowa Medical Society* (March 1964).
2. J.E. James, "Symptoms of Alcoholism in Women: A Preliminary Survey of A.A. Members," *Journal of Studies of Alcohol* 36 (1975).

Appendix B: The Twelve Steps

1. *Alcoholics Anonymous*, p. 59.

Index

About the Authors

Joseph Nowinski, Ph.D. is associate adjunct professor of psychology at the University of Connecticut and supervising psychologist, Correctional Health Care Division, University of Connecticut Health Center. In addition to *The Twelve-Step Facilitation Handbook*, Dr. Nowinski is the author of *Substance Abuse in Adolescents and Young Adults: A Guide To Treatment*, and *Family Recovery and Substance Abuse*. He and his family live in Tolland, Connecticut.

Stuart Baker works for the APT Foundation and Yale University as a clinical supervisor and trainer in a wide range of substance abuse treatment research studies, including a position as a primary clinical supervisor for Twelve Step Facilitation therapists in Project MATCH at Yale, as well as providing direct clinical care in a variety of outpatient settings. He consults internationally as a trainer and supervisor on applying Twelve Step Facilitation therapy. He is author of the "Twelve Step Facilitation Therapy for Drug Abuse and Dependence" manual (published by NIDA) and Web-based training program. He has a private practice in Middletown, Connecticut, and is licensed and certified as a drug and alcohol counselor.